Media Planning Workbook

Fifth Edition

With Discussions and Problems

William B. Goodrich
University of South Carolina

Jack Z. Sissors
Northwestern University

NTC College Division
NTC/Contemporary Publishing Group
Lincolnwood, Illinois USA

Library of Congress Cataloging-in-Publication Data

Goodrich, William B.
Media planning workbook : with discussions and problems / William B. Goodrich, Jack Z. Sissors. -- 5th ed.
p. cm.
ISBN 0-8442-3502-4 (alk. paper)
1. Advertising media planning. I. Sissors, Jack Zanville
. II. Title.
HF5826.5.G66 1995
659.1'11--dc20 95-39649
CIP

ISBN-13: 978-0-8442-3502-8
ISBN-10: 0-8442-3502-4

Published by NTC/Contemporary Publishing Group, Inc.,
4255 West Touhy Avenue,
Lincolnwood (Chicago), Illinois 60712-1975 U.S.A.

Manufactured in the United States of America.

11 12 13 14 15 WDD 14 13 12 11 10

Contents

Section One Marketing Analysis Problems

Section Two Media Analysis Problems

Section Three Media Strategy Planning Problems

Section Four Miscellaneous Problems

Appendix Media Rates and Other Data

Exhibits

Tables

Introduction

This workbook was written to help you put into practice some of the more important concepts discussed in your textbook and lectures in an advertising media planning course. Specific problems dealing with media planning are the focal point of the workbook.

It is important to note that this workbook does not try to prepare you to take a job in a media department of an advertising agency (or company), even though you could probably do well in such a job after having successfully passed a media planning course. Rather, one of our objectives is to help you understand how to solve media planning problems, instead of how to do some of the many clerical tasks performed in a media department (such as filling out worksheets or purchase orders).

Another objective is to present the kinds of problems that occur in more sophisticated advertising agencies. These problems tend to be more difficult, and solving them requires more intellectual effort. Aside from their academic value, these problems also have a practical value in that they help you think logically. Nevertheless, these problems are within the capability of college students majoring in marketing and advertising.

A third objective is to help you develop a method of dealing with media problems. Conceivably, many people can make media decisions without any formal training. But they might not be able to justify their decisions. Our method is to have you analyze the available research data and then, when necessary, have you modify these data on the basis of logic and reason. The result is a decision that will stand the test of inquiry. We want to help you not only to make the informed decision, but also to build a rationale to defend it. The rationale for making media decisions is somewhat like the rationale that a lawyer uses in building a case. We hope that when you arrive at solutions to the assignments, your decisions will be based on the best evidence and logical thinking.

To make the discussion and assignments more meaningful, we start each general topic by explaining its purpose, because you ought to know what you are about to be asked to do and why it is important. As a result, you should find your work on the solutions to be more meaningful.

To help you further, chapter and page references are given for the book *Advertising Media Planning,* by Sissors and Bumba. You will find it helpful to read this textbook before you do an assignment.

Finally, in addition to the assignments, we also present some media data that might be helpful in other courses, whether in media planning or other areas of marketing. The sources we present are those usually available to a professional media planner.

William B. Goodrich
Jack Z. Sissors

Acknowledgments

The authors wish to acknowledge and thank the following companies and their representatives for the use of materials in this workbook:

Advanced Media Systems; The Arbitron Company; Charleston Tea Plantation; Grey Advertising, Inc.; Leading National Advertisers, Inc.; *Marketer's Guide to Media* from the publisher of *ADWEEK*; Mediamark Research, Inc.; Nielsen Media Research; Simmons Market Research Bureau, Inc.; Sp5 Quotations and Data, Inc. (SQAD); and SRDS (Standard Rate and Data Service).

Thanks also to Geoff McClelland, DDB Needham Worldwide (Chicago); Bill Reynolds, Henderson Advertising (Greenville, SC); and Ralph Morgan, University of South Carolina for their help in tracking down media source materials and to *Advertising Age* for data that came from its media workshops.

We are especially grateful to Louise Gainey at the University of Miami School of Communication for her close scrutiny of the manuscript for this edition.

W. B. G.
J. Z. S.

How to Use This Book

Please note that nearly all the assignments are divided into two sections: (1) Discussion and (2) Problem(s). Carefully read the discussion section before you try to solve the problem(s).

The *Media Planning Workbook* is divided into four sections, as follows:

1. Marketing Analysis Problems
2. Media Analysis Problems
3. Media Strategy Planning Problems
4. Miscellaneous Problems

As you proceed through the book, you will find each set of problems slightly more difficult than the preceding set. Furthermore, the solutions to problems in some assignments depend on lessons learned in previous assignments. For this reason, it is important to do the assignments in their proper order.

Section One

Marketing Analysis Problems

Assignment 1

Using Demographic and Index Numbers

Objective: To provide a discussion beyond the textbook that will help you understand and use demographic usage data. The main purpose of such data is to help the planner select primary prospects to whom advertising will be addressed. Media that reaches those prospects will then be selected. Specifically, this discussion will help you do the following: (1) read data from major syndicated research sources that report product usage; and (2) determine which numbers are the most meaningful for marketing and media planning analysis.

Discussion

One of the first steps in planning media is to identify precisely who the target audience is. This audience is generally made up of people who are most likely to buy or use the product and the brand being advertised.

Major syndicated research services such as Simmons Market Research Bureau, Inc., and Mediamark Research, Inc. (MRI) report user-usage data for many product categories. The data in such reports show product usage patterns for various demographic categories. The data also show how users are exposed to the various kinds of media.

Review of these and other research data that help to identify the best prospects is a critical step in the media planning process. An excellent media plan that is aimed at the wrong targets is worse than a mediocre plan that reaches the correct targets.

Refer to *Advertising Media Planning,* 5th ed., by Sissors and Bumba, Chapter 8.

How to Read Product Usage Data

Both Simmons and MRI report product usage data in much the same way. When you learn to understand MRI data, such as are shown in Exhibit 1–1, you will also have a good understanding of how to read Simmons data. Different tables will report on male, female, female homemaker, or principal shopper users, depending on the type of product. Always determine the base that is being used by checking the boldface heading at the top of the column of demographic characteristics at the upper left-hand corner of the table. Exhibit 1–1 reports the usage of female homemakers.

The column of figures under the heading "Total U.S. '000" reports the total number of persons in the United States in each demographic group. The numbers are reported in thousands (000), so you will have to keep in mind this shorthand method of reporting. In Exhibit 1–1, 85,337 female homemakers stands for 85,337,000 (or 85.3 million) female homemakers.

Exhibit 1–1 MRI: Gelatin and Gelatin Desserts Users (Female Homemakers)

		ALL				PACKAGES/LAST 30 DAYS: HEAVY MORE THAN 3				MEDIUM 2 - 3				LIGHT LESS THAN 2			
BASE: FEMALE HOMEMAKERS	TOTAL U.S. '000	A '000	B % DOWN	C % ACROSS	D INDEX	A '000	B % DOWN	C % ACROSS	D INDEX	A '000	B % DOWN	C % ACROSS	D INDEX	A '000	B % DOWN	C % ACROSS	D INDEX
All Female Homemakers	85337	37750	100.0	44.2	100	8686	100.0	10.2	100	11802	100.0	13.8	100	17262	100.0	20.2	100
Women	85337	37750	100.0	44.2	100	8686	100.0	10.2	100	11802	100.0	13.8	100	17262	100.0	20.2	100
Household Heads	32518	13076	34.6	40.2	91	2907	33.5	8.9	88	4241	35.9	13.0	94	5929	34.3	18.2	90
Homemakers	85337	37750	100.0	44.2	100	8686	100.0	10.2	100	11802	100.0	13.8	100	17262	100.0	20.2	100
Graduated College	14828	6344	16.8	42.8	97	910	10.5	6.1	60	1581	13.4	10.7	77	3854	22.3	26.0	128
Attended College	15832	7283	19.3	46.0	104	1426	16.4	9.0	88	2264	19.2	14.3	103	3593	20.8	22.7	112
Graduated High School	35787	16057	42.5	44.9	101	3879	44.7	10.8	106	5439	46.1	15.2	110	6739	39.0	18.8	93
Did not Graduate High School	18890	8065	21.4	42.7	97	2471	28.4	13.1	129	2518	21.3	13.3	96	3077	17.8	16.3	81
18-24	7537	2502	6.6	33.2	75	*410	4.7	5.4	53	656	5.6	8.7	63	1436	8.3	19.1	94
25-34	20103	8216	21.8	40.9	92	1329	15.3	6.6	65	2450	20.8	12.2	88	4436	25.7	22.1	109
35-44	18425	8436	22.3	45.8	104	1851	21.3	10.0	99	2516	21.3	13.7	99	4069	23.6	22.1	109
45-54	12510	5873	15.6	46.9	106	1424	16.4	11.4	112	1649	14.0	13.2	95	2800	16.2	22.4	111
55-64	10767	4726	12.5	43.9	99	1363	15.7	12.7	124	1526	12.9	14.2	102	1837	10.6	17.1	84
65 or Over	15997	7998	21.2	50.0	113	2309	26.6	14.4	142	3005	25.5	18.8	136	2683	15.5	16.8	83
18-34	27640	10717	28.4	38.8	88	1739	20.0	6.3	62	3106	26.3	11.2	81	5872	34.0	21.2	105
18-49	52912	22162	58.7	41.9	95	4249	48.9	8.0	79	6474	54.9	12.2	88	11438	66.3	21.6	107
25-54	51037	22525	59.7	44.1	100	4604	53.0	9.0	89	6615	56.0	13.0	94	11306	65.5	22.2	110
Employed Full Time	36699	14682	38.9	40.0	90	2722	31.3	7.4	73	4318	36.6	11.8	85	7642	44.3	20.8	103
Part-time	9765	4539	12.0	46.5	105	972	11.2	10.0	98	1240	10.5	12.7	92	2327	13.5	23.8	118
Sole Wage Earner	12396	4806	12.7	38.8	88	820	9.4	6.6	65	1475	12.5	11.9	86	2511	14.5	20.3	100
Not Employed	38874	18530	49.1	47.7	108	4993	57.5	12.8	126	6245	52.9	16.1	116	7293	42.2	18.8	93
Professional	7570	3127	8.3	41.3	93	496	5.7	6.6	64	858	7.3	11.3	82	1773	10.3	23.4	116
Executive/Admin./Managerial	5564	2178	5.8	39.1	88	*375	4.3	6.7	66	640	5.4	11.5	83	1163	6.7	20.9	103
Clerical/Sales/Technical	19711	8084	21.4	41.0	93	1364	15.7	6.9	68	2476	21.0	12.6	91	4243	24.6	21.5	106
Precision/Crafts/Repair	1062	370	1.0	34.8	79	*62	.7	5.8	57	*122	1.0	11.5	83	*187	1.1	17.6	87
Other Employed	12556	5461	14.5	43.5	98	1396	16.1	11.1	109	1462	12.4	11.6	84	2603	15.1	20.7	102
H/D Income $75,000 or More	9247	3862	10.2	41.8	94	755	8.7	8.2	80	1024	8.7	11.1	80	2083	12.1	22.5	111
$60,000 - 74,999	6134	2735	7.2	44.6	101	432	5.0	7.0	69	814	6.9	13.3	96	1490	8.6	24.3	120
$50,000 - 59,999	6831	3055	8.1	44.7	101	685	7.9	10.0	99	854	7.2	12.5	90	1516	8.8	22.2	110
$40,000 - 49,999	9554	4412	11.7	46.2	104	829	9.5	8.7	85	1334	11.3	14.0	101	2250	13.0	23.6	116
$30,000 - 39,999	12056	5252	13.9	43.6	98	1021	11.8	8.5	83	1572	13.3	13.0	94	2660	15.4	22.1	109
$20,000 - 29,999	14114	6804	18.0	48.2	109	1622	18.7	11.5	113	2344	19.9	16.6	120	2838	16.4	20.1	99
$10,000 - 19,999	14945	6496	17.2	43.5	98	1880	21.6	12.6	124	2082	17.6	13.9	101	2534	14.7	17.0	84
Less than $10,000	12456	5133	13.6	41.2	93	1463	16.8	11.7	115	1778	15.1	14.3	103	1891	11.0	15.2	75
Census Region: North East	17660	8581	22.7	48.6	110	2427	27.9	13.7	135	2487	21.1	14.1	102	3667	21.2	20.8	103
North Central	20650	11311	30.0	54.8	124	2747	31.6	13.3	131	3651	30.9	17.7	128	4913	28.5	23.8	118
South	30442	12140	32.2	39.9	90	2351	27.1	7.7	76	4067	34.5	13.4	97	5723	33.2	18.8	93
West	16586	5719	15.1	34.5	78	1162	13.4	7.0	69	1598	13.5	9.6	70	2959	17.1	17.8	88
Marketing Reg.: New England	4884	2466	6.5	50.5	114	734	8.5	15.0	148	760	6.4	15.6	113	972	5.6	19.9	98
Middle Atlantic	14800	6872	18.2	46.4	105	1870	21.5	12.6	124	1930	16.4	13.0	94	3072	17.8	20.8	103
East Central	11958	5867	15.5	49.1	111	1436	16.5	12.0	118	1751	14.8	14.6	106	2680	15.5	22.4	111
West Central	13141	7045	18.7	53.6	121	1659	19.1	12.6	124	2399	20.3	18.3	132	2988	17.3	22.7	112
South East	16710	6699	17.7	40.1	91	1038	12.0	6.2	61	2455	20.8	14.7	106	3206	18.6	19.2	95
South West	9760	4088	10.8	41.9	95	964	11.1	9.9	97	1196	10.1	12.3	89	1928	11.2	19.8	98
Pacific	14083	4712	12.5	33.5	76	984	11.3	7.0	69	1312	11.1	9.3	67	2417	14.0	17.2	85
County Size A	34391	13841	36.7	40.2	91	3311	38.1	9.6	95	3680	31.2	10.7	77	6850	39.7	19.9	98
County Size B	25027	11371	30.1	45.4	103	2393	27.6	9.6	94	3381	28.6	13.5	98	5597	32.4	22.4	111
County Size C	12805	6030	16.0	47.1	106	1246	14.3	9.7	96	2111	17.9	16.5	119	2672	15.5	20.9	103
County Size D	13113	6509	17.2	49.6	112	1736	20.0	13.2	130	2630	22.3	20.1	145	2142	12.4	16.3	81
MSA Central City	30623	12944	34.3	42.3	96	2659	30.6	8.7	85	3681	31.2	12.0	87	6605	38.3	21.6	107
MSA Suburban	35692	15577	41.3	43.6	99	3658	42.1	10.2	101	4436	37.6	12.4	90	7482	43.3	21.0	104
Non-MSA	19022	9229	24.4	48.5	110	2369	27.3	12.5	122	3685	31.2	19.4	140	3176	18.4	16.7	83
Single	11851	3799	10.1	32.1	72	721	8.3	6.1	60	1101	9.3	9.3	67	1977	11.5	16.7	82
Married	51571	24503	64.9	47.5	107	5763	66.3	11.2	110	7457	63.2	14.5	105	11284	65.4	21.9	108
Other	21915	9448	25.0	43.1	97	2202	25.4	10.0	99	3245	27.5	14.8	107	4001	23.2	18.3	90
Parents	34515	16668	44.2	48.3	109	3531	40.7	10.2	101	4795	40.6	13.9	100	8342	48.3	24.2	119
Working Parents	21701	10557	28.0	48.6	110	1949	22.4	9.0	88	3191	27.0	14.7	106	5417	31.4	25.0	123
Household Size: 1 Person	14215	5712	15.1	40.2	91	1311	15.1	9.2	91	1984	16.8	14.0	101	2417	14.0	17.0	84
2 Persons	26840	11270	29.9	42.0	95	2683	30.9	10.0	98	3750	31.8	14.0	101	4837	28.0	18.0	89
3 or More	44283	20768	55.0	46.9	106	4692	54.0	10.6	104	6068	51.4	13.7	99	10008	58.0	22.6	112
Any Child in Household	37360	17869	47.3	47.8	108	3840	44.2	10.3	101	5208	44.1	13.9	101	8820	51.1	23.6	117
Under 2 Years	7908	3581	9.5	45.3	102	624	7.2	7.9	78	1058	9.0	13.4	97	1899	11.0	24.0	119
2-5 Years	14287	6594	17.5	46.2	104	1155	13.3	8.1	79	2147	18.2	15.0	109	3291	19.1	23.0	114
6-11 Years	18515	8990	23.8	48.6	110	2030	23.4	11.0	108	2533	21.5	13.7	99	4426	25.6	23.9	118
12-17 Years	15623	7644	20.2	48.9	111	2011	23.2	12.9	126	1994	16.9	12.8	92	3639	21.1	23.3	115
White	72894	33294	88.2	45.7	103	7650	88.1	10.5	103	10619	90.0	14.6	105	15026	87.0	20.6	102
Black	9966	3577	9.5	35.9	81	758	8.7	7.6	75	981	8.3	9.8	71	1838	10.6	18.4	91
Spanish Speaking	5802	2270	6.0	39.1	88	919	10.6	15.8	156	582	4.9	10.0	73	769	4.5	13.3	66
Home Owned	57540	27491	72.8	47.8	108	6442	74.2	11.2	110	9077	76.9	15.8	114	11972	69.4	20.8	103
Daily Newspapers: Read Any	49061	22440	59.4	45.7	103	5133	59.1	10.5	103	7089	60.1	14.4	104	10218	59.2	20.8	103
Read One Daily	40836	18841	49.9	46.1	104	4126	47.5	10.1	99	6104	51.7	14.9	108	8611	49.9	21.1	104
Read Two or More Dailies	8225	3599	9.5	43.8	99	1007	11.6	12.2	120	985	8.3	12.0	87	1607	9.3	19.5	97
Sunday Newspapers: Read Any	56000	25854	68.5	46.2	104	5672	65.3	10.1	100	8086	68.5	14.4	104	12096	70.1	21.6	107
Read One Sunday	49916	22893	60.6	45.9	104	5014	57.7	10.0	99	7257	61.5	14.5	105	10622	61.5	21.3	105
Read Two or More Sundays	6084	2962	7.8	48.7	110	659	7.6	10.8	106	829	7.0	13.6	99	1474	8.5	24.2	120
Quintile I - Outdoor	16789	7164	19.0	42.7	96	1523	17.5	9.1	89	2483	21.0	14.8	107	3158	18.3	18.8	93
Quintile II	17026	7493	19.8	44.0	99	1538	17.7	9.0	89	1963	16.6	11.5	83	3992	23.1	23.4	116
Quintile III	17384	8114	21.5	46.7	106	2027	23.3	11.7	115	2442	20.7	14.0	102	3645	21.1	21.0	104
Quintile IV	17306	7905	20.9	45.7	103	1714	19.7	9.9	97	2517	21.3	14.5	105	3675	21.3	21.2	105
Quintile V	16833	7074	18.7	42.0	95	1884	21.7	11.2	110	2397	20.3	14.2	103	2793	16.2	16.6	82
Quintile I - Magazines	16671	7758	20.6	46.5	105	1765	20.3	10.6	104	2549	21.6	15.3	111	3445	20.0	20.7	102
Quintile II	17247	7837	20.8	45.4	103	1944	22.4	11.3	111	2405	20.4	13.9	101	3488	20.2	20.2	100
Quintile III	17140	7356	19.5	42.9	97	1403	16.2	8.2	80	2297	19.5	13.4	97	3656	21.2	21.3	105
Quintile IV	17108	7555	20.0	44.2	100	1708	19.7	10.0	98	2354	19.9	13.8	99	3493	20.2	20.4	101
Quintile V	17171	7245	19.2	42.2	95	1867	21.5	10.9	107	2198	18.6	12.8	93	3180	18.4	18.5	92
Quintile I - Newspapers	17008	8041	21.3	47.3	107	1819	20.9	10.7	105	2354	19.9	13.8	100	3867	22.4	22.7	112
Quintile II	17523	8551	22.7	48.8	110	1933	22.3	11.0	108	2820	23.9	16.1	116	3798	22.0	21.7	107
Quintile III	17113	7258	19.2	42.4	96	1670	19.2	9.8	96	2301	19.5	13.4	97	3286	19.0	19.2	95
Quintile IV	16903	7043	18.7	41.7	94	1409	16.2	8.3	82	2122	18.0	12.6	91	3512	20.3	20.8	103
Quintile V	16790	6858	18.2	40.8	92	1854	21.3	11.0	108	2205	18.7	13.1	95	2799	16.2	16.7	82
Tercile I - Yellow Pages	14064	6591	17.5	46.9	106	1407	16.2	10.0	98	2015	17.1	14.3	104	3169	18.4	22.5	111
Tercile II	13615	6539	17.3	48.0	109	1771	20.4	13.0	128	1837	15.6	13.5	98	2931	17.0	21.5	106
Tercile III	13809	6205	16.4	44.9	102	1167	13.4	8.5	83	1812	15.4	13.1	95	3225	18.7	23.4	115

Spring

1. **The estimated number of users (column A).** These data report the number of adults who have used the product. Like the numbers in the Total U.S. column, they are reported in thousands (000). In Exhibit 1–1, 37,750,000 (or 37.8 million) female homemakers are users of gelatin or gelatin desserts.
2. **Users as a percentage of total.** Both MRI and Simmons report percentages in two ways:

   (a) **Column B: Percentage of a user category who fall into a specific demographic group.** Examples: 21.8 percent of all users of gelatin and gelatin desserts are female homemakers aged 25–34, and 15.3 percent of heavy users are female homemakers aged 25–34.

   Column B is headed "Down" because when the percentages for a demographic category—such as place of residence—are added vertically, they will total 100 percent. Example: Census Region for heavy users: 27.9 + 31.6 + 27.1 + 13.4 = 100. Keep in mind that the demographic segments within the category must be mutually exclusive or the total can exceed 100 percent.

   (b) **Column C: Percentage of a demographic segment who are in a certain usage group.** Examples: 40.9 percent of all female homemakers aged 25–34 are users, and 6.6 percent of all female homemakers aged 25–34 are heavy users.

   Column C is headed "Across" because when the percentages for heavy, medium, and light users are added across, they total the percentage in column C for all users. Example: For female homemakers aged 25–34: 6.6 (heavy users) + 12.2 (medium users) + 22.1 (light users) = 40.9 (all users).
3. **Index numbers (column D).** The index numbers in column D are based on the percentages in column C and are used to compare the percentage of users (all, heavy, medium, or light) in a demographic segment to the percentage of users (all, heavy, medium, or light) in the base population or universe.

   Think of an index number of 100 as average. An index number of 100 indicates that the usage rate for a demographic segment is the same as in the population or universe. An index number over 100 is better than average, and one under 100 is below average.

   Example: In Exhibit 1–1 under all users, female homemakers aged 18–24 have an index of 75. This means that gelatin/gelatin desserts usage by female homemakers aged 18–24 is only 75% as much as the usage by all female homemakers. Put another way, usage by female homemakers aged 18–24 is 25 percent below average (100−75 = 25). Female homemakers aged 45–54 have an index of 106, which means that usage by this group is 6 percent above average.

If you don't understand how to read the data (or if the pages begin to look like numerical alphabet soup—and you are looking at data on cake mixes or soap), don't worry. Remember that many professionals must refamiliarize themselves with a data page before analyzing it, especially if it is a source that they use infrequently. It is better to double-check the meaning of numbers and how to read them than to use the wrong numbers or misinterpret their meaning.

The following points may help the beginner who is lost in the numbers:

1. The key to understanding the usage numbers is to recheck headings of columns and items for rows. These descriptions identify the numbers and what they represent.
2. Look for totals and averages (if you wish, look for "the 100s"). The "100s" (at the top of columns in both MRI and Simmons) either stand for 100 percent (total of a category) or 100 index (the average rate for all users).
3. Differentiate between percentages and index numbers. All percentages mean some proportion of the total, and each number will be lower than 100 percent. All index numbers show how much above or below average (index 100) the usage rate for a specific demographic segment is when compared with total users, or with population in that segment.
   Or put another way: If it is a percentage, 67 percent means two-thirds of users or usage within the segment (this would generally be a very high percentage). If it an index number, 67 is at only two-thirds the average rate (this would be a relatively low index number).
4. Look for one group of numbers and reread and think about what the numbers in that group mean. Once you understand "the system," again, you will find it much easier to understand the total page.
5. Of course, "When all else fails, read the directions" provided in all sources of information. The interested student should develop the good practice of reviewing instructions for use of each data source before using it.

What the Usage Numbers Tell You

For a given period, the numbers tell you:

1. How many homemakers (or adults, etc.) use or purchase a product
2. How many times they use or purchase the product
3. How certain segments of users compare with other user segments

Generally, data show use of the generic product class, such as cake mixes. However, information for major brands is also given in most product categories.

Please note that the data do not show the volume of any product used. Whereas you can learn that 33 percent of homemakers use a product at a certain rate (such as four times a month), this information indicates only the frequency of use, not the actual volume used.

If you want to make a rough estimate of the amount of a product used (or volume), you can do the following:

1. Find the number of persons who use the product from a table.
2. Multiply that number by the number of times those persons use the product during a given period.
3. Multiply that number by an estimate of how much of that product is used on an average occasion. For example, in the situation of dishwashing detergents, you might estimate that each sinkful of dishwashing requires an average of one ounce of liquid.

Further, remember that the data only report past usage as indicated by respondents in a selected sample. The data do not report current or actual product usage.

How to Determine Which Numbers Are Most Important

The analysis of usage data generally raises several questions, such as which numbers are most important and how broadly or narrowly you should define the targets for your media plan. The following considerations will help you when you review usage data.

1. **Look at all the numbers.** Do not look at only the high numbers. Low and intermediate numbers might be just as helpful to your evaluation of prospect groups. A student of media planning operating without computer support might emphasize only three or four key demographic segments, but it is important to understand all the numbers and how certain demographic data support findings reported for other demographic groups.
2. **Be aware of shortcomings in concentrating on only the highest index numbers.** For example, a group with a high index usage rate might represent either a small number of users, a small population base, or both.
3. **Review above-average index numbers (those above 100) as possibly a good starting point.** This will tell you in which groups incidence of use is better than average. Because media are purchased to deliver messages to X thousands of audience members, there should be an adequate number of prospects (or a reasonably high rate of incidence of use) within the selected audience.
4. **List and rank the key demographic groups.** Analysis of other marketing information/factors can provide direction about whether heavy or light users are the key prospects for your brand. Heavy users might not be receptive to your brand's advertising, or they might be difficult to convince; light users might not represent a profitable share of the market.
5. **Determine priority, or rank, of demographic groups in the order of their importance.** Understand which groups are most important and how much more important they are than other groups. Your first reaction might be, "I knew that would be the higher user group," but it is important to provide statistical evidence that one group is more important than another. This analysis may be subjective, but it should be defendable.
6. **Review data to determine how broadly or narrowly you should define the target audience.** Should you key on one age segment, or two or three? Look for numbers that confirm each other—does a "composite" begin to emerge (large-size households; teenage children; homemakers 35–49; etc.)? Do the numbers suggest different usage categories (very young and very old)? Do numbers suggest something that does not make sense, indicating that perhaps more research is needed?
7. **Determine how important the reported differences in usage really are.** Obviously, the difference between an index of 99 and one of 101 is not at all meaningful. However, even in product categories with very broad or general

use, there are usually some meaningful differences reported. Perhaps at first glance the difference of 91 and 109 does not seem important (a difference of only 9 percent for each from the average 100 index), yet the reported difference between the two indexes is 18 percentage points (almost one-fifth of the average usage rate). Because each marketing situation is different, you must use your judgment to determine when to ignore and when to emphasize the reported differences.

Problems

Using the data contained in Exhibit 1–1, answer the following questions regarding users of gelatin/gelatin desserts:

1. What percentage of all users are aged 45–54? ________________
2. What percentage of heavy users live in County Size A? ________________
3. How many female homemakers aged 35–44 are there in the United States? ________________
4. How many female homemakers who graduated from college are heavy users? ________________
5. What percentage of female homemakers aged 35–44 are light users? ________________
6. What percentage of female homemakers living in County Size C are medium users? ________________
7. Are female homemakers living in the New England marketing region more or less likely to be heavy users of gelatin/gelatin desserts? ________________
8. By what percentage are the homemakers in the above question more or less likely to be heavy users? ________________
9. How many female homemakers aged 18–49 do *not* use gelatin/gelatin desserts? ________________
10. Looking at the data on the presence of children in the household, explain why the column B percentages total over 100 percent when added vertically.

Assignment 2

Misleading Index Numbers

Objective: To help you become aware that you might use index numbers incorrectly if you are not careful. Most often beginners tend to select the demographic targets with the largest index numbers.

Discussion

You should always check the amount of usage and the population size of any demographic group that has a large index number. It should be obvious that if either or both are small, then you will want to find some other demographic segment with a higher usage or larger population base, even if it has a smaller index number.

In addition, you might also err when using index numbers if you look only at total usage volume generated in a given market without also considering the size of the audience that must be reached to deliver ads to an adequate number of users. Depending on distribution, size, and quality of the sales force, competition, and other marketing factors, in some situations it can be more productive to advertise in three or four smaller geographic (or demographic) markets rather than in one large market.

Refer to *Advertising Media Planning,* 5th ed., by Sissors and Bumba, Chapter 9.

Problems

1. You are given the following marketing data for an unidentified product.

Geographic region	U.S. population in each segment (%)	U.S. product volume in each segment (%)	Usage index
A	24.3	25.5	105
B	29.9	29.9	100
C	38.7	36.8	95
D	7.1	7.8	110
Total U.S.	100.0	100.0	100

Rank these market regions in order of "best potential" for the product, indicating the most important piece of data used in each selection. Be sure to briefly explain your reasoning.

Rank	Region	Data used	Explanation
1.	__________	__________	__________
2.	__________	__________	__________
3.	__________	__________	__________
4.	__________	__________	__________

2. You are given the following data on metropolitan markets for another product.

Metro market	U.S. population in each market (%)	U.S. product usage in each market (%)	Usage index
A	6.7	3.6	54
B	3.1	3.2	103
C	1.5	1.9	127
D	1.1	1.8	164

Suppose that your agency is considering placing advertising in these four markets:

(a) Should your agency avoid placing advertising in market A because it has a low index number? Briefly explain.

(b) Why might we want to advertise in all four markets and heavy-up markets B, C, and D? In your explanation, ignore index numbers. Briefly explain.

Assignment 3

Using Simmons for Selecting Primary Target Demographics

Objective: To analyze and understand the use of some of the Simmons Market Research Bureau data for planning purposes. Simmons provides syndicated research reports that are widely used for media planning.

Discussion

Simmons provides data on product, brand, and media usage. These data are often used to find specific demographic segments that could become the target audiences of a media plan.

Product and brand usage are reported not only by demographics, but also in cross-tabulated form that shows the rate of usage. In order to conserve space, printed data often show demographics only for all users and heavy users; however, subscribers to Simmons Market Research Bureau reports can get data on medium and light users via online computer access.

Exhibit 3–1 shows Simmons product usage data for diet or sugar free cola drinks. Here is some specific information on how to read the data.

The left-hand column lists the demographic categories—in this case for adults. The next column lists the total number of adults in each category (e.g., there are 23,951,000 adults aged 18–24). Note that the figures in this column are reported in thousands (i.e., you must add three zeros to each number as indicated by the notation at the head of the column—'000).

For adults aged 18–24 who are heavy users of diet or sugar free cola, the data would be interpreted as follows:

Column A: 1,820,000 adults aged 18–24 are heavy users of the product.

Column B: 10.3 percent of heavy users are aged 18–24 (1,820 ÷ 17,594 = .1034 or 10.3 percent). Column B totals 100 percent for all of the demographic segments in each category when the segments are mutually exclusive. Column B percentages for age groups 18–24 through 65 or older total 100 percent.

Column C: 7.6 percent of all adults aged 18–24 are heavy users (1,820 ÷ 23,951 = .0759 or 7.6 percent).

Column D: Adults aged 18–24 are 19 percent less likely to be heavy users of the product compared to all adults. This is an index number comparing the column C percentage for the demographic group to the percentage for all adults at the top of column C (7.6 ÷ 9.4 × 100 = 80.85 or 81).

Refer to *Advertising Media Planning,* 5th ed., by Sissors and Bumba, Chapter 0.

Exhibit 3–1 Simmons: Diet or Sugar Free Cola Drinks (Adults)

0025
P 15

DIET OR SUGAR FREE COLA DRINKS (CARBONATED): ALL USERS, USERS IN LAST 7 DAYS AND KINDS
(ADULTS)

0025
P 15

	TOTAL U.S. '000	ALL USERS A '000	ALL USERS B % DOWN	ALL USERS C % ACROSS	ALL USERS D INDX	HEAVY USERS 11 OR MORE A '000	HEAVY USERS 11 OR MORE B % DOWN	HEAVY USERS 11 OR MORE C % ACROSS	HEAVY USERS 11 OR MORE D INDX	BOTTLED A '000	BOTTLED B % DOWN	BOTTLED C % ACROSS	BOTTLED D INDX	CANNED A '000	CANNED B % DOWN	CANNED C % ACROSS	CANNED D INDX
TOTAL ADULTS	187747	75561	100.0	40.2	100	17594	100.0	9.4	100	39203	100.0	20.9	100	54225	100.0	28.9	100
MALES	90070	32652	43.2	36.3	90	7496	42.6	8.3	89	16795	42.8	18.6	89	22814	42.1	25.3	88
FEMALES	97676	42909	56.8	43.9	109	10098	57.4	10.3	110	22408	57.2	22.9	110	31410	57.9	32.2	111
PRINCIPAL SHOPPERS	115901	47340	62.7	40.8	101	10711	60.9	9.2	99	24771	63.2	21.4	102	33751	62.2	29.1	101
18 - 24	23951	8192	10.8	34.2	85	1820	10.3	7.6	81	4873	12.4	20.3	97	5779	10.7	24.1	84
25 - 34	41492	15502	20.5	37.4	93	4617	26.2	11.1	119	8246	21.0	19.9	95	11232	20.7	27.1	94
35 - 44	40678	16783	22.2	41.3	103	4496	25.6	11.1	118	9019	23.0	22.2	106	12723	23.5	31.3	108
45 - 54	29045	12891	17.1	44.4	110	3482	19.8	12.0	128	7217	18.4	24.8	119	9409	17.4	32.4	112
55 - 64	21263	9703	12.8	45.6	113	1654	9.4	7.8	83	4601	11.7	21.6	104	6732	12.4	31.7	110
65 OR OLDER	31318	12491	16.5	39.9	99	1524	8.7	4.9	52	5247	13.4	16.8	80	8349	15.4	26.7	92
18 - 34	65443	23694	31.4	36.2	90	6437	36.6	9.8	105	13119	33.5	20.0	96	17011	31.4	26.0	90
18 - 49	122143	47562	62.9	38.9	97	12910	73.4	10.6	113	26284	67.0	21.5	103	34861	64.3	28.5	99
25 - 54	111215	45176	59.8	40.6	101	12595	71.6	11.3	121	24482	62.4	22.0	105	33364	61.5	30.0	104
35 - 49	56701	23868	31.6	42.1	105	6473	36.8	11.4	122	13165	33.6	23.2	111	17850	32.9	31.5	109
50 OR OLDER	65603	27999	37.1	42.7	106	4684	26.6	7.1	76	12919	33.0	19.7	94	19364	35.7	29.5	102
GRADUATED COLLEGE	37353	17195	22.8	46.0	114	3942	22.4	10.6	113	9908	25.3	26.5	127	13231	24.4	35.4	123
ATTENDED COLLEGE	39301	16056	21.2	40.9	102	4012	22.8	10.2	109	7713	19.7	19.6	94	12203	22.5	31.0	108
GRADUATED HIGH SCHOOL	73139	29403	38.9	40.2	100	6765	38.5	9.2	99	15414	39.3	21.1	101	20405	37.6	27.9	97
DID NOT GRADUATE HIGH SCHOOL	37954	12906	17.1	34.0	84	2875	16.3	7.6	81	6168	15.7	16.3	78	8387	15.5	22.1	77
EMPLOYED MALES	62041	21728	28.8	35.0	87	5711	32.5	9.2	98	11858	30.2	19.1	92	15727	29.0	25.3	88
EMPLOYED FEMALES	53100	23959	31.7	45.1	112	6516	37.0	12.3	131	12903	32.9	24.3	116	18109	33.4	34.1	118
EMPLOYED FULL-TIME	99735	39078	51.7	39.2	97	10526	59.8	10.6	113	21636	55.2	21.7	104	28642	52.8	28.7	99
EMPLOYED PART-TIME	15406	6610	8.7	42.9	107	1701	9.7	11.0	118	3126	8.0	20.3	97	5195	9.6	33.7	117
NOT EMPLOYED	72606	29874	39.5	41.1	102	5367	30.5	7.4	79	14441	36.8	19.9	95	20388	37.6	28.1	97
PROFESSIONAL/MANAGER	32308	13811	18.3	42.7	106	3352	19.1	10.4	111	7608	19.4	23.5	113	11011	20.3	34.1	118
TECHNICAL/CLERICAL/SALES	35568	15463	20.5	43.5	108	4007	22.8	11.3	120	8237	21.0	23.2	111	11385	21.0	32.0	111
PRECISION/CRAFT	12562	4576	6.1	36.4	91	1446	8.2	11.5	123	2614	6.7	20.8	100	3240	6.0	25.8	89
OTHER EMPLOYED	34704	11837	15.7	34.1	85	3421	19.4	9.9	105	6302	16.1	18.2	87	8202	15.1	23.6	82
SINGLE	41125	14625	19.4	35.6	88	4048	23.0	9.8	105	8319	21.2	20.2	97	9905	18.3	24.1	83
MARRIED	111354	47835	63.3	43.0	107	10805	61.4	9.7	104	24428	62.3	21.9	105	35370	65.2	31.8	110
DIVORCED/SEPARATED/WIDOWED	35268	13102	17.3	37.1	92	2741	15.6	7.8	83	6456	16.5	18.3	88	8949	16.5	25.4	88
PARENTS	61860	25247	33.4	40.8	101	7212	41.0	11.7	124	13673	34.9	22.1	106	19246	35.5	31.1	108
WHITE	159985	66228	87.6	41.4	103	15672	89.1	9.8	105	34109	87.0	21.3	102	48609	89.6	30.4	105
BLACK	21570	7641	10.1	35.4	88	1498	8.5	6.9	74	4210	10.7	19.5	93	4489	8.3	20.8	72
OTHER	6191	1692	2.2	27.3	68	*425	2.4	6.9	73	883	2.3	14.3	68	1126	2.1	18.2	63
NORTHEAST-CENSUS	38611	15284	20.2	39.6	98	2910	16.5	7.5	80	9925	25.3	25.7	123	9313	17.2	24.1	84
MIDWEST	45021	19057	25.2	42.3	105	4816	27.4	10.7	114	8534	21.8	19.0	91	15126	27.9	33.6	116
SOUTH	65246	26467	35.0	40.6	101	6643	37.8	10.2	109	14308	36.5	21.9	105	17939	33.1	27.5	95
WEST	38869	14753	19.5	38.0	94	3225	18.3	8.3	89	6437	16.4	16.6	79	11847	21.8	30.5	106
COUNTY SIZE A	76945	30518	40.4	39.7	99	6912	39.3	9.0	96	16755	42.7	21.8	104	21490	39.6	27.9	97
COUNTY SIZE B	55516	22398	29.6	40.3	100	5374	30.5	9.7	103	11277	28.8	20.3	97	16400	30.2	29.5	102
COUNTY SIZE C	27293	10529	13.9	38.6	96	2179	12.4	8.0	85	5337	13.6	19.6	94	7495	13.8	27.5	95
COUNTY SIZE D	27993	12116	16.0	43.3	108	3128	17.8	11.2	119	5833	14.9	20.8	100	8840	16.3	31.6	109
METRO CENTRAL CITY	58084	21737	28.8	37.4	93	5137	29.2	8.8	94	11138	28.4	19.2	92	15357	28.3	26.4	92
METRO SUBURBAN	88940	38779	48.7	41.4	103	8281	47.1	9.3	99	19678	50.2	22.1	106	26464	48.8	29.8	103
NON METRO	40722	17045	22.6	41.9	104	4176	23.7	10.3	109	8387	21.4	20.6	99	12404	22.9	30.5	105
TOP 5 ADI'S	42410	16497	21.8	38.9	97	3515	20.0	8.3	88	9181	23.4	21.6	104	11461	21.1	27.0	94
TOP 10 ADI'S	59256	23503	31.1	39.7	99	5081	28.9	8.6	91	13461	34.3	22.7	109	16482	30.4	27.8	96
TOP 20 ADI'S	81977	32998	43.7	40.3	100	6796	38.6	8.3	88	18085	46.1	22.1	106	23435	43.2	28.6	99
HSHLD. INC. $75,000 OR MORE	26237	11955	15.8	45.5	113	2653	15.1	10.1	108	6124	15.6	23.3	112	8908	16.4	33.9	117
$60,000 OR MORE	43694	19853	26.3	45.4	113	4648	26.4	10.6	114	10565	26.9	24.2	116	14963	27.6	34.2	119
$50,000 OR MORE	61638	27026	35.8	43.8	109	6496	36.9	10.5	112	14425	36.8	23.4	112	20580	38.0	33.4	116
$40,000 OR MORE	83714	36892	48.8	44.1	109	8955	50.9	10.7	114	19610	50.0	23.4	112	28083	51.8	33.5	116
$30,000 OR MORE	110173	47291	62.5	42.9	107	11715	66.6	10.6	113	24904	63.5	22.6	108	35562	65.6	32.3	112
$30,000 - $39,999	26459	10399	13.8	39.3	98	2761	15.7	10.4	111	5294	13.5	20.0	96	7479	13.8	28.3	98
$20,000 - $29,999	28910	10953	14.5	37.9	94	2257	12.8	7.8	83	5452	13.9	18.9	90	7615	14.0	26.3	91
$10,000 - $19,999	29666	10537	13.9	35.5	88	1932	11.0	6.5	70	5334	13.6	18.0	86	6959	12.8	23.5	81
UNDER $10,000	18998	6780	9.0	35.7	89	1690	9.6	8.9	95	3513	9.0	18.5	89	4088	7.5	21.5	75
HOUSEHOLD OF 1 PERSON	23989	8726	11.5	36.4	90	1813	10.3	7.6	81	4531	11.6	18.9	90	5603	10.3	23.4	81
2 PEOPLE	61625	25763	34.1	41.8	104	4984	28.3	8.1	86	12335	31.5	20.0	96	18462	34.0	30.0	104
3 OR 4 PEOPLE	75459	30353	40.2	40.2	100	7808	44.4	10.3	110	16726	42.7	22.2	106	22156	40.9	29.4	102
5 OR MORE PEOPLE	26674	10720	14.2	40.2	100	2989	17.0	11.2	120	5610	14.3	21.0	101	8003	14.8	30.0	104
NO CHILD IN HSHLD	113318	44964	59.5	39.7	99	8896	50.6	7.9	84	22824	58.2	20.1	96	31455	58.0	27.8	96
CHILD(REN) UNDER 2 YEARS	13676	5607	7.4	41.0	102	1524	8.7	11.1	119	2988	7.6	21.8	105	3991	7.4	29.2	101
2 - 5 YEARS	27475	11040	14.6	40.2	100	3039	17.3	11.1	118	6209	15.8	22.6	108	7955	14.7	29.0	100
6 - 11 YEARS	35656	13969	18.5	39.2	97	4036	22.9	11.3	121	7479	19.1	21.0	100	10632	19.6	29.8	103
12 - 17 YEARS	34050	14120	18.7	41.5	103	4270	24.3	12.5	134	7345	18.7	21.6	103	10938	20.2	32.1	111
RESIDENCE OWNED	129490	55699	73.7	43.0	107	12167	69.2	9.4	100	28441	72.5	22.0	105	40885	75.4	31.6	109
VALUE: $70,000 OR MORE	80885	36033	47.7	44.5	111	7678	43.6	9.5	101	18974	48.4	23.5	112	26768	49.4	33.1	115
VALUE: UNDER $70,000	48605	19666	26.0	40.5	101	4489	25.5	9.2	99	9467	24.1	19.5	93	14117	26.0	29.0	101
RESIDENCE RENTED	52590	17799	23.6	33.8	84	4934	28.0	9.4	100	9591	24.5	18.2	87	12124	22.4	23.1	80

SIMMONS MARKET RESEARCH BUREAU, INC. 1994

PROJECTION RELATIVELY UNSTABLE BECAUSE OF SAMPLE BASE-USE WITH CAUTION
*NUMBER OF CASES TOO SMALL FOR RELIABILITY-SHOWN FOR CONSISTENCY ONLY

Problems

Shown here is a small portion of a Simmons page.

CAFFEINATED INSTANT & FREEZE-DRIED COFFEE: ALL USERS, USERS ON AVERAGE DAY AND TYPES (PRINCIPAL SHOPPERS)

	TOTAL U.S. '000	ALL USERS A '000	B % DOWN	C % ACROSS	D INDX	HEAVY USERS FOUR OR MORE A '000	B % DOWN	C % ACROSS	D INDX
TOTAL PRINCIPAL SHOPPERS	115901	26832	100.0	23.2	100	8223	100.0	7.1	100
18 - 24	8751	1840	6.9	21.0	91	617			
25 - 34	25859	5171	19.3	20.0	86	1968			
35 - 44	26564	6172	23.0	23.2	100	1899			
45 - 54	19076	4322	16.1	22.7	98	766			
55 - 64	14120	3504	13.1	24.8	107	1264			
65 OR OLDER	21532	5824	21.7	27.0	117	1708			

1. Calculate the missing percentages and index numbers for heavy users in the data above. Record your answers in the spaces below.

Demographic group	Column B %	Column C %	Index
Adults aged			
18–24	______	______	______
25–34	______	______	______
35–44	______	______	______
45–54	______	______	______
55–64	______	______	______
65 or older	______	______	______

Show your calculations for female homemakers aged 25–34.

2. Given the data provided in Exhibit 3–1, and assuming heavy users are key targets, which age groups are the most important? Use only the age groups 18–24 through 65 or older at the top of the page. Rank each group from most important (1) to least important (6).

Rank	Demographic age segment
1	______________________
2	______________________
3	______________________
4	______________________
5	______________________
6	______________________

3. Looking at the household size data for heavy users in Exhibit 3–1, what do the data indicate?

   Looking at the data on the presence of children in the household, what conclusion can be drawn?

4. Again, looking at Exhibit 3–1, is there a relationship between heavy use of diet or sugar free cola and household income? What is that relationship?

Assignment 4

Analyzing Product Usage Data of Media Audiences

Objective: To help you understand and use product usage data reported by major syndicated research sources for specific media vehicle audiences. When these data exist and are reliable for your product, they provide the most direct method of evaluating alternative media against reach of key user groups.

Discussion

Simmons and MRI report product usage by media type and also by specific vehicles. MRI data for magazines are shown in Exhibit 4–1. Usage data for radio and TV dayparts, radio formats, and networks and cable networks are shown in Exhibit 4–2.

The media planner usually evaluates product usage data to define key target demographic groups and then selects media that most effectively and efficiently reach those demographic targets. However, planners could use product usage data reported for the specific media types and vehicles, which enable them to compare heavy users versus light users reached by the media. It is desirable to review both types of usage information when they are available.

Media vehicles frequently publish both types of data, often based on their own research. However, it is usually easier and more reliable to use the data reported by sources like Simmons and MRI, because usage data for demographic groups and all media reported by these sources are obtained from the same sample of respondents.

Exhibits 4–1 and 4–2 are read much the same as Exhibit 1–1 discussed in Assignment 1 of this workbook. In Exhibit 4–1, the data would be interpreted as follows:

Top row:	There are 85,337,000 female homemakers in the United States (at the time of the survey).
Column A:	77,468,000 of the 85.3 million use paper towels.
Column B:	All users (77,468,000) are equal to 100 percent.
Column C:	All users represent 90.8 percent of all U.S. adults.
Column D:	All users also represent a 100 index number.
Second row:	For *American Baby,* there are 3,623,000 female homemakers who are readers of that magazine.
Column A:	3,298,000 readers of *American Baby* are users of paper towels.

Exhibit 4–1 MRI: Paper Towels Users (Female Homemakers)—Magazines

BASE: FEMALE HOMEMAKERS	TOTAL U.S. '000	ALL A '000	ALL B % DOWN	ALL C % ACROSS	ALL D INDEX	HEAVY (MORE THAN 4) A '000	HEAVY B % DOWN	HEAVY C % ACROSS	HEAVY D INDEX	MEDIUM (3 - 4) A '000	MEDIUM B % DOWN	MEDIUM C % ACROSS	MEDIUM D INDEX	LIGHT (LESS THAN 3) A '000	LIGHT B % DOWN	LIGHT C % ACROSS	LIGHT D INDEX
						ROLLS/LAST 30 DAYS											
All Female Homemakers	85337	77468	100.0	90.8	100	18114	100.0	21.2	100	25436	100.0	29.8	100	33918	100.0	39.7	100
American Baby	3623	3298	4.3	91.0	100	806	4.4	22.2	105	1195	4.7	33.0	111	1297	3.8	35.8	90
American Health	2787	2542	3.3	91.2	100	726	4.0	26.0	123	942	3.7	33.8	113	874	2.6	31.4	79
American Hunter	652	628	.8	96.3	106	•92	.5	14.1	66	•272	1.1	41.7	140	•264	.8	40.5	102
American Legion	1468	1394	1.8	95.0	105	•338	1.9	23.0	108	•474	1.9	32.3	108	583	1.7	39.7	100
American Rifleman	787	758	1.0	96.3	106	•150	.8	19.1	90	•291	1.1	37.0	124	•317	.9	40.3	101
American Way	466	•386	.5	82.8	91	•33	.2	7.1	33	•112	.4	24.0	81	•241	.7	51.7	130
American Way/SW Spirit (Gr)	608	528	.7	86.8	96	•48	.3	7.9	37	•177	.7	29.1	98	•304	.9	50.0	126
Architectural Digest	1841	1561	2.0	84.8	93	•367	2.0	19.9	94	613	2.4	33.3	112	582	1.7	31.6	80
Atlantic	523	437	.6	83.6	92	•100	.6	19.1	90	•164	.6	31.4	105	•173	.5	33.1	83
Audubon	999	928	1.2	92.9	102	•182	1.0	18.2	86	•217	.9	21.7	73	529	1.6	53.0	133
Baby Talk	2480	2184	2.8	88.1	97	•567	3.1	22.9	108	764	3.0	30.8	103	853	2.5	34.4	87
Barron's	•252	•176	.2	-	-	•31	.2	-	-	•34	.1	-	-	•110	.3	-	-
Bassmaster	•449	•400	.5	-	-	•102	.6	-	-	•166	.7	-	-	•133	.4	-	-
Better Homes & Gardens	23288	21138	27.3	90.8	100	5084	28.1	21.8	103	7398	29.1	31.8	107	8657	25.5	37.2	94
BHG/LHJ Combo (Gr)	38258	34922	45.1	91.3	101	8589	47.4	22.5	106	12069	47.4	31.5	106	14264	42.1	37.3	94
Black Enterprise	1206	1129	1.5	93.6	103	•269	1.5	22.3	105	•302	1.2	25.0	84	•558	1.6	46.3	116
Bon Appetit	3277	3006	3.9	91.7	101	706	3.9	21.5	101	985	3.9	30.1	101	1314	3.9	40.1	101
Bridal Guide	1750	1554	2.0	88.8	98	•485	2.7	27.7	131	•432	1.7	24.7	83	636	1.9	36.3	91
Bride's and Your New Home	1754	1595	2.1	90.9	100	•444	2.5	25.3	119	514	2.0	29.3	98	637	1.9	36.3	91
Business Week	1431	1309	1.7	91.5	101	•302	1.7	21.1	99	416	1.6	29.1	98	591	1.7	41.3	104
Byte	•299	•277	.4	-	-	•79	.4	-	-	•70	.3	-	-	•128	.4	-	-
Cable Guide/Total TV (Gr)	7391	6692	8.6	90.5	100	1744	9.6	23.6	111	2638	10.4	35.7	120	2310	6.8	31.3	79
Car and Driver	637	533	.7	83.7	92	•135	.7	21.2	100	•161	.6	25.3	85	•236	.7	37.0	93
Car Craft	•215	•203	.3	-	-	•8	-	-	-	•57	.2	-	-	•138	.4	-	-
Colonial Homes	1965	1811	2.3	92.2	102	•451	2.5	23.0	108	623	2.4	31.7	106	736	2.2	37.5	94
Compute	•266	•229	.3	-	-	•25	.1	-	-	•68	.3	-	-	•137	.4	-	-
Conde Nast Select (Gr)	33440	30043	38.8	89.8	99	6977	38.5	20.9	98	10971	43.1	32.8	110	12096	35.7	36.2	91
Conde Nast Traveler	905	763	1.0	84.3	93	•144	.8	15.9	75	•259	1.0	28.6	96	360	1.1	39.8	100
Consumers Digest	2503	2312	3.0	92.4	102	518	2.9	20.7	97	731	2.9	29.2	98	1063	3.1	42.5	107
Cooking Light	2588	2289	3.0	88.4	97	635	3.5	24.5	116	694	2.7	26.8	90	960	2.8	37.1	93
Cosmopolitan	10414	9386	12.1	90.1	99	2128	11.7	20.4	96	3170	12.5	30.4	102	4088	12.1	39.3	99
Country Home	5708	5243	6.8	91.9	101	1246	6.9	21.8	103	1909	7.5	33.4	112	2088	6.2	36.6	92
Country Living	8187	7657	9.9	93.5	103	1938	10.7	23.7	112	2724	10.7	33.3	112	2995	8.8	36.6	92
Country Music	2599	2360	3.0	90.8	100	713	3.9	27.4	129	808	3.2	31.1	104	839	2.5	32.3	81
Delta's SKY Magazine	544	488	.6	89.7	99	•65	.4	11.9	56	•159	.6	29.2	98	•264	.8	48.5	122
Discover	1785	1649	2.1	92.4	102	•408	2.3	22.9	108	493	1.9	27.6	93	747	2.2	41.8	105
Disney Channel Magazine	3191	2936	3.8	92.0	101	900	5.0	28.2	133	1001	3.9	31.4	105	1035	3.1	32.4	82
Easyriders	•431	•416	.5	-	-	•108	.6	-	-	•141	.6	-	-	•167	.5	-	-
Ebony	5851	5154	6.7	88.1	97	1237	6.8	21.1	100	1549	6.1	26.5	89	2369	7.0	40.5	102
Elle	2413	2086	2.7	86.4	95	640	3.5	26.5	125	687	2.7	28.5	96	760	2.2	31.5	79
Endless Vacation	682	637	.8	93.4	103	•101	.6	14.8	70	•197	.8	28.9	97	•339	1.0	49.7	125
Entertainment Weekly	1953	1725	2.2	88.3	97	•387	2.1	19.8	93	•569	2.2	29.1	98	768	2.3	39.3	99
Entrepreneur	334	327	.4	97.9	108	•91	.5	27.2	128	•94	.4	28.1	94	•143	.4	42.8	108
Episodes	1552	1321	1.7	85.1	94	•445	2.5	28.7	135	•360	1.4	23.2	78	516	1.5	33.2	84
Esquire	1000	883	1.1	88.3	97	•172	.9	17.2	81	•317	1.2	31.7	106	•394	1.2	39.4	99
Essence	3515	3151	4.1	89.6	99	708	3.9	20.1	95	993	3.9	28.3	95	1451	4.3	41.3	104
Family Circle	22065	20203	26.1	91.6	101	5253	29.0	23.8	112	7106	27.9	32.2	108	7844	23.1	35.5	89
Family Circle/McCall's (Gr)	36509	33460	43.2	91.6	101	8539	47.1	23.4	110	11833	46.5	32.4	109	13088	38.6	35.8	90
Family Handyman	1232	1188	1.5	96.4	106	•299	1.7	24.3	114	•437	1.7	35.5	119	453	1.3	36.8	93
Field & Stream	3107	2878	3.7	92.6	102	814	4.5	26.2	123	1022	4.0	32.9	110	1042	3.1	33.5	84
First For Women	4256	3766	4.9	88.5	97	1063	5.9	25.0	118	1313	5.2	30.9	104	1391	4.1	32.7	82
Flower & Garden	2658	2321	3.0	87.3	96	659	3.6	24.8	117	744	2.9	28.0	94	918	2.7	34.5	87
Flower & Grdn/Workbench (Gr)	3647	3246	4.2	89.0	98	936	5.2	25.7	121	1048	4.1	28.7	96	1262	3.7	34.6	87
Food & Wine	1626	1507	1.9	92.7	102	•406	2.2	25.0	118	495	1.9	30.4	102	606	1.8	37.3	94
Forbes	1222	1126	1.5	92.1	102	•327	1.8	26.8	126	•377	1.5	30.9	104	422	1.2	34.5	87
Fortune	1029	881	1.1	85.6	94	•191	1.1	18.6	87	•264	1.0	25.7	86	426	1.3	41.4	104
4 Wheel & Off Road	•236	•176	.2	-	-	•47	.3	-	-	•61	.2	-	-	•68	.2	-	-
Four Wheeler	•295	•251	.3	-	-	•28	.2	-	-	•109	.4	-	-	•114	.3	-	-
FW/Financial World	•332	•288	.4	-	-	•78	.4	-	-	•81	.3	-	-	•128	.4	-	-
Glamour	7642	6880	8.9	90.0	99	1670	9.2	21.9	103	2618	10.3	34.3	115	2593	7.6	33.9	85
Golf Digest	1134	1045	1.3	92.2	102	•250	1.4	22.0	104	•378	1.5	33.3	112	417	1.2	36.8	93
Golf Digest/Tennis (Gr)	1599	1451	1.9	90.7	100	•387	2.1	24.2	114	478	1.9	29.9	100	586	1.7	36.6	92
Golf Illustrated	622	550	.7	88.4	97	•200	1.1	32.2	151	•143	.6	23.0	77	•206	.6	33.1	83
Golf Magazine	892	805	1.0	90.2	99	•210	1.2	23.5	111	•328	1.3	36.8	123	•267	.8	29.9	75
Good Housekeeping	20746	19075	24.6	91.9	101	4848	26.8	23.4	110	6566	25.8	31.6	106	7661	22.6	36.9	93
Gourmet	2807	2541	3.3	90.5	100	736	4.1	26.2	124	808	3.2	28.8	97	997	2.9	35.5	89
GQ (Gentlemen's Quarterly)	1329	1211	1.6	91.1	100	•194	1.1	14.6	69	594	2.3	44.7	150	422	1.2	31.8	80
Guns & Ammo	501	•454	.6	90.6	100	•128	.7	25.5	120	•174	.7	34.7	117	•152	.4	30.3	76
Hachette Magazine Ntwk (Gr)	28957	26293	33.9	90.8	100	6921	38.2	23.9	113	8950	35.2	30.9	104	10419	30.7	36.0	91
Hachette Men's Package (Gr)	3365	2892	3.7	85.9	95	654	3.6	19.4	92	1088	4.3	32.3	108	1148	3.4	34.1	86
Harper's Bazaar	2264	1966	2.5	86.8	96	602	3.3	26.6	125	759	3.0	33.5	112	605	1.8	26.7	67
Hearst Combo Power (Gr)	31339	28761	37.1	91.8	101	7182	39.6	22.9	108	9921	39.0	31.7	106	11658	34.4	37.2	94
Hearst Homes (Gr)	17440	16087	20.8	92.2	102	4065	22.4	23.3	110	5879	23.1	33.7	113	6142	18.1	35.2	89
Hemispheres (United)	491	463	.6	94.3	104	•82	.5	16.7	79	•104	.4	21.2	71	•276	.8	56.2	141
HG (House & Garden)	3702	3377	4.4	91.2	100	875	4.8	23.6	111	1095	4.3	29.6	99	1407	4.1	38.0	96
Home	2401	2073	2.7	86.3	95	499	2.8	20.8	98	805	3.2	33.5	112	769	2.3	32.0	81
Home Mechanix	•421	•369	.5	-	-	•89	.5	-	-	•144	.6	-	-	•136	.4	-	-
Hot Rod	729	•628	.8	86.1	95	•101	.6	13.9	65	•226	.9	31.0	104	•302	.9	41.4	104
House Beautiful	4910	4478	5.8	91.2	100	1214	6.7	24.7	116	1706	6.7	34.7	117	1558	4.6	31.7	80
Hunting	•495	•395	.5	-	-	•113	.6	-	-	•151	.6	-	-	•130	.4	-	-
Inc.	675	617	.8	91.4	101	•132	.7	19.6	92	•230	.9	34.1	114	•255	.8	37.8	95
Inside Sports	•342	•262	.3	-	-	•74	.4	-	-	•38	.1	-	-	•150	.4	-	-
Jet	3923	3473	4.5	88.5	98	915	5.1	23.3	110	1080	4.2	27.5	92	1479	4.4	37.7	95
Kiplinger's Personal Finance	1125	1072	1.4	95.3	105	•250	1.4	22.2	105	•374	1.5	33.2	112	449	1.3	39.9	100
Ladies' Home Journal	14970	13784	17.8	92.1	101	3505	19.3	23.4	110	4671	18.4	31.2	105	5607	16.5	37.5	94
Lear's	835	797	1.0	95.4	105	•148	.8	17.7	84	•246	1.0	29.5	99	403	1.2	48.3	121
Life	7565	6775	8.7	89.6	99	1561	8.6	20.6	97	2341	9.2	30.9	104	2873	8.5	38.0	96
Mademoiselle	3665	3330	4.3	90.9	100	727	4.0	19.8	93	1376	5.4	37.5	126	1227	3.6	33.5	84
McCall's	14444	13257	17.1	91.8	101	3286	18.1	22.7	107	4727	18.6	32.7	110	5244	15.5	36.3	91
Men's Fitness	•110	•107	.1	-	-	•27	.1	-	-	•57	.2	-	-	•22	.1	-	-
Men's Health	•365	•349	.5	-	-	•127	.7	-	-	•63	.2	-	-	•159	.5	-	-
Metropolitan Home	1453	1320	1.7	90.8	100	•154	.9	10.6	50	636	2.5	43.8	147	529	1.6	36.4	92
Metro-Puck Comics Network	20822	19028	24.6	91.4	101	4637	25.6	22.3	105	5984	23.5	28.7	96	8407	24.8	40.4	102

Spring

Exhibit 4–1 (continued)

BASE: FEMALE HOMEMAKERS	TOTAL U.S. '000	ALL A '000	ALL B % DOWN	ALL C % ACROSS	ALL D INDEX	HEAVY (MORE THAN 4) A '000	HEAVY B % DOWN	HEAVY C % ACROSS	HEAVY D INDEX	MEDIUM (3 - 4) A '000	MEDIUM B % DOWN	MEDIUM C % ACROSS	MEDIUM D INDEX	LIGHT (LESS THAN 3) A '000	LIGHT B % DOWN	LIGHT C % ACROSS	LIGHT D INDEX
						ROLLS/LAST 30 DAYS											
All Female Homemakers	85337	77468	100.0	90.8	100	18114	100.0	21.2	100	25436	100.0	29.8	100	33918	100.0	39.7	100
Midwest Living	1467	1407	1.8	95.9	106	•315	1.7	21.5	101	512	2.0	34.9	117	580	1.7	39.5	99
Mirabella	1485	1304	1.7	87.8	97	•267	1.5	18.0	85	503	2.0	33.9	114	535	1.6	36.0	91
Modern Bride	2221	1917	2.5	86.3	95	•502	2.8	22.6	106	668	2.6	30.1	101	747	2.2	33.6	85
Modern Maturity	20114	18676	24.1	92.9	102	4135	22.8	20.6	97	6076	23.9	30.2	101	8465	25.0	42.1	106
Money	3229	2984	3.9	92.4	102	663	3.7	20.5	97	963	3.8	29.8	100	1358	4.0	42.1	106
Motor Trend	•386	•313	.4	-	-	•67	.4	-	-	•131	.5	-	-	•114	.3	-	-
Muscle & Fitness	1230	1122	1.4	91.2	100	•235	1.3	19.1	90	•314	1.2	25.5	86	572	1.7	46.5	117
National Enquirer	11110	9955	12.9	89.6	99	2596	14.3	23.4	110	3388	13.3	30.5	102	3970	11.7	35.7	90
National Geographic	12740	11605	15.0	91.1	100	2706	14.9	21.2	100	3737	14.7	29.3	98	5162	15.2	40.5	102
National Geographic Traveler	1378	1211	1.6	87.9	97	•387	2.1	28.1	132	•324	1.3	23.5	79	501	1.5	36.4	91
Natural History	648	588	.8	90.7	100	•134	.7	20.7	97	•158	.6	24.4	82	•296	.9	45.7	115
Newsweek	7892	7154	9.2	90.6	100	1627	9.0	20.6	97	2490	9.8	31.6	106	3037	9.0	38.5	97
New Woman	3885	3464	4.5	89.2	98	1021	5.6	26.3	124	1110	4.4	28.6	96	1333	3.9	34.3	86
New York Magazine	733	581	.7	79.3	87	•146	.8	19.9	94	•144	.6	19.6	66	•291	.9	39.7	100
New York Times (Daily)	1256	993	1.3	79.1	87	•215	1.2	17.1	81	323	1.3	25.7	86	455	1.3	36.2	91
New York Times Magazine	1937	1608	2.1	83.0	91	355	2.0	18.3	86	537	2.1	27.7	93	717	2.1	37.0	93
The New Yorker	1206	1077	1.4	89.3	98	•178	1.0	14.8	70	444	1.7	36.8	124	455	1.3	37.7	95
North American Fisherman	583	•523	.7	89.7	99	•125	.7	21.4	101	•199	.8	34.1	115	•199	.6	34.1	86
North American Hunter	•457	•450	.6	-	-	•164	.9	-	-	•201	.8	-	-	•85	.3	-	-
Omni	908	819	1.1	90.2	99	•173	1.0	19.1	90	•267	1.0	29.4	99	•379	1.1	41.7	105
Organic Gardening	2076	1859	2.4	89.5	99	•373	2.1	18.0	85	900	3.5	43.4	145	586	1.7	28.2	71
Outdoor Life	1446	1277	1.6	88.3	97	•373	2.1	25.8	122	•389	1.5	26.9	90	•515	1.5	35.6	90
Parade	33029	30511	39.4	92.4	102	7772	42.9	23.5	111	10344	40.7	31.3	105	12395	36.5	37.5	94
Parenting	4166	3599	4.6	86.4	95	975	5.4	23.4	110	1110	4.4	26.6	89	1514	4.5	36.3	91
Parents' Magazine	7886	7030	9.1	89.1	98	1865	10.3	23.6	111	2360	9.3	29.9	100	2806	8.3	35.6	90
PC Computing	1020	913	1.2	89.5	99	•202	1.1	19.8	93	•391	1.5	38.3	129	•320	.9	31.4	79
PC Magazine	937	900	1.2	96.1	106	•242	1.3	25.8	122	•229	.9	24.4	82	429	1.3	45.8	115
PC World	825	686	.9	83.2	92	•127	.7	15.4	73	•166	.7	20.1	68	393	1.2	47.6	120
Penthouse	•438	•425	.5	-	-	•148	.8	-	-	•82	.3	-	-	•196	.6	-	-
Penton Executive Netwk (Gr)	3197	2844	3.7	89.0	98	796	4.4	24.9	117	809	3.2	25.3	85	1241	3.7	38.8	98
People	20232	18263	23.6	90.3	99	4607	25.4	22.8	107	5924	23.3	29.3	98	7732	22.8	38.2	96
Petersen Magazine Netwk (Gr)	4579	3940	5.1	86.0	95	924	5.1	20.2	95	1493	5.9	32.6	109	1522	4.5	33.2	84
Playboy	1812	1592	2.1	87.9	97	•332	1.8	18.3	86	565	2.2	31.2	105	695	2.0	38.4	97
Popular Hot Rodding	•327	•238	.3	-	-	•77	.4	-	-	•89	.3	-	-	•72	.2	-	-
Popular Mechanics	1151	1054	1.4	91.6	101	•424	2.3	36.8	174	•367	1.4	31.9	107	•263	.8	22.8	57
Popular Science	1089	1015	1.3	93.2	103	•305	1.7	28.0	132	•408	1.6	37.5	126	•303	.9	27.8	70
Practical Homeowner	710	593	.8	83.5	92	•100	.6	14.1	66	•281	1.1	39.6	133	•212	.6	29.9	75
Premiere	649	563	.7	86.7	96	•107	.6	16.5	78	•205	.8	31.6	106	•251	.7	38.7	97
Prevention	6686	6139	7.9	91.8	101	1527	8.4	22.8	108	1890	7.4	28.3	95	2723	8.0	40.7	102
Reader's Digest	26147	24126	31.1	92.3	102	5816	32.1	22.2	105	7957	31.3	30.4	102	10353	30.5	39.6	100
Redbook	10593	9686	12.5	91.4	101	2334	12.9	22.0	104	3355	13.2	31.7	106	3997	11.8	37.7	95
Road & Track	•451	•340	.4	-	-	•73	.4	-	-	•136	.5	-	-	•131	.4	-	-
Rodale Active Network (Gr)	1739	1477	1.9	84.9	94	425	2.3	24.4	115	•516	2.0	29.7	100	536	1.6	30.8	78
Rolling Stone	2091	1881	2.4	90.0	99	•523	2.9	25.0	118	662	2.6	31.7	106	696	2.1	33.3	84
Runner's World	571	490	.6	85.8	95	•101	.6	17.7	83	•235	.9	41.2	138	•154	.5	27.0	68
Saturday Evening Post	2093	1899	2.5	90.7	100	•556	3.1	26.6	125	740	2.9	35.4	119	603	1.8	28.8	72
Scientific American	599	569	.7	95.0	105	•154	.9	25.7	121	•169	.7	28.2	95	•247	.7	41.2	104
Self	2601	2351	3.0	90.4	100	422	2.3	16.2	76	839	3.3	32.3	108	1090	3.2	41.9	105
Sesame Street Magazine	4562	4090	5.3	89.7	99	1193	6.6	26.2	123	1406	5.5	30.8	103	1491	4.4	32.7	82
Seventeen	3347	2982	3.8	89.1	98	1100	6.1	32.9	155	1144	4.5	34.2	115	738	2.2	22.0	55
Shape	1978	1735	2.2	87.7	97	•378	2.1	19.1	90	578	2.3	29.2	98	778	2.3	39.3	99
Ski	541	487	.6	90.0	99	•113	.6	20.9	98	•128	.5	23.7	79	•246	.7	45.5	114
Skiing	371	•339	.4	91.4	101	•45	.2	12.1	57	•122	.5	32.9	110	•171	.5	46.1	116
Smithsonian	3604	3286	4.2	91.2	100	839	4.6	23.3	110	1006	4.0	27.9	94	1442	4.3	40.0	101
Soap Opera Digest	5084	4684	6.0	92.1	101	1371	7.6	27.0	127	1517	6.0	29.8	100	1796	5.3	35.3	89
Soap Opera Weekly	3337	3117	4.0	93.4	103	1001	5.5	30.0	141	1166	4.6	34.9	117	950	2.8	28.5	72
Southern Living	7889	7399	9.6	93.8	103	2064	11.4	26.2	123	2647	10.4	33.6	113	2689	7.9	34.1	86
Spin	•251	•215	.3	-	-	•28	.2	-	-	•68	.3	-	-	•119	.4	-	-
Sport	•472	•351	.5	-	-	•123	.7	-	-	•76	.3	-	-	•151	.4	-	-
The Sporting News	625	551	.7	88.2	97	•123	.7	19.7	93	•195	.8	31.2	105	•233	.7	37.3	94
Sports Afield	•538	•475	.6	-	-	•104	.6	-	-	•153	.6	-	-	•218	.6	-	-
Sports Illustrated	4423	3865	5.0	87.4	96	942	5.2	21.3	100	1455	5.7	32.9	110	1468	4.3	33.2	84
Star	6219	5643	7.3	90.7	100	1517	8.4	24.4	115	1797	7.1	28.9	97	2330	6.9	37.5	94
Sunday Mag/Net	14624	13143	17.0	89.9	99	3075	17.0	21.0	99	4224	16.6	28.9	97	5845	17.2	40.0	101
Sunset	2658	2382	3.1	89.6	99	•330	1.8	12.4	58	847	3.3	31.9	107	1204	3.5	45.3	114
Tennis	465	406	.5	87.3	96	•137	.8	29.5	139	•100	.4	21.5	72	•169	.5	36.3	91
Texas Monthly	904	852	1.1	94.2	104	•205	1.1	22.7	107	•295	1.2	32.6	109	352	1.0	38.9	98
Time	9223	8392	10.8	91.0	100	2061	11.4	22.3	105	2829	11.1	30.7	103	3502	10.3	38.0	96
Town & Country	1802	1697	2.2	94.2	104	•496	2.7	27.5	130	618	2.4	34.3	115	583	1.7	32.4	81
Travel & Leisure	1559	1436	1.9	92.1	101	•246	1.4	15.8	74	512	2.0	32.8	110	678	2.0	43.5	109
True Story	3481	3177	4.1	91.3	101	897	5.0	25.8	121	1107	4.4	31.8	107	1173	3.5	33.7	85
TV Guide	21868	19998	25.8	91.4	101	5288	29.2	24.2	114	6666	26.2	30.5	102	8044	23.7	36.8	93
USAir	883	767	1.0	86.9	96	•98	.5	11.1	52	•297	1.2	33.6	113	•372	1.1	42.1	106
U.S. News & World Report	3891	3571	4.6	91.8	101	746	4.1	19.2	90	1362	5.4	35.0	117	1463	4.3	37.6	95
Us	2470	2263	2.9	91.6	101	462	2.6	18.7	88	782	3.1	31.7	106	1020	3.0	41.3	104
USA Today	1454	1332	1.7	91.6	101	•311	1.7	21.4	101	441	1.7	30.3	102	579	1.7	39.8	100
USA Weekend	13573	12530	16.2	92.3	102	3193	17.6	23.5	111	4013	15.8	29.6	99	5324	15.7	39.2	99
Vanity Fair	2183	1934	2.5	88.6	98	441	2.4	20.2	95	732	2.9	33.5	112	762	2.2	34.9	88
Victoria	2378	2141	2.8	90.0	99	462	2.6	19.4	92	826	3.2	34.7	117	853	2.5	35.9	90
Vogue	6852	6061	7.8	88.5	97	1324	7.3	19.3	91	2136	8.4	31.2	105	2601	7.7	38.0	96
Walking Magazine	750	616	.8	82.1	90	•134	.7	17.9	84	•177	.7	23.6	79	•305	.9	40.7	102
Wall Street Journal	1172	1005	1.3	85.8	94	•161	.9	13.7	65	•315	1.2	26.9	90	529	1.6	45.1	114
Weight Watchers	3623	3243	4.2	89.5	99	915	5.1	25.3	119	1050	4.1	29.0	97	1278	3.8	35.3	89
Woman's Day	19325	17922	23.1	92.7	102	4974	27.5	25.7	121	5734	22.5	29.7	100	7213	21.3	37.3	94
Woman's World	5178	4633	6.0	89.5	99	1343	7.4	25.9	122	1490	5.9	28.8	97	1800	5.3	34.8	87
Workbasket	2468	2278	2.9	92.3	102	•612	3.4	24.8	117	635	2.5	25.7	86	1030	3.0	41.7	105
Workbench	989	925	1.2	93.5	103	•277	1.5	28.0	132	•304	1.2	30.7	103	•344	1.0	34.8	88
Working Mother	2588	2251	2.9	87.0	96	615	3.4	23.8	112	958	3.8	37.0	124	678	2.0	26.2	66
Working Woman	3383	3029	3.9	89.5	99	830	4.6	24.5	116	1067	4.2	31.5	106	1132	3.3	33.5	84
WWF Magazine	514	•473	.6	92.0	101	•183	1.0	35.6	168	•101	.4	19.6	66	•189	.6	36.8	93
Yankee	1434	1295	1.7	90.3	99	•315	1.7	22.0	103	429	1.7	29.9	100	551	1.6	38.4	97
YM	997	837	1.1	84.0	92	•250	1.4	25.1	118	•254	1.0	25.5	85	•333	1.0	33.4	84

Spring

Exhibit 4–2 MRI: Paper Towels Users (Female Homemakers)—Broadcast

		ALL				ROLLS/LAST 30 DAYS: HEAVY MORE THAN 4				MEDIUM 3 - 4				LIGHT LESS THAN 3			
BASE: FEMALE HOMEMAKERS	TOTAL U.S. '000	A '000	B % DOWN	C % ACROSS	D INDEX	A '000	B % DOWN	C % ACROSS	D INDEX	A '000	B % DOWN	C % ACROSS	D INDEX	A '000	B % DOWN	C % ACROSS	D INDEX
All Female Homemakers	85337	77468	100.0	90.8	100	18114	100.0	21.2	100	25436	100.0	29.8	100	33918	100.0	39.7	100
Quintile I - Radio	16542	14780	19.1	89.3	98	3598	19.9	21.8	102	5168	20.3	31.2	105	6015	17.7	36.4	91
Quintile II	16596	14836	19.2	89.4	98	3535	19.5	21.3	100	5075	20.0	30.6	103	6226	18.4	37.5	94
Quintile III	17395	16079	20.8	92.4	102	3683	20.3	21.2	100	5211	20.5	30.0	101	7184	21.2	41.3	104
Quintile IV	17590	16148	20.8	91.8	101	3902	21.5	22.2	105	5290	20.8	30.1	101	6955	20.5	39.5	99
Quintile V	17213	15625	20.2	90.8	100	3395	18.7	19.7	93	4692	18.4	27.3	91	7538	22.2	43.8	110
Quintile I - TV (Total)	17784	15896	20.5	89.4	98	3759	20.8	21.1	100	5387	21.2	30.3	102	6750	19.9	38.0	95
Quintile II	17517	15897	20.5	90.8	100	3566	19.7	20.4	96	5188	20.4	29.6	99	7143	21.1	40.8	103
Quintile III	17174	15683	20.2	91.3	101	3663	20.2	21.3	100	4980	19.6	29.0	97	7040	20.8	41.0	103
Quintile IV	16410	14900	19.2	90.8	100	3727	20.6	22.7	107	4600	18.1	28.0	94	6572	19.4	40.0	101
Quintile V	16452	15093	19.5	91.7	101	3399	18.8	20.7	97	5280	20.8	32.1	108	6414	18.9	39.0	98
Radio Wkday: 6-10:00 am Cume	48872	44346	57.2	90.7	100	10374	57.3	21.2	100	15073	59.3	30.8	103	18900	55.7	38.7	97
10:00 am - 3:00 pm	30743	27699	35.8	90.1	99	7015	38.7	22.8	107	9328	36.7	30.3	102	11356	33.5	36.9	93
3:00 pm - 7:00 pm	34106	31074	40.1	91.1	100	7426	41.0	21.8	103	10824	42.6	31.7	106	12823	37.8	37.6	95
7:00 pm - Midnight	12876	11476	14.8	89.1	98	2276	12.6	17.7	83	4036	15.9	31.3	105	5164	15.2	40.1	101
Radio Average Weekday Cume	66710	60678	78.3	91.0	100	14513	80.1	21.8	102	20329	79.9	30.5	102	25837	76.2	38.7	97
Radio Avg. Weekend Day Cume	53963	48932	63.2	90.7	100	11179	61.7	20.7	98	16248	63.9	30.1	101	21505	63.4	39.9	100
Radio Formats: Adult Contemp	17642	16152	20.8	91.6	101	3754	20.7	21.3	100	5320	20.9	30.2	101	7078	20.9	40.1	101
All News	3598	3221	4.2	89.5	99	746	4.1	20.7	98	982	3.9	27.3	92	1493	4.4	41.5	104
AOR/Progressive Rock	9687	8719	11.3	90.0	99	1654	9.1	17.1	80	2768	10.9	28.6	96	4296	12.7	44.3	112
Black	2293	1979	2.6	86.3	95	*616	3.4	26.9	127	*456	1.8	19.9	67	907	2.7	39.6	100
CHR/Rock	13057	11815	15.3	90.5	100	2848	15.7	21.8	103	3908	15.4	29.9	100	5059	14.9	38.7	97
Classic Rock	4177	3744	4.8	89.6	99	833	4.6	19.9	94	1171	4.6	28.0	94	1739	5.1	41.6	105
Classical	1848	1586	2.0	85.8	95	293	1.6	15.9	75	522	2.1	28.2	95	771	2.3	41.7	105
Country	18672	17411	22.5	93.2	103	3876	21.4	20.8	98	6041	23.7	32.4	109	7494	22.1	40.1	101
Easy Listening	1479	1325	1.7	89.6	99	*260	1.4	17.6	83	496	1.9	33.5	113	569	1.7	38.5	97
Full Service	1641	1444	1.9	88.0	97	315	1.7	19.2	90	354	1.4	21.6	72	774	2.3	47.2	119
Golden Oldies	8719	7970	10.3	91.4	101	1751	9.7	20.1	95	2518	9.9	28.9	97	3701	10.9	42.4	107
MOR/Nostalgia	3012	2748	3.5	91.2	101	592	3.3	19.7	93	901	3.5	29.9	100	1255	3.7	41.7	105
News/Talk	11476	10452	13.5	91.1	100	2203	12.2	19.2	90	3316	13.0	28.9	97	4932	14.5	43.0	108
Soft Contemporary	4067	3743	4.8	92.0	101	905	5.0	22.3	105	1379	5.4	33.9	114	1458	4.3	35.8	90
Urban Contemporary	5275	4511	5.8	85.5	94	1292	7.1	24.5	115	1411	5.5	26.7	90	1809	5.3	34.3	86
Radio Networks: ABC Excel	4096	3642	4.7	88.9	98	764	4.2	18.7	88	1061	4.2	25.9	87	1817	5.4	44.4	112
ABC Galaxy	3649	3293	4.3	90.2	99	574	3.2	15.7	74	1245	4.9	34.1	114	1475	4.3	40.4	102
ABC Genesis	7040	6226	8.0	88.4	97	1479	8.2	21.0	99	2242	8.8	31.8	107	2505	7.4	35.6	90
ABC Platinum	10459	9586	12.4	91.7	101	1802	9.9	17.2	81	3326	13.1	31.8	107	4459	13.1	42.6	107
ABC Prime	15465	14419	18.6	93.2	103	3345	18.5	21.6	102	4654	18.3	30.1	101	6419	18.9	41.5	104
AURN	1960	1611	2.1	82.2	91	*535	3.0	27.3	129	*381	1.5	19.4	65	694	2.0	35.4	89
CBS	6923	6325	8.2	91.4	101	1270	7.0	18.3	86	1862	7.3	26.9	90	3193	9.4	46.1	116
CBS Spectrum	10316	9309	12.0	90.2	99	2167	12.0	21.0	99	2693	10.6	26.1	88	4449	13.1	43.1	109
Concert Music Network	904	785	1.0	86.8	96	*135	.7	14.9	70	245	1.0	27.1	91	405	1.2	44.8	113
Internet	37022	33379	43.1	90.2	99	7873	43.5	21.3	100	10857	42.7	29.3	98	14650	43.2	39.6	100
Katz Radio Group	32884	29972	38.7	91.1	100	6582	36.3	20.0	94	9927	39.0	30.2	101	13463	39.7	40.9	103
Mutual	8865	8131	10.5	91.7	101	1801	9.9	20.3	96	2556	10.0	28.8	97	3774	11.1	42.6	107
NBC	5263	4886	6.3	92.8	102	1118	6.2	21.2	100	1672	6.6	31.8	107	2096	6.2	39.8	100
Power	4943	4380	5.7	88.6	98	1218	6.7	24.6	116	1626	6.4	32.9	110	1537	4.5	31.1	78
The Source	4535	3991	5.2	88.0	97	1043	5.8	23.0	108	1225	4.8	27.0	91	1723	5.1	38.0	96
STRZ Entertainment	1253	1110	1.4	88.6	98	*375	2.1	29.9	141	*187	.7	14.9	50	547	1.6	43.7	110
Super	7056	6423	8.3	91.0	100	1293	7.1	18.3	86	2200	8.6	31.2	105	2930	8.6	41.5	104
Ultimate	7308	6703	8.7	91.7	101	1472	8.1	20.1	95	2164	8.5	29.6	99	3068	9.0	42.0	106
Wall Street Journal Network	3183	2813	3.6	88.4	97	539	3.0	16.9	80	904	3.6	28.4	95	1370	4.0	43.0	108
Compuserve	*242	*230	.3	-	-	*78	.4	-	-	*30	.1	-	-	*122	.4	-	-
Prodigy	768	724	.9	94.3	104	*225	1.2	29.3	138	*250	1.0	32.6	109	*250	.7	32.6	82
TV Wkday Av 1/2 Hr:7-9:00am	9173	8204	10.6	89.4	99	2229	12.3	24.3	114	2569	10.1	28.0	94	3406	10.0	37.1	93
9:00 am - 4:00 pm	12812	11471	14.8	89.5	99	2935	16.2	22.9	108	3641	14.3	28.4	95	4895	14.4	38.2	96
4:00 pm - 7:30 pm	22495	20355	26.3	90.5	100	4465	24.6	19.8	94	6736	26.5	29.9	100	9154	27.0	40.7	102
7:30 pm - 8:00 pm	34099	30928	39.9	90.7	100	6902	38.1	20.2	95	9759	38.4	28.6	96	14267	42.1	41.8	105
8:00 pm - 11:00 pm	39148	35453	45.8	90.6	100	7910	43.7	20.2	95	11874	46.7	30.3	102	15669	46.2	40.0	101
11:00 pm - 11:30 pm	22744	20713	26.7	91.1	100	4661	25.7	20.5	97	6710	26.4	29.5	99	9342	27.5	41.1	103
11:30 pm - 1:00 am	6720	6035	7.8	89.8	99	1393	7.7	20.7	98	1928	7.6	28.7	96	2713	8.0	40.4	102
TV Prime Time Cume	70414	64006	82.6	90.9	100	15132	83.5	21.5	101	20975	82.5	29.8	100	27899	82.3	39.6	100
Program-Types:Comedy/Variety	10917	9942	12.8	91.1	100	2885	15.9	26.4	124	3101	12.2	28.4	95	3956	11.7	36.2	91
Early Eve. Netwk News - M-F	11348	10500	13.6	92.5	102	2772	15.3	24.4	115	3647	14.3	32.1	108	4081	12.0	36.0	90
Feature Films - Prime	8173	7678	9.9	93.9	103	2074	11.4	25.4	120	2538	10.0	31.1	104	3066	9.0	37.5	94
General Drama - Prime	7595	6992	9.0	92.1	101	1716	9.5	22.6	106	2367	9.3	31.2	105	2909	8.6	38.3	96
Police Docudrama	8713	8091	10.4	92.9	102	2428	13.4	27.9	131	2985	11.7	34.3	115	2678	7.9	30.7	77
Pvt Det/Susp/Myst/Pol.-Prime	13663	12786	16.5	93.6	103	3117	17.2	22.8	107	4500	17.7	32.9	110	5169	15.2	37.8	95
Situation Comedies - Prime	8921	8359	10.8	93.7	103	2006	11.1	22.5	106	2630	10.3	29.5	99	3722	11.0	41.7	105
Cable TV	49057	44986	58.1	91.7	101	11475	63.3	23.4	110	15202	59.8	31.0	104	18309	54.0	37.3	94
Pay TV	20698	19024	24.6	91.9	101	5209	28.8	25.2	119	6522	25.6	31.5	106	7293	21.5	35.2	89
Heavy Cable Viewing (15+ Hr)	22515	21032	27.1	93.4	103	5390	29.8	23.9	113	7127	28.0	31.7	106	8516	25.1	37.8	95
Cable Networks:																	
A&E (Arts & Entertainment)	11731	10798	13.9	92.0	101	2466	13.6	21.0	99	3829	15.1	32.6	110	4502	13.3	38.4	97
American Movie Classics	8785	8087	10.4	92.1	101	1804	10.0	20.5	97	2666	10.5	30.3	102	3616	10.7	41.2	104
BET (Black Entertainment TV)	2569	2278	2.9	88.7	98	590	3.3	23.0	108	732	2.9	28.5	96	956	2.8	37.2	94
CMT (Country Music TV)	4837	4513	5.8	93.3	103	1167	6.4	24.1	114	1564	6.1	32.3	108	1782	5.3	36.8	93
CNBC	3458	3192	4.1	92.3	102	827	4.6	23.9	113	1062	4.2	30.7	103	1303	3.8	37.7	95
CNN	28393	26117	33.7	92.0	101	6703	37.0	23.6	111	8971	35.3	31.6	106	10443	30.8	36.8	93
Comedy Central	3174	2930	3.8	92.3	102	755	4.2	23.8	112	1059	4.2	33.4	112	1116	3.3	35.2	88
Court TV	1249	1130	1.5	90.5	100	*239	1.3	19.1	90	*255	1.0	20.4	68	636	1.9	50.9	128
The Discovery Channel	18731	17093	22.1	91.3	101	4183	23.1	22.3	105	6073	23.9	32.4	109	6836	20.2	36.5	92
E! Entertainment Television	2451	2289	3.0	93.4	103	673	3.7	27.5	129	698	2.7	28.5	96	918	2.7	37.5	94
ESPN	13218	12344	15.9	93.4	103	3188	17.6	24.1	114	4195	16.5	31.7	106	4961	14.6	37.5	94
The Family Channel	15013	13892	17.9	92.5	102	3713	20.5	24.7	117	4868	19.1	32.4	109	5312	15.7	35.4	89
Headline News	10614	9907	12.8	93.3	103	2648	14.6	24.9	118	3404	13.4	32.1	108	3854	11.4	36.3	91
Lifetime	11785	10864	14.0	92.2	102	2649	14.6	22.5	106	3904	15.3	33.1	111	4311	12.7	36.6	92
MTV	8325	7423	9.6	89.2	98	2200	12.1	26.4	124	2218	8.7	25.6	89	3005	8.9	36.1	91
Nick at Nite	7496	6917	8.9	92.3	102	2005	11.1	26.7	126	2485	9.8	33.2	111	2427	7.2	32.4	81
Nickelodeon	9180	8328	10.8	90.7	100	2437	13.5	26.5	125	2868	11.3	31.2	105	3023	8.9	32.9	83
Nostalgia Channel	1079	984	1.3	91.2	100	*216	1.2	20.0	94	*337	1.3	31.2	105	*431	1.3	39.9	100
Prevue Guide Channel	4418	4154	5.4	94.0	104	1171	6.5	26.5	125	1645	6.5	37.2	125	1338	3.9	30.3	76
TBS	17159	15662	20.2	91.3	101	4334	23.9	25.3	119	5369	21.1	31.3	105	5958	17.6	34.7	87
The Travel Channel	1725	1616	2.1	93.7	103	*187	1.0	10.8	51	577	2.3	33.4	112	852	2.5	49.4	124
TLC: The Learning Channel	2364	2300	3.0	97.3	107	628	3.5	26.6	125	781	3.1	33.0	111	890	2.6	37.6	95
TNN: The Nashville Network	11299	10522	13.6	93.1	103	2654	14.7	23.5	111	3700	14.5	32.7	110	4168	12.3	36.9	93
TNT (Turner Network TV)	18209	16793	21.7	92.2	102	4642	25.6	25.5	120	5575	21.9	30.6	103	6576	19.4	36.1	91
USA Network	17169	15958	20.6	92.9	102	4017	22.2	23.4	110	5539	21.8	32.3	108	6402	18.9	37.3	94
VH-1	5352	4853	6.3	90.7	100	1429	7.9	26.7	126	1381	5.4	25.8	87	2043	6.0	38.2	96
The Weather Channel	18025	16795	21.7	93.2	103	4360	24.1	24.2	114	5887	23.1	32.7	110	6547	19.3	36.3	91

Spring

Column B: *American Baby* reaches 4.3 percent of all users of paper towels (3,298 ÷ 77,468 = .0425 or 4.3%).

Column C: 91.0 percent of *American Baby* readers are users of paper towels (3,298 ÷ 3,623 = .9102 or 91.0%).

Column D: *American Baby* readers are on a par with all female homemakers in the use of paper towels. The index number 100 is based on the percentage at the top of column C (91.0 ÷ 90.8 × 100 = 100.2 or 100).

Refer to *Advertising Media Planning,* 5th ed., by Sissors and Bumba, Chapter 0.

Problems

1. Review the usage data in Exhibit 4–1. If cost-per-thousand considerations are not a factor, which three would you recommend if reach of all paper towels users is your most important objective?

   How many and what percentage of heavy users would you reach with each of these publications?

2. Assume that all other considerations are comparable for each publication listed in Exhibit 4–1. Further assume that cost-per-thousand total audience is very close for all publications. Which three would you recommend if the objective is to achieve the lowest cost-per-thousand heavy users of paper towels?

How many and what percentage of heavy users would each of the above publications reach?

3. Reviewing the data in Exhibit 4–2, which three radio networks would you select to reach the greatest number of users of paper towels?

4. Assume that all other considerations are comparable for each radio network listed in Exhibit 4–2. Further assume that cost-per-thousand total audience is very close for all networks. Which three radio networks would you recommend if the objective is to achieve the lowest CPM for heavy users of paper towels?

How many and what percentage of users would each of the above networks reach?

5. Again using Exhibit 4–2, which network TV program type would deliver the highest reach of heavy users of paper towels?

   How many and what percentage of heavy users would it deliver?

6. Which cable TV network would deliver the highest reach of all users of paper towels?

   How many and what percentage of users would it deliver?

Assignment 5

Analyzing Market Data

Objective: To give you the opportunity to see and use marketing data that do not come from either MRI or Simmons. The data shown come from Nielsen's Food & Drug Audit or similar kinds of research. The problem of using the data is that of relating them to media planning decisions.

Refer to *Advertising Media Planning,* 5th ed., by Sissors and Bumba, Chapter 7.

Discussion

Media decisions are based on many different kinds of marketing and media data. The following tables are primarily marketing data that can be of value to a media planner in the following two ways:

1. It can be helpful in understanding the nature of the market and competitive brands.
2. Some of it could directly affect market strategy planning, which in turn can affect media planning.

Problem

Build a picture of the market and the relative differences of brands A, B, and C. In building a picture, state only significant facts that are revealed in the tables, and then explain briefly how they could play a role in planning marketing and media.

Bimonthly Industry Sales
(in millions of pounds)

	1992	1993	1994	1995
Jan.–Feb.	16.5	18.8	18.7	20.5
Mar.–Apr.	12.7	13.7	14.8	15.2
May–June	10.7	11.8	11.6	12.5
July–Aug.	11.3	12.5	12.8	14.3
Sept.–Oct.	15.5	16.5	17.2	17.9
Nov.–Dec.	18.8	20.6	19.7	20.9
Totals	85.5	93.9	94.8	101.3

Yearly Average Market Shares

	1992	1993	1994	1995	1995 percentage of national distribution
Brand A	57.9%	60.7%	61.4%	61.7%	97%
Brand B	14.8	13.8	12.9	12.2	82
Brand C	9.7	10.3	10.6	10.3	64
All others	17.6	15.1	15.0	15.8	86
	100.0%	99.9%	99.9%	100.0%	

Monthly Market Shares, 1995
(pound basis)

	Jan.–Feb.	Mar.–Apr.	May–June	July–Aug.	Sept.–Oct.	Nov.–Dec.
Brand A	58.5%	61.1%	64.2%	64.9%	62.1%	59.3%
All others	41.5	38.9	35.8	35.1	37.9	40.7
	100.0%	100.0%	100.0%	100.0%	100.0%	100.0%

Brand A Advertising Expenditures
(000s)

	Jan.–Feb.	Mar.–Apr.	May–June	July–Aug.	Sept.–Oct.	Nov.–Dec.	Totals
Spot TV	$ 88	$ 68	$ 48	$ 16	$ 4	$ 1	$ 225
Radio							
Newspaper							
Magazine	26	—	32	21	—	—	79
Network TV	346	302	151	242	549	390	1,980
	$460	$370	$231	$279	$553	$391	$2,284

Importance of Cents-Off Promotions and Premium Offers
(percentage of brand's volume in deals)

	Jan.–Feb.	Mar.–Apr.	May–June	July–Aug.	Sept.–Oct.	Nov.–Dec.
Brand A	41.5%	48.1%	19.3%	33.3%	58.1%	25.3%
Brand B	53.0	55.4	49.3	46.9	27.0	12.5
Brand C	89.0	88.5	78.5	66.0	79.2	84.9

Assignment 6

Using Sales & Marketing Management Survey of Buying Power Data

Objective: To help you become familiar with some of the data contained in the Sales & Marketing Management Survey of Buying Power—in particular, how to build a marketing index for your own brand. This index would be helpful in selecting markets in which to place advertising and in assigning weight to markets on the basis of sales potential.

Discussion

Market selection and weighting, as practiced by major advertisers and agencies, is a very sophisticated process. Huge sums are spent to collect competitive sales information on a market-by-market basis to help establish market potential and select those areas that merit special attention. Many advertisers, however, cannot afford the luxury of special surveys and audits and must rely on some less costly source of data on which to make market selection decisions.

Sales & Marketing Management's Survey of Buying Power is one source that is within the budget of even the smallest advertisers. Although it does not provide competitive brand sales information, the Survey of Buying Power does contain data that are useful in determining market sales potential.

One widely used market measure is the Buying Power Index (BPI). This weighted index combines three basic elements—population, effective buying income, and retail sales—into a measurement of a market's ability to buy. In addition to the BPI, the Survey of Buying Power also includes tables of market-by-market sales in broad retail categories such as food stores, drugstores, and automotive dealers.

Refer to *Advertising Media Planning*, 5th ed., by Sissors and Bumba, Chapter 7.

How to Create Your Own Index

You might want to create your own index, however, if you believe that the Buying Power Index is too general for your purposes. To build your index you will have to select the factors reported by the Survey of Buying Power that best reflect the sales potential of your kind of market. An example follows.

Suppose that you wanted to introduce a new product in Georgia markets. You chose one state only because you did not have enough funds to cover more markets. Perhaps you can do a better job in fewer markets with the limited financial resources you have. Your product is a line of medium- to high-priced furniture.

In order to build your index, you might select population, effective buying income, and retail sales of furniture/furnishings/appliances. You would probably select population because you want markets in which there are many people available to buy your products. Effective buying income is like disposable income. Therefore, markets in which there is a greater amount of disposable income might be better suited than those with smaller amounts. Obviously, retail sales of furniture/furnishings/appliances are directly related to retail sales of furniture.

So you gather data from the survey and build the index as described below. In doing so it is important to understand two practices:

- It is possible to add numbers that represent unlike measurements, such as adding population to income dollars to retail sales dollars. Beginners often are surprised that this can be done. In this situation, it is appropriate. It is not appropriate in most others.
- Sales & Marketing Management uses weighted factors for its Buying Power Index. You should be careful when weighting factors unless you have adequate evidence to help you decide the relative importance of each factor. Thus, for this assignment no weighting has been given.

Steps in building the index:

1. Select the factors.
2. Find data for all markets that could be used.
3. Arrange the data in a table, such as the sample here, entitled Three-Factor Index. Note that population data are listed in thousands (000), and effective buying income and retail sales are shown in millions (000,000).

Three-Factor Index

Market	Population[a] (000)	Effective buying income (EBI)[a] (000,000)	Retail sales of furniture/ furnishings/ appliances[a] (000,000)	Sum of factors	Market value index (%)	Allocation of $250,000 budget
Albany	107.6	689.8[b]	25.9[c]	823.3		
Athens	108.5	607.8	21.2	737.5		
Atlanta	1,906.7	14,773.3	293.9	16,973.9[d]	75.7	$189,250
Augusta	292.9	1,797.7	52.9	2,143.5[d]	9.6	24,000
Columbus	227.1	1,286.3	40.4	1,553.8		
Macon	248.4	1,436.0	36.7	1,721.1[d]	7.7	19,250
Savannah	219.9	1,304.3	57.7	1,581.9[d]	7.0	17,500
Totals				22,420.4	100.0	$250,000

[a]Reprinted with permission of Sales & Marketing Management.

[b]This number was reported in Survey of Buying Power as 689,849 and was rounded to 689.8 million for use in developing an index.

[c]This number was reported in Survey of Buying Power as 25,922 and was rounded to 25.9 million for use in developing an index.

[d]Markets selected.

4. Add the three factors for each market horizontally. The sum of the three factors is noted in the "Sum of factors" column.
5. Select the four markets to be used based on the sum of factors.
6. Add together the sums of factors *for the four markets you have selected.*
7. Divide the sum of factors for each market you have selected by the base. (The base is the total of the sum of factors you developed in step 6.)
8. Enter the market value index for each market selected.
9. If you have a budget, multiply the budget by the market value index for each selected market to find the amount allocated to each market based on sales potential.

Problem

Assume you have a new fast-food chain as a client in your advertising agency. Your client plans to open outlets in the state of Iowa. Because the budget is somewhat limited, the initial introduction will be limited to four markets that offer the highest sales potential.

Using the Sales & Marketing Management Survey of Buying Power for the state of Iowa (Exhibit 6–1), create a multiple-factor index and then select the top four metro areas. Show your work in the space provided.

Also, assume you have a budget of $400,000 for advertising. Allocate that budget to the four markets on the basis of the sales potential for each metro market area.

Exhibit 6–1 Sales & Marketing Management Survey of Buying Power

Iowa

S&MM ESTIMATES: 1/1/94

POPULATION

METRO AREA / County / City	Total Population (Thousands)	% Of U.S.	Median Age Of Pop.	% of Population by Age Group: 18-24 Years	25-34 Years	35-49 Years	50 & Over	Households (Thousands)
CEDAR RAPIDS	**174.7**	**.0673**	**34.1**	**10.1**	**15.9**	**22.9**	**25.7**	**68.0**
Linn	174.7	.0673	34.1	10.1	15.9	22.9	25.7	68.0
• Cedar Rapids	113.0	.0435	34.2	10.6	16.3	22.2	26.5	45.3
SUBURBAN TOTAL	61.7	.0238	34.0	9.3	14.9	24.2	24.3	22.7
DAVENPORT-MOLINE-ROCK ISLAND	**353.3**	**.1361**	**34.9**	**8.8**	**14.3**	**22.4**	**27.5**	**138.6**
Scott	154.9	.0597	33.2	9.1	15.3	22.9	24.4	59.4
• Davenport	97.0	.0374	32.5	10.2	16.3	20.6	25.3	38.0
Henry, Ill.	*50.5*	*.0194*	*37.0*	*7.1*	*12.7*	*22.4*	*30.8*	*19.4*
Rock Island, Ill.	*147.9*	*.0570*	*35.9*	*8.9*	*14.0*	*21.8*	*29.5*	*59.8*
• Moline	*43.1*	*.0166*	*36.4*	*7.9*	*14.8*	*21.7*	*30.5*	*18.5*
• Rock Island	*40.3*	*.0155*	*35.4*	*11.6*	*12.8*	*19.4*	*31.2*	*16.3*
SUBURBAN TOTAL	172.9	.0666	35.7	7.5	13.7	24.2	27.0	65.8
DES MOINES	**414.8**	**.1598**	**33.4**	**10.0**	**16.8**	**22.9**	**24.5**	**161.8**
Dallas	31.4	.0121	35.6	6.5	11.6	22.9	28.0	11.9
Polk	345.3	.1330	33.2	10.4	17.3	22.7	24.2	136.5
• Des Moines	195.0	.0751	33.1	11.3	17.4	20.9	25.8	79.4
Warren	38.1	.0147	33.7	9.5	13.9	24.1	24.1	13.4
SUBURBAN TOTAL	219.8	.0847	33.7	8.9	16.1	24.7	23.4	82.4
DUBUQUE	**87.3**	**.0337**	**33.9**	**10.1**	**14.2**	**20.9**	**27.5**	**31.4**
Dubuque	87.3	.0337	33.9	10.1	14.2	20.9	27.5	31.4
• Dubuque	59.0	.0227	35.0	10.9	14.1	20.3	29.6	22.1
SUBURBAN TOTAL	28.3	.0110	31.8	8.5	14.1	22.4	23.1	9.3
IOWA CITY	**100.6**	**.0388**	**28.1**	**23.4**	**18.9**	**20.5**	**16.5**	**37.8**
Johnson	100.6	.0388	28.1	23.4	18.9	20.5	16.5	37.8
• Iowa City	60.3	.0232	25.1	32.2	18.2	18.0	14.0	22.2
SUBURBAN TOTAL	40.3	.0156	32.3	10.2	19.7	24.3	20.4	15.6
SIOUX CITY	**118.4**	**.0456**	**33.5**	**8.9**	**14.5**	**20.6**	**27.2**	**44.4**
Woodbury	101.1	.0390	33.8	8.9	14.4	20.5	27.8	38.2
• Sioux City	82.9	.0319	33.4	9.7	14.7	20.2	27.5	31.6
Dakota, Neb.	*17.3*	*.0066*	*31.9*	*8.4*	*15.7*	*21.1*	*24.1*	*6.2*
SUBURBAN TOTAL	35.5	.0137	33.7	6.8	14.4	21.6	26.5	12.8
WATERLOO-CEDAR FALLS	**124.1**	**.0478**	**33.7**	**13.2**	**12.9**	**21.3**	**27.0**	**47.4**
Black Hawk	124.1	.0478	33.7	13.2	12.9	21.3	27.0	47.4
• Cedar Falls	35.0	.0135	27.4	26.1	11.1	19.4	22.2	12.0
• Waterloo	66.3	.0255	35.7	8.6	13.8	21.3	29.9	27.3
SUBURBAN TOTAL	22.8	.0088	35.1	6.5	13.8	24.4	25.9	8.1

RETAIL SALES BY STORE GROUP

METRO AREA / County / City	Total Retail Sales ($000)	Food ($000)	Eating & Drinking Places ($000)	General Mdse. ($000)	Furniture/ Furnish. Appliance ($000)	Automotive ($000)	Drug ($000)
CEDAR RAPIDS	**1,859,647**	**308,896**	**192,598**	**296,610**	**101,080**	**467,463**	**61,576**
Linn	1,859,647	308,896	192,598	296,610	101,080	467,463	61,576
• Cedar Rapids	1,513,974	248,487	164,388	288,362	67,993	345,368	52,855
SUBURBAN TOTAL	345,673	60,409	28,210	8,248	33,087	122,095	8,721
DAVENPORT-MOLINE-ROCK ISLAND	**3,386,678**	**588,628**	**356,488**	**483,242**	**173,872**	**776,397**	**178,103**
Scott	1,721,273	300,872	161,670	239,736	93,698	409,260	70,707
• Davenport	1,239,092	203,713	113,523	173,357	80,597	331,348	53,058
Henry, Ill.	*337,181*	*60,776*	*30,509*	*40,247*	*15,593*	*97,433*	*17,365*
Rock Island, Ill.	*1,328,224*	*226,980*	*164,309*	*203,259*	*64,581*	*269,704*	*90,031*
• Moline	*644,533*	*76,356*	*81,245*	*151,519*	*51,249*	*107,912*	*31,334*
• Rock Island	*249,726*	*45,460*	*33,324*	*28,005*	*6,263*	*50,991*	*20,078*
SUBURBAN TOTAL	1,253,327	263,099	128,396	130,361	35,763	286,148	73,633
DES MOINES	**4,612,330**	**908,549**	**428,105**	**595,498**	**252,225**	**1,086,058**	**157,576**
Dallas	182,625	43,799	9,251	10,139	5,452	63,589	4,506
Polk	4,204,695	814,378	408,209	579,449	245,655	907,079	148,543
• Des Moines	2,590,828	514,732	268,377	348,145	173,842	545,660	89,386
Warren	225,010	50,372	8,645	5,910	1,118	115,390	4,527
SUBURBAN TOTAL	2,021,502	393,817	157,728	247,353	78,383	540,398	68,190
DUBUQUE	**905,790**	**164,881**	**87,618**	**160,516**	**42,644**	**210,676**	**40,438**
Dubuque	905,790	164,881	87,618	160,516	42,644	210,676	40,438
• Dubuque	793,650	143,581	79,600	148,500	36,638	165,807	37,285
SUBURBAN TOTAL	112,140	21,300	8,018	12,016	6,006	44,869	3,153
IOWA CITY	**940,866**	**210,962**	**109,396**	**123,604**	**64,784**	**171,252**	**38,621**
Johnson	940,866	210,962	109,396	123,604	64,784	171,252	38,621
• Iowa City	677,086	156,054	81,389	99,217	48,016	109,946	32,105
SUBURBAN TOTAL	263,780	55,908	28,007	24,387	16,768	61,306	6,516
SIOUX CITY	**1,137,239**	**238,435**	**114,699**	**185,229**	**50,500**	**204,764**	**32,035**
Woodbury	1,060,630	222,061	99,917	184,157	44,525	186,293	28,705
• Sioux City	1,015,526	214,676	89,985	174,752	44,091	182,004	28,213
Dakota, Neb.	*76,609*	*17,374*	*14,782*	*1,072*	*5,975*	*18,471*	*3,330*
SUBURBAN TOTAL	121,713	24,759	24,714	10,477	6,409	22,760	3,792
WATERLOO-CEDAR FALLS	**1,222,170**	**194,232**	**107,254**	**222,187**	**40,136**	**356,726**	**48,041**
Black Hawk	1,222,170	194,232	107,254	222,187	40,136	356,726	48,041
• Cedar Falls	427,101	41,583	38,704	62,503	12,725	178,245	14,090
• Waterloo	717,984	131,675	62,991	158,126	25,590	148,159	32,340
SUBURBAN TOTAL	77,085	20,974	5,559	1,558	1,821	30,322	1,611

EFFECTIVE BUYING INCOME

% of Hslds. by EBI Group:
(A) $10,000-$19,999
(B) $20,000-$34,999
(C) $35,000-$49,999
(D) $50,000 & Over

METRO AREA / County / City	Total EBI ($000)	Median Hsld. EBI	A	B	C	D	Buying Power Index
CEDAR RAPIDS	**3,056,653**	**39,064**	**13.5**	**21.8**	**22.0**	**34.2**	**.0769**
Linn	3,056,653	39,064	13.5	21.8	22.0	34.2	.0769
• Cedar Rapids	2,020,277	38,181	13.9	21.7	22.0	32.9	.0648
SUBURBAN TOTAL	1,036,376	40,865	12.6	22.2	22.2	36.7	.0221
DAVENPORT-MOLINE-ROCK ISLAND	**5,327,509**	**32,738**	**17.3**	**23.9**	**19.9**	**26.7**	**.1398**
Scott	2,324,241	33,948	16.5	23.5	20.4	28.0	.0646
• Davenport	1,352,273	29,883	18.4	25.0	18.9	23.0	.0416
Henry, Ill.	*696,456*	*30,248*	*19.8*	*26.6*	*20.0*	*22.1*	*.0169*
Rock Island, Ill.	*2,306,812*	*32,420*	*17.1*	*23.9*	*19.2*	*26.9*	*.0583*
• Moline	*755,137*	*33,334*	*16.7*	*25.4*	*19.2*	*28.2*	*.0217*
• Rock Island	*591,945*	*28,924*	*19.0*	*23.3*	*18.6*	*22.6*	*.0138*
SUBURBAN TOTAL	2,628,154	35,262	16.2	23.3	21.0	29.4	.0627
DES MOINES	**7,401,181**	**38,856**	**13.6**	**22.5**	**21.4**	**34.4**	**.1873**
Dallas	457,711	32,691	17.5	26.1	21.9	24.4	.0106
Polk	6,364,286	39,254	13.3	22.3	21.2	35.2	.1636
• Des Moines	3,244,406	33,968	16.2	24.4	21.3	27.1	.0913
Warren	579,184	40,323	12.9	21.3	23.2	35.2	.0131
SUBURBAN TOTAL	4,156,775	44,001	11.1	20.5	21.6	41.5	.0960
DUBUQUE	**1,242,707**	**33,531**	**17.1**	**25.2**	**21.6**	**26.0**	**.0347**
Dubuque	1,242,707	33,531	17.1	25.2	21.6	26.0	.0347
• Dubuque	846,989	31,978	18.5	25.3	21.0	24.0	.0262
SUBURBAN TOTAL	395,718	37,225	14.0	24.9	22.8	30.8	.0085
IOWA CITY	**1,724,871**	**35,850**	**15.8**	**21.8**	**18.0**	**33.2**	**.0420**
Johnson	1,724,871	35,850	15.8	21.8	18.0	33.2	.0420
• Iowa City	972,772	31,660	18.4	21.8	15.8	29.8	.0261
SUBURBAN TOTAL	752,099	40,829	12.2	21.8	21.0	38.0	.0159
SIOUX CITY	**1,747,322**	**32,357**	**17.6**	**24.8**	**20.6**	**25.3**	**.0464**
Woodbury	1,499,784	31,826	17.9	25.1	20.4	24.7	.0410
• Sioux City	1,241,270	31,555	18.0	25.1	20.8	24.0	.0359
Dakota, Neb.	*247,538*	*35,400*	*15.6*	*23.4*	*21.5*	*29.1*	*.0054*
SUBURBAN TOTAL	506,052	34,180	16.4	24.1	20.2	28.5	.0105
WATERLOO-CEDAR FALLS	**1,741,525**	**30,330**	**18.7**	**23.9**	**18.5**	**24.7**	**.0480**
Black Hawk	1,741,525	30,330	18.7	23.9	18.5	24.7	.0480
• Cedar Falls	481,786	32,633	18.3	21.7	17.1	29.8	.0146
• Waterloo	940,380	28,060	20.1	24.4	18.2	21.2	.0268
SUBURBAN TOTAL	319,359	35,437	15.0	25.0	21.5	29.2	.0086

Source: Reprinted from the 1994 Survey of Buying Power published by Sales & Marketing Management and produced by Market Statistics, both companies of Bill Communications.

Assignment 7

Competitive Media Expenditure Analysis

Objective: To provide an opportunity to extract and analyze media expenditure data and to consider what implications the data have for media strategy planning.

Discussion

Several companies provide information on the amount of money national advertisers spend in various classes of media. Two of those companies are Leading National Advertisers (LNA) and MediaWatch. Their data are published quarterly by Competitive Media Reporting and reports advertising spending in ten major media. LNA data covers expenditures in magazines, Sunday magazines, newspapers, outdoor, and national spot radio. MediaWatch covers expenditures in network television, spot television, syndicated television, cable television, and network radio.

Exhibit 7–1 contains selected data from LNA/MediaWatch Multi-Media Service for category H122, Mattresses. It shows quarterly (Q1, Q2, Q3, Q4) and full-year (94 YTD) data for 1994 as well as full-year 1993 data (93 YTD) for each advertiser. Note that expenditure figures are reported in thousands (000).

Refer to *Advertising Media Planning,* 5th ed., by Sissors and Bumba, Chapter 7.

Problems

1. Assume that you have a mattress company client and are getting ready to develop next year's advertising plan. You are interested in knowing the annual spending of your primary competitors, whether their budgets are increasing, and, if so, by how much. Use the form below to organize your data. Use brand totals, *not* company totals.

Brand	1993	1994	Percentage change Y/A
Sealy	____	____	________
Select Comfort	____	____	________
Serta	____	____	________
Simmons	____	____	________
Sleepys	____	____	________
Spring Air	____	____	________

Exhibit 7–1 LNA/Media/Watch Multi-Media Service YTD (1994)

CLASS/BRAND $

LNA/MEDIAWATCH MULTI-MEDIA SERVICE

January - December 1994

CLASS/COMPANY/BRAND		CLASS CODE	QUARTERLY AND YEAR-TO-DATE ADVERTISING DOLLARS (000)										
			10 MEDIA TOTAL	MAGAZINES	SUNDAY MAGAZINES	NEWSPAPERS	OUTDOOR	NETWORK TELEVISION	SPOT TELEVISION	SYNDICATED TELEVISION	CABLE TV NETWORKS	NETWORK RADIO	NATIONAL SPOT RADIO
H122 MATTRESSES													
SEALY CORP													
SEALY MATTRESSES		H122											
	Q1		14,718.5	163.5	116.7	126.4	- -	9,393.6	1,170.4	2,805.1	942.8	- -	- -
	Q2		10,225.2	152.9	106.9	36.3	- -	5,330.2	973.1	2,735.7	890.1	- -	- -
	Q3		4,794.8	- -	- -	- -	- -	2,498.5	455.1	1,451.7	389.5	- -	- -
	Q4		113.1	- -	- -	25.4	- -	- -	37.2	50.5	- -	- -	- -
	94 YTD		29,851.6	316.4	223.6	188.1	- -	17,222.3	2,635.8	7,043.0	2,222.4	- -	- -
	93 YTD		22,799.8	174.5	147.9	383.9	- -	12,109.3	1,996.7	6,227.5	1,760.0	- -	- -
STEARNS & FOSTER MATTRESS		H122											
	Q4		4.6	- -	- -	- -	- -	- -	4.6	- -	- -	- -	- -
	94 YTD		4.6	- -	- -	- -	- -	- -	4.6	- -	- -	- -	- -
	93 YTD		1,022.5	873.8	148.0	0.7	- -	- -	- -	- -	- -	- -	- -
COMPANY TOTAL													
	Q1		14,718.5	163.5	116.7	126.4	- -	9,393.6	1,170.4	2,805.1	942.8	- -	- -
	Q2		10,225.2	152.9	106.9	36.3	- -	5,330.2	973.1	2,735.7	890.1	- -	- -
	Q3		4,794.8	- -	- -	- -	- -	2,498.5	455.1	1,451.7	389.5	- -	- -
	Q4		117.7	- -	- -	25.4	- -	- -	41.8	50.5	- -	- -	- -
	94 YTD		29,856.2	316.4	223.6	188.1	- -	17,222.3	2,640.4	7,043.0	2,222.4	- -	- -
	93 YTD		23,822.3	1,048.3	295.9	384.6	- -	12,1[illegible].3	1,996.7	6,227.5	1,[illegible]0.0		- -
SELECT COMFORT													
SELECT COMFORT MATTRESSES		H122											
	Q1		1,040.7	968.5	7.9	17.5	6.6	- -	8.6	- -	- -	31.6	- -
	Q2		890.4	881.1	7.9	- -	- -	- -	0.9	- -	0.5	- -	- -
	Q3		1,520.3	1,481.4	12.0	8.8	- -	- -	15.7	- -	2.4	- -	- -
	Q4		1,445.3	1,256.7	- -	41.7	- -	- -	4.9	120.8	21.2	- -	- -
	94 YTD		4,896.7	4,587.7	27.8	68.0	6.6	- -	30.1	120.8	24.1	31.6	- -
	93 YTD		3,237.8	3,034.5	183.9	- -	- -	- -	- -	- -	- -	19.4	- -
SERTA INC													
SERTA MATTRESSES		H122											
	Q1		4,245.3	- -	- -	3.2	- -	3,842.2	116.2	- -	283.7	- -	- -
	Q2		82.2	- -	- -	23.2	- -	- -	59.0	- -	- -	- -	- -
	Q3		4,576.6	- -	- -	0.3	13.9	3,547.3	256.1	- -	759.0	- -	- -
	Q4		187.1	- -	- -	0.5	12.5	- -	174.1	- -	- -	- -	- -
	94 YTD		9,091.2	- -	- -	27.2	26.4	7,389.5	605.4	- -	1,042.7	- -	- -
	93 YTD		7,599.1	- -	32.0	57.0	3.0	5,576.5	619.1	478.5	833.0	- -	- -
SERTA LOCAL DEALER/DISTRIBUTOR													
SERTA MATTRESSES LOCAL DEALER/DIST		H122											
	Q4		26.8	- -	- -	- -	- -	- -	26.8	- -	- -	- -	- -
	94 YTD		26.8	- -	- -	- -	- -	- -	26.8	- -	- -	- -	- -
SIMMONS CO													
SIMMONS MATTRESSES		H122											
	Q1		235.2	- -	- -	110.2	- -	- -	90.7	- -	34.3	- -	- -
	Q2		2,590.3	1,596.9	- -	81.7	- -	- -	702.1	- -	209.6	- -	- -
	Q3		3,461.8	1,603.2	- -	- -	- -	- -	1,428.2	- -	430.4	- -	- -
	Q4		1,428.7	1,168.0	- -	6.0	- -	- -	217.6	- -	37.1	- -	- -
	94 YTD		7,716.0	4,368.1	- -	197.9	- -	- -	2,438.6	- -	711.4	- -	- -
	93 YTD		6,714.7	6,021.8	- -	47.5	- -	- -	623.4	- -	- -	- -	22.0
SLEEPYS													
SLEEPYS MATTRESSES		H122											
	Q1		1,234.7	- -	- -	1,234.7	- -	- -	- -	- -	- -	- -	- -
	Q2		1,076.5	- -	- -	1,076.5	- -	- -	- -	- -	- -	- -	- -
	Q3		1,857.1	- -	- -	1,857.1	- -	- -	- -	- -	- -	- -	- -
	Q4		1,388.6	- -	- -	1,388.6	- -	- -	- -	- -	- -	- -	- -
	94 YTD		5,556.9	- -	- -	5,556.9	- -	- -	- -	- -	- -	- -	- -
	93 YTD		4,457.6	- -	19.4	4,438.2	- -	- -	- -	- -	- -	- -	- -
SPRING AIR CO													
SPRING AIR MATTRESS		H122											
	Q1		14.3	- -	- -	- -	- -	- -	11.8	- -	- -	- -	2.5
	Q2		671.0	35.2	- -	- -	- -	172.2	24.9	- -	127.2	311.5	- -
	Q3		395.7	- -	- -	- -	- -	103.2	20.9	- -	271.6	- -	- -
	Q4		29.0	- -	- -	- -	- -	- -	29.0	- -	- -	- -	- -
	94 YTD		1,110.0	35.2	- -	- -	- -	275.4	86.6	- -	398.8	311.5	2.5
	93 YTD		1,133.6	- -	- -	- -	- -	- -	72.8	- -	- -	1,059.6	1.2

2. Looking at the quarterly spending by Serta and Simmons, how are the two spending strategies different?

3. Using the data in Exhibit 7–1, complete the form below showing the dollar amount and the percentage each listed brand spends in each medium. Show dollar amounts in thousands (000). Use brand figures, *not* company totals.

Brand	Total	Magazines	Sunday Magazines	Newspapers	Outdoor	Network TV	Spot TV	Syndicated TV	Cable TV	Network Radio	Spot Radio
Sealy											
% of brand total											
Select											
% of brand total											
Serta											
% of brand total											
Simmons											
% of brand total											
Sleepys											
% of brand total											
Spring Air											
% of brand total											
Totals 6 Brands											
% of 6 brands total											

4. Based on the data above, if you were to launch a new national brand with a modest (under $3,000,000) budget, what media classes might you consider? Why?

5. Looking again at the above data, how do the media expenditures by Sleepys differ from the other brands? What does this difference suggest in terms of Sleepys marketing area?

Assignment 8

Using SRDS Media Information

Objective: To help you become familiar with the media information published by SRDS (Standard Rate and Data Service) by having you extract specific pieces of information from sample data. SRDS provides some of the most important data that media planners have at their disposal.

Discussion

SRDS publishes a number of rates and data books each month covering the major media, with the exception of outdoor. Media planners and buyers rely on these publications for information regarding rates, discounts, mechanical requirements, closing dates, etc.

Sample pages from the February 1995 editions of SRDS Newspaper, Consumer Magazine and Agri-Media, and Business Publication books are presented in Exhibits 8–1 through 8–3. Examine these pages carefully to become familiar with the information presented before you begin this assignment.

It should be noted that assignments related to spot television and spot radio SRDS books are not included. This is because media people generally work directly with TV and radio station representatives (and in some cases with the stations) in negotiating a spot TV or spot radio buy.

Problems

Magazine

You are planning to run a series of six full-page, four-color ads nationally in *McCall's*. The ads will be scheduled in alternate months, beginning in January. In addition, you are planning to run three full-page, black-and-white ads in a custom region comprised of the East Central and Southeast areas.

1. What is the total cost for the national ads? (Be sure to take advantage of all applicable discounts.) ________________

2. What is the total circulation for the regional ads? ____________________
   a. What is the CPM for the regional ads? ________________
   b. What is the cost of each regional ad? ________________

Exhibit 8–1 SRDS: *McCall's* Magazine

McCall's

A Gruner + Jahr Company Publication

Location ID: 8 MLST 49 — Mid 001260-000

Published monthly by G + J USA Publishing, 110 Fifth Ave., New York, NY 10011. Phone 212-463-1000. Fax 212-463-1269FAX: 212-463-1023 (Production).

For shipping info., see Print Media Production Source.

PUBLISHER'S EDITORIAL PROFILE

McCALL'S editorial focuses on the issues that women face today. Articles on fashion, beauty, health, parenting, home and food give McCall's readers practical, useful information that helps them take positive action in their lives. Rec'd 11/22/94.

1. PERSONNEL

Pub—Barbara Litrell.
Prod Dir—Catherine Merolle.

2. REPRESENTATIVES and/or BRANCH OFFICES

New York, NY 10011—Madelyn Alpert Roberts, VP/Assoc Pub, Phone 212-463-1261; Lucy Kuhn, Assoc N.Y. Mgr, Phone 212-463-1279; Linda James, Assoc N.Y. Mgr,Risa Cradall, Assoc N.Y. Mgr. Phone 212-463-1279, 110 5th Ave.
Chicago, IL 60601—Caryn Grippe, Chicago Mgr, 111 East Wacker Dr., Suite 529. Phone 312-616-2630.
Los Angeles, CA 90048—Patricia Kaufmann Rose, West Coast Mgr, 11766 Wilshire Blvd., Ste 800. Phone 213-938-3946.
San Francisco, CA 94111—Gail Sonn, San Francisco Sales Mgr, 601 Montgomery St., Ste 850. Phone 415-986-2455.
Troy—Meyers, Laine, Inc.
Atlanta—Himmelsbach Communications.
New York—M & G Communications. (Direct Response).
Odessa, FL—Swain and Eversole.

3. COMMISSION AND CASH DISCOUNT

15% commission is allowed to recognized advertising agencies placing accepted copy and assuming credit risk. Advertising billed to advertising agencies with credit on 1st of month preceding month of issue, due and payable 20 days thereafter.
Make up requirements may cause on-page coupons to be backed with other ads. When this is necessary, at publisher's discretion, an additional discount will be earned.

ADVERTISING RATES
Effective January 1, 1995. (Issue)
Rates received October 17, 1994.

5. BLACK/WHITE RATES

1 page	87,560.
2/3 page	63,240.
Floating digest	57,005.
1/2 page or digest	54,290.
1/3 page	33,535.
1/4 page (Sq)	30,340.
Agate line	346.76

Volume Discount

Natl advertisers earn discounts based on natl equivalent page volume without regard to coloration. Supplied inserts do not earn discounts. Discounts based on contract year of 12 consecutive months.

Equivalents	Discount	Equivalents	Discount
3 pages	7%	36 pages	20%
6 pages	10%	48 pages	22%
12 pages	12%	60 pages	25%
18 pages	16%	72 pages	30%
24 pages	18%		

Seasonal Discount

Full page advertisement in the Jan, Jul, or Aug issues earns a seasonal discount. Seasonal discounts are additive to volume discounts to a maximum of 30%.

Frequency	Discount
1 seasonal month	5%
2 seasonal months	7%
3 Seasonal months	10%

Consecutive Page Discount

Four or more consecutive full-run, four color pages in same issue (covers/copy change ads excluded) earns discount.*

Total pages	Discount
4-5 consecutive pages	20%
6-7 consecutive pages	25%
8+ consecutive pages	30%

(*) Unless earned discount is higher.

6. COLOR RATES

Black & 1-Color:

1 page	100,070.
2/3 page	71,295.
Floating digest	63,060.
1/2 page or digest	60,055.
1/3 page	37,535.
1/4 page (Sq)	34,030.

4-Color:

1 page	103,305.
2/3 page	78,330.
Floating digest	64,610.
1/2 page or digest	61,530.
1/3 page	43,420.
1/4 page (Sq)	34,870.

7. COVERS

4-Color:

2nd cover	129,385.	4th cover	148,510.
3rd cover	124,195.		

8. INSERTS

Available.

9. BLEED

No charge.

11. CLASSIFIED/MAIL ORDER/SPECIALTY RATES

Publisher's Discount

Publishers are offered a 15% discount in lieu of all other discounts.

12. SPLIT-RUN

GEOGRAPHIC COPY SPLITS

Advertisers may split copy in a national ad along McCall's standard regional lines. Rates are based on the national cost with an additional charge for each change in copy.
Additional for each copy change:
Black and white .... 2450. 4-Color .... 3195.
2-Color .... 2660.

COPY SPLITS IN TEST MARKETS

If a national advertisement splits copy into McCall's test markets, the following net setup charges apply. These costs are additive to the geographic copy split costs listed above and apply to each region in which test markets are used.

	Copy Split Charge
Nat'l split in test market per region	1065.

TWO-WAY RANDOM SPLIT

Advertisers may use 2 different ads of equal size, each ad appearing in 50% of McCall's circulation, at random. National rates with an additional charge for copy change.
Additional for each copy change:
Black and white .... 2450. 4-Color .... 3195.
2-Color .... 2660.

NEWSSTAND/SUBSCRIPTION SPLIT

Advertisers may use different ads of equal size in newsstand and subscription copies. National rates with an additional charge of 3,195.00.
Split run copy charges are net manufacturing costs. They neither contribute to nor earn discounts or agency commissions. Closing dates for Split Runs are the same as Regional editions.

SUBSCRIPTION CIRCULATION

An edition consisting of subscription copies only is offered to advertisers subject to availability. Rates are based on national open CPM plus a 3,195.00 premium.

13a. GEOGRAPHIC and/or DEMOGRAPHIC EDITIONS

National advertisers that run a schedule of 6 or more national pages get the national CPM for complete regions (22.45). Advertisers that don't meet the national page criteria have the following regional rates.

BLACK AND WHITE RATES:

	1 page	2/3 page	1/2 page	1/3 page
Under 600,000 circ.	25.05	18.73	14.22	9.84
600,000-1,399,999	23.80	17.78	13.51	9.36
1,400,000-1,999,999	22.55	16.85	13.27	8.87
2,000,000-2,999,999	21.30	15.91	12.09	8.38
3,000,000-3,999,999	20.03	14.97	11.38	7.88
4,000,000 or more	18.78	14.03	10.67	7.38

COLOR RATES:

Black & 1 color:	1 page	2/3 page	1/2 page	1/3 page
Under 600,000 circ.	27.78	20.55	15.92	10.88
600,000-1,399,999	26.34	19.52	15.13	10.34
1,400,000-1,999,999	24.99	18.50	14.34	9.79
2,000,000-2,999,999	23.62	17.46	13.55	9.25
3,000,000-3,999,999	22.23	16.43	12.73	8.71
4,000,000 or more	20.84	15.41	11.94	8.16

4-Color:	1 page	2/3 page	1/2 page	1/3 page
Under 600,000 circ.	31.00	22.55	17.50	11.73
600,000-1,399,999	29.16	21.42	16.62	11.15
1,400,000-1,999,999	27.62	21.42	16.62	11.15
2,000,000-2,999,999	26.10	19.17	14.88	9.98
3,000,000-3,999,999	24.57	18.02	14.01	9.39
4,000,000 or more	23.02	16.91	13.12	8.81

Circ (000)		Circ (000)	
California	371	East Central	550
Western	270	Southeast	876
West Central	459	Middle Atlantic	476
Southwest	464	Metro New York	209
Central	263	New England	226

TEST MARKETS

In addition to regional editions, 127 standard test markets, based on subscription circulation only, are available. First page any color, 34.10 CPM or 3,195.00 per region; second page 22.45 CPM or 2,660.00 per region whichever is grater. A 450.00 net set-up charge applies to each region that the advertiser is running a test market in. National advertisers that run a schedule of 6 of more national pages get the national CPM for test markets (22.45). Minimum charges apply.

Circulation figures for Regions, Test Markets, Silver Edition and Newsstand are current estimated averages. A 5% variation must be allowed for the circulation and distribution of these editions.

SILVER EDITION

See listing in Classification 28a.
Circulation figures for Regions, Test Markets, Silver. Newsstand and subscription editions are current estimated averages. A 5% variation must be allowed for the circulation and distribution of the editions.

14. CONTRACT AND COPY REGULATIONS

See Contents page for location—items 1, 2, 3, 7, 8, 9, 10, 16, 18, 19, 20, 21, 24, 25, 26, 28, 30, 32, 33, 35, 36, 38, 39.

15. GENERAL REQUIREMENTS

Also see SRDS Print Media Production Source.
Printing Process: Rotogravure Full Run
Trim Size: 7-13/16 x 10-1/2; No./Cols. 3.
Binding Method: Perfect.
Colors Available: 4-color process.
Covers: 4-color process.

AD PAGE DIMENSIONS

1 pg	7 x 10	1/3 v	2-3/16 x 10
2/3 v	4-1/2 x 10	1/3 sq	4-1/2 x 4-1/2
2/3 h	7 x 6-1/2	Digest	4-1/2 x 6-3/4
1/2 v	3-7/16 x 10	Island Unit	4-3/8 x 6-1/2
1/2 h	7 x 4-1/2		

16. ISSUE AND CLOSING DATES

Published monthly.

Issue:	On sale	Closing	(**)
Jan '95	12/13	10/14	10/4
Feb	1/10	11/15	11/1
Mar	2/14	12/15	12/6
Apr	3/14	1/13	1/3
May	4/11	2/15	2/7
Jun	5/9	3/15	3/7
Jul	6/13	4/14	4/4
Aug	7/11	5/15	5/2
Sep	8/8	6/15	6/6
Oct	9/12	7/14	7/5
Nov	10/10	8/15	8/1
Dec	11/7	9/15	9/5

(**) Regional/Copy Splits
Closing applies to National/Covers.
Cancellations or changes in orders not accepted after closing date.

17. SPECIAL SERVICES

A.B.C. Supplemental Data Report released January 1991 issue.

18. CIRCULATION

Established 1876. Single copy 1.95; per year 13.94.
Summary data—for detail see Publisher's Statement.

A.B.C. 6-30-94 (6 mos. aver.—Magazine Form)

Tot. Pd.	(Subs)	(Single)	(Assoc)
4,636,022	4,169,489	466,533	--

Average Non-Analyzed Non-Paid Circulation (not incl. above):
Total 151,512

TERRITORIAL DISTRIBUTION 3/94—4,663,480

N.Eng.	Mid.Atl.	E.N.Cen.	W.N.Cen.	S.Atl.
236,830	664,967	807,094	384,373	892,048
E.S.Cen.	W.S.Cen.	Mtn.St.	Pac.St.	Canada
361,103	481,773	255,506	547,573	21,915
Foreign	Other			
5,723	4,575			

Consumer Magazine and Agri-Media Rates and Data

Exhibit 8–2 SRDS: Denver Newspapers

Denver

(2 LISTINGS)
Denver County—Map Location F-3

THE DENVER POST

1560 Broadway, Denver, CO 80202.
Phone 303-820-1070. Fax: 303-820-1469.

ABC

Location ID: 1 NSNL CO Mid 016248-000
Member: ABC Coupon Distribution Verification Service; ACB, Inc.; NAA.
MORNING, SATURDAY AND SUNDAY.

1. PERSONNEL
Sr VP Sales/Mktg—Kirk MacDonald.
VP/Adv—Allen J. Walters.
Natl Adv Mgr—Gil Borelli.

2. REPRESENTATIVES and/or BRANCH OFFICES
Newspapers First.
Mexico—Towmar.
Canada—McGown/Intermac.

3. COMMISSION AND CASH DISCOUNT
15% to agencies; no cash discount.

4. POLICY-ALL CLASSIFICATIONS
Newspaper reserves right to revise advertising rates at any time.
Alcoholic beverage advertising accepted.

ADVERTISING RATES
Effective October 1, 1994.
Received July 18, 1994.

5. BLACK/WHITE RATES

	Morn	Sun.
Sau open, per inch	136.00	177.00

Inches charged full depth: col. 21 pg. 126.

BULK CONTRACT RATES

Per col. inch	Daily	Sunday
31.5"	128.00	170.00
126"	127.00	166.00
250"	126.00	162.00
500"	124.00	161.00
1,000"	121.00	154.00
2,000"	120.00	153.00
3,500"	114.00	152.00
5,000"	111.00	146.00
7,500"	107.00	144.00
10,000"	105.00	143.00

7. COLOR RATES AND DATA
Use b/w rate plus the following applicable costs:

	b/w 1 c	b/w 2 c	b/w 3 c
Daily extra	1,550.00	1,725.00	1,900.00
Sunday extra	1,900.00	2,070.00	2,185.00

Special color incks add 350.00 to above premiums.
Closing dates: reservations, printing material and cancellations, 7 days before publication.

9. SPLIT RUN
No charge for 50-50 black/white split. 31.5 inch minimum.

11. SPECIAL DAYS/PAGES/FEATURES
Best Food Days: Wednesday.

12. R.O.P. DEPTH REQUIREMENTS
Ads over 19 inches deep charged full col.

13. CONTRACT AND COPY REGULATIONS
See Contents page for location of regulations—items 1, 3, 5, 6, 7, 8, 9, 10, 11, 13, 14, 15, 16, 17, 18, 19, 20, 23, 25, 26, 29.

14. CLOSING TIME
Published Morning, Saturday and Sunday.

Day	Time	Closes	Day	Time	Closes
Sun	noon	Wed	Thu	5 pm	Mon
Mon	5 pm	Thu	Fri	5 pm	Tue
Tue	noon	Fri	Sat	5 pm	Wed
Wed	5 pm	Fri			

SPECIAL SECTIONS

Day	Time	Closes	Day	Time	Closes
Travel	12 n	Mon	Food	5 pm	Thu

15. MECHANICAL MEASUREMENTS
PRINTING PROCESS: Offset.
6 col; ea 2-1/16"; 1/8" betw col.
Inches charged full depth: col. 21; pg. 126.

16. SPECIAL CLASSIFICATIONS/RATES
Repeat ads-50% discount, no change in copy or size, must run same week, Monday through Sunday. No minimum size, commissionable.
Political, Traveling Sales Shows (cashier's check in advance)—general rates apply.
Sports Today, Full size, daily and Sunday—general rate applies.
Sunday, Travel full size separate section, Entertainment, (broadsheet)—general rate applies.

17. CLASSIFIED RATES
For complete data refer to classified rate section.

18. COMICS
POLICY—ALL CLASSIFICATIONS
When orders placed through Metro-Puck comics Network-see that listing.
Effective October 1, 1994.
Received July 18, 1994.
COLOR RATES AND DATA
Black and 3 colors:

	1 Time		1 Time
Full Page	13,296.00	1/3 pg	5,914.00
2/3 pg	11,892.00	1/6 pg	4,547.00
1/2 pg	7,946.00		

CLOSING TIMES
Reservations: 6 weeks before publication. No cancellations after reservation deadline.
MECHANICAL MEASUREMENTS
PRINTING PROCESS: Rotary Flexographic.
Page size 13" wide x 20- 1/8" deep.
Colors available: ANPA/AAAA: black and 3 colors: standard red, yellow and blue.
Double truck available: no charge for gutter.

19. MAGAZINES

Denver Post Magazine

SUNDAY.
Effective October 1, 1994.
Received July 18, 1994.
BLACK/WHITE RATES

Open, per inch	177.00

Bulk contract rates same as ROP.
COLOR RATES AND DATA
Use b/w rate plus the following applicable costs:

	b/w 1 c	b/w 2 c	b/w 3 c
Extra	1,900.00	2,070.00	2,185.00

SPECIAL DAYS/PAGES/FEATURES
Denver Post Magazine, Women's, Society and Lifestyle.
CLOSING TIMES
Reservations Noon, Monday.
Mechanical Measurements
PRINTING PROCESS: OFFSET.
5 cols. x 13" x 65" to page.
Modular sizes only, 3 1/4", 6 1/2", 9 3/4", 13".

TV/Cable Week

SUNDAY.
Effective October 1, 1994.
Received July 18, 1994.
BLACK/WHITE RATES

	Open	7 ti	13 ti	26 ti	52 ti
Full Page	3,479.00	2,758.00	2,623.00	2,563.00	2,443.00
3/4 pg	2,800.00	2,205.00	2,096.00	2,054.00	1,977.00
1/2 pg	1,893.00	1,485.00	1,425.00	1,390.00	1,332.00
1/4 pg	1,120.00	875.00	848.00	823.00	797.00
1/8 pg	789.00	637.00	619.00	559.00	553.00
1/16 pg	417.00	339.00	332.00	314.00	306.00

COLOR RATES AND DATA
Use b/w rate plus the following applicable costs:

	b/w 1 c	b/w 2 c	b/w 3 c
Extra	575.00	675.00	775.00

CLOSING TIMES
B/W: Reservations 21 days in advance of publication.
Camaera-ready 11 days preceding publication date.
Color: Camera-ready 20 days preceding publication date.
MECHANICAL MEASUREMENTS
PRINTED PROCESS: Web Offset.
Page size 6 3/4" x 9 3/4".

20. CIRCULATION
Established 1892, per copy daily .25; Sunday .75.
Net Paid—A.B.C. 3-31-94* (Newspaper Form)

	NEWSPAPER DESIGNATED MARKET		
	Total	NDM	Outside
Morn	293,777	239,426	54,351
Sun	450,483	336,439	114,044

(*) 26 weeks.
Unpaid dist. (not included above):
Morn Total 3,457; Sun Total 4,771
For county, MSA & DMA data, see CIRCULATION 95.

Exhibit 8–2 (continued)

DENVER
Rocky Mountain News

(Tabloid)
400 W. Colfax Ave., Denver, CO 80204.
Phone 303-892-5413/, 5227. Fax 303-892-5208

ADSAT
ABC

Location ID: 1 NSNL CO Mkt 016249-000
Member: NAA; ABC Coupon Distribution Verification Service; ACB, Inc.
MORNING, SATURDAY AND SUNDAY.

1. PERSONNEL
Pub—Larry D. Strutton.
Sr V.P. Circ/Adv—Elizabeth F. Brenner.
Display Adv Dir—Rick Avery.
Mgr Gen Adv—Susan Duchin.

2. REPRESENTATIVES and/or BRANCH OFFICES
Sawyer-Ferguson-Walker Co., Inc.

3. COMMISSION AND CASH DISCOUNT
15% to agencies; no cash discount.

4. POLICY-ALL CLASSIFICATIONS
No notice given of any rate revision.
Alcoholic beverage advertising accepted (daily & Sunday).

ADVERTISING RATES
Effective January 1, 1995.
Received December 21, 1994.
(Rates Pending Approval)

5. BLACK/WHITE RATES

	Morn.	Sun.
SAU open, per inch	173.75	188.75

Inches charged full depth col. 14; pg. 70; dbl truck 140.
Food Fare: Inches charged full depth: col. 22; pg. 132; dbl truck 264.

BULK CONTRACT RATES

Within 1 year:	Morn.	Sun.
31.5"	169.75	185.50
70"	165.50	181.00
132"	165.00	177.75
250"	161.25	175.75
500"	159.25	172.75
750"	157.25	169.50
1,200"	155.75	168.25
1,600"	153.50	167.50
3,200"	149.50	162.75
5,800"	129.25	139.50
7,000"	115.75	123.50

Rates apply within contract year. In absence of contract all advertising billed at open rate. Master contracts of multiple product advertisers should include all product names in contracts. Advertisers signing specific bulk contracts will be billed at applicable contract rate and rebilled at earned rate if contract is not fulfilled, or refunded if lower rate is earned.

7. COLOR RATES AND DATA
Use b/w rate plus the following applicable costs:

	b/w 1 c	b/w 2 c	b/w 3 c
Daily, extra	1,385.00	1,800.00	2,240.00
Sunday	1,517.00	1,950.00	2,390.00

Colors other than ANPA process red, yellow, blue or bright red charged at additional 25% per color. PMS colors are an additional 50% per color. Tabloid page production material for black plus 2 or 3 colors may not exceed 10-3/8" in width.
Food Fare double truck 264 inches.

8a. INSERTS
PREPRINTED INSERTS

Tab page:	Cost/M	Tab page:	Cost/M
1-6	54.00	26-36	61.75
8-14	56.25	38-50	63.75
15-24	60.25	52 or more	66.75

Frequency discounts available.

9. SPLIT RUN
Daily or Sunday in b/w or b/w 1c 300.00 make-over charge.
Minimum ad size b/w 20 inches, 150.00 extra for each additional plate for color or more than one split.
Closing 1 day in advance of regular closings.

11. SPECIAL DAYS/PAGES/FEATURES
Best Food Day: Wednesday.
Las Noticias, Sports Plus, Monday; Business, Tuesday; Style, Thursday; Weekend, Friday; Auto, Saturday; Homes, Real Estate, Sat. & Sun; Magazine & Travel, Sunday.

12. R.O.P. DEPTH REQUIREMENTS
Tabloid: Ads over 11-3/4 inches charged full column.
Saturday & Sunday Homes and Travel: Ads over 19 inches deep charged full col.

13. CONTRACT AND COPY REGULATIONS
See Contents page for location of regulations—items 1, 3, 5, 6, 7, 9, 13, 14, 15, 16, 17, 18, 19, 20, 21, 23, 25, 26, 17, 18, 29.

14. CLOSING TIME
Published Morning, Saturday and Sunday.

Day	Time	Closes
Mon	5 pm	Thu
Tue	5 pm	Fri
Wed	5 pm	fri
Thu	5 pm	Mon
Fri	5 pm	Mon
Sat	5 pm	Wed
Sun	5 pm	Wed
SPECIAL SECTIONS		
Food	5 pm	Fri
Colo. People (Sunday Magazine)	noon	Mon
Sunday Travel	2 nd	Pre/Fri
Style	5 pm	Mon

15. MECHANICAL MEASUREMENTS
PRINTING PROCESS: Photo Composition, Offset.

5 col; ea 2-1/16; 1/8" betw col.
Inches charged full depth: col. 14; pg. 70; dbl truck 140.
Food Fare—Wednesday; Style—Thursday.

5 col; ea 2-1/16"; 1/8" betw col.
Inches charged full depth: col. 22; pg. 132; dbl truck 264.

17. CLASSIFIED RATES
For complete data refer to classified rate section.

18. COMICS

POLICY—ALL CLASSIFICATION
When orders are placed through Metro-Puck Comics Network—see that listing.
Effective January 1, 1995.
Received December 21, 1994.

COLOR RATES AND DATA
Black and 2 standard colors:

1 page	7,440.00
2/3 page	6,050.00
1/2 page	4,055.00
1/3 page	3,150.00

50% Repeat Discount, ad must repeat within 7 days of original insertion.

CLOSING TIMES
Reservations and copy 5 weeks in advance. Advertiser to furnish Veloxes or negatives. Forms close 5 weeks in advance.

MECHANICAL MEASUREMENTS
PRINTING PROCESS: Photo Composition
Direct Letterpress (NAPP.)
Tabloid page size: 9-1/2" x 13".
For ad sizes see Metro-Puck Comic Network listing
Colors available: ANPA/AAAA; 4 Colors.
All printing material to be sent to the American Color, 302 Grote St., Buffalo, NY. 14207.

19. MAGAZINES

Colorado People Travel
SUNDAY.
Effective January 1, 1995.
Received December 21, 1994.

BLACK/WHITE RATES
Flat, per inch 188.75
Bulk linage contract rates ame as R.O.P.

COLOR RATES AND DATA
Use b/w rate plus the following applicable costs:

	b/w 1 c	b/w 2 c	b/w 3 c
Extra	1,515.00	1.950.00	2,390.00

Above rates apply for ANPA process red, yellow, blue and bright red only. Other ANPA colors, additional 25%, PMS colors 50%.
Closing time: Reservations 10 days before publication; printing material, 4 days before publication.
B/w 3 c Thursday 10 days preceding publication.
As many inches deep as columns wide.

CLOSING TIMES
Noon, Friday 9 days before publication.

MECHANICAL MEASUREMENTS
Photo Composition, Offset.
Page size 13" wide x 22" deep. 65 cols to page.
Inches to: col. 22; page 132.
Color available: ANPA/AAAA: 4 Colors.

TV DIAL
SUNDAY.
Effective January 1, 1995.
Received December 21, 1994.

BLACK/WHITE RATES
Sold in units; 10 per page, ea unit 1-3/8" x 5"

1 unit	618.00	5 units	1,612.00
2 units	853.00	6 units	1.850.00
3 units	1,145.00	10 units	3,025.00
4 units	1,405.00		

FREQUENCY CONTRACT DISCOUNTS

Within 1 year:	Discounts	Within 1 year:	Discounts
6 weeks	10%	26 weeks	20%
13 weeks	15%	52 weeks	25%

COLOR RATES AND DATA
Use b/w rate plus the following applicable costs:

	b/w 1 c	b/w 2 c	b/w 3 c
Extra	690.00	990.00	1,265.00

ANPA process colors only; red, yellow and blue. Minimum 4 units.
Colors other than stated are an additional 120.00.

CLOSING TIMES
3rd Thursday before publication. B/w 3 c: 3rd Wednesday before publication.

MECHANICAL MEASUREMENTS
PRINTING PROCESS: Offset.
5/8-6/6—5 cols/ea 8 picas-6 pts/6 pts betw col.
Prime Time 1/4 pg (horiz) 7-3/8" x 2-3/8"

20. CIRCULATION
Established 1859. Per copy daily, .35; Sunday .75.
Net Paid—A.B.C. 9-30-94 (Newspaper Form)

NEWSPAPER DESIGNATED MARKET

	Total	NDM	Outside
Morn	344,585	313,382	31,203
Sun	446,866	402,536	44,330

Total City Zone: Morn 263,384; Sun 334,486.

Unpaid dist. (not included above)
Morn Total 4,548; Sun Total 6,293
A.B.C. Zip Code Analysis available from publisher.
For county, MSA & DMA data, see CIRCULATION 95.

Exhibit 8–3 SRDS: Trade Magazines

Gourmet News

The Business Newspaper For The Gourmet Industry
A United Publications, Inc. Publication

BPA ABP

Location ID: 7 BLST 61 Mid 003421-000
Published 12 times a year by United Publications, Inc., P.O. Box 1056, 38 Lafayette St., Yarmouth, ME 04096. Phone 207-846-0600. Fax 207-846-0657

PUBLISHER'S EDITORIAL PROFILE

GOURMET NEWS is a business newspaper for the gourmet industry. The publication reports the news affecting Independent gourmet/specialty food stores; Gourmet distributors, wholesalers, brokers, importers; Supermarket gourmet departments/specialty food store chains; Gourmet cookware and gift shops; Department store gourmet departments and other key industry segments. In addition to publishing leading news stories, Gourmet News contains separate news sections to Specialty Retailers; Supermarkets and Department Stores; Distributors, Brokers and Wholesalers; and Supplier Business. Rec'd 12/30/91.

1. PERSONNEL
Pub—Christopher Crocker.
Adv Acct Mgr—Sue Babin.
Adv Acct Mgr—Lenore Grant.
Adv Acct Mgr—Bonnie Nelson.
Classif Adv Sales—Jo-Ellen Reed.

2. REPRESENTATIVES and/or BRANCH OFFICES
Yarmouth, ME 04096—Jo-Ellen Reed, Classif Adv Sales. PO Box 1056. Phone 207-846-0600. FAX: 207-846-0657.
Los Gatos, CA 95031-0395—Lenore Grant, P.O. Box 395. Phone 408-377-6462. FAX 408-377-3582.
New York, NY 10706—Bonnie Nelson, 55 Scenic Dr., Hastings on the Hudson. Phone 914-478-4408. FAX: 914-478-4916.
Chicago, IL 60660—Sue Babin, 6033 N. Sheridan, Ste. 13J. Phone 312-275-4020. FAX: 312-275-3438.

3. COMMISSION AND CASH DISCOUNT
15% to agencies on space, color and position only. 2% 10 days.

4. GENERAL RATE POLICY
When new rates are announced, current advertisers will be protected at their current rate for 90 days after the effective date of the new rate. Orders may be cancelled at the time the change in rates becomes effective without incurring a short rate adjustment on insertions already run, provided the contract has been earned up to date for cancellation.
Cancellations not accepted after closing date.

ADVERTISING RATES
Effective January 1, 1995. (Issue/Card)
Rates received September 12, 1994.

5. BLACK/WHITE RATES
Tabloid:

	1 ti	3 ti	6 ti	12 ti	18 ti	24 ti
1 page	3880.	3530.	2990.	2715.	2600.	2485.

Junior:

	1 ti	3 ti	6 ti	12 ti	18 ti	24 ti
1 page	3180.	2895.	2450.	2225.	2130.	2035.
2/3 page	2385.	2170.	1835.	1670.	1600.	1525.
1/2 page	2065.	1880.	1590.	1445.	1385.	1320.
1/3 page	1335.	1215.	1030.	935.	895.	855.
1/4 page	1080.	985.	830.	755.	725.	690.
1/6 page	765.	695.	550.	535.	515.	490.

6. COLOR RATES

	Page or less	Sprd
2-color process, extra	350.	510.
2-color matched, extra	480.	670.
4-color sprd. extra	—	1275.

Tabloid:

	1 ti	3 ti	6 ti	12 ti	18 ti	24 ti
4-Color:						
1 page	4805.	4455.	3915.	3640.	3525.	3410.

Junior:

	1 ti	3 ti	6 ti	12 ti	18 ti	24 ti
4-Color:						
1 page	4105.	3820.	3375.	3150.	3055.	2960.
2/3 page	3310.	3095.	2760.	2595.	2525.	2450.
1/2 page	2990.	2805.	2515.	2370.	2310.	2245.
1/3 page	2260.	2140.	1955.	1860.	1820.	1780.
1/4 page	2005.	1910.	1755.	1680.	1650.	1615.
1/6 page	1690.	1620.	1515.	1460.	1440.	1415.

7. COVERS
Includes 4-Color:
Non-cancellable:

	1 ti	3 ti	6 ti	12 ti	18 ti	24 ti
2nd cover	5060.	4690.	4110.	3820.	3695.	3570.
3rd cover	4900.	4545.	3990.	3705.	3590.	3470.
4th cover	5375.	4980.	4355.	4040.	3905.	3775.

8. INSERTS
Available.

9. BLEED
No charge.

10. SPECIAL POSITION
Non-cancellable.
Extra 10%

	1 ti	6 ti	12 ti
Product Wrap-ups (4-color only)	495.	455.	430.

11. CLASSIFIED/MAIL ORDER
See Business Publication Advertising Source Classified section.

13. SPECIAL ISSUE RATES AND DATA
NATONAL DIRECTORY OF GOURMET BASKET RETAILERS
Published annually; issue July.
Special rates apply.
Space closes June 20; Material June 27.

14. CONTRACT AND COPY REGULATIONS
See Contents page for location—items 1 thru 32.

15. GENERAL REQUIREMENTS
Also see SRDS Print Media Production Source.
Printing Process: Offset Full Run
Trim Size: 10-5/8 x 14-3/4; No./Cols. 4 & 5.
Binding Method: Saddle Stitched.
Colors Available: 4-color process; Matched.
Covers: 4-color process; Matched.

TABLOID AD PAGE DIMENSIONS
1 pg 9-5/8 x 13-3/4

JR AD PAGE DIMENSIONS

1 pg	7 x 10	1/3 v	2-3/16 x 10
2/3 v	4-9/16 x 10	1/3 sq	4-9/16 x 4-7/8
1/2 isl	4-9/16 x 7-1/2	1/4 v	3-3/8 x 4-7/8
1/2 v	3-3/8 x 10	1/6 v	2-3/16 x 4-7/8
1/2 h	7 x 4-7/8		

16. ISSUE AND CLOSING DATES
Published 12 times a year.

Issue:	Closing (+)	Closing (*)	Issue:	Closing (+)	Closing (*)
Jan	12/7	12/9	Jul	6/7	6/9
Feb	1/4	1/6	Aug	7/5	7/7
Mar	2/8	2/10	Sep	8/9	8/11
Apr	3/8	3/10	Oct	9/6	9/8
May	4/5	4/7	Nov	10/11	10/13
Jun	5/10	5/12	Dec	11/8	11/10

(+) Space
(*) Material

18. CIRCULATION
Established 1935. Single copy 2.50; per year 35.00.
Summary data—for detail see Publisher's Statement.
B.P.A. 6-30-94 (6 mos. aver. qualified)

Total	Non-Pd	Paid
20,100	20,100	...

Non-qualified paid subscriptions and or non-paid requests 203
Average Non-Qualified (not incl. elsewhere):
Total 4,430
TERRITORIAL DISTRIBUTION 5/94—20,100

N.Eng.	Mid.Atl.	E.N.Cen.	W.N.Cen.	S.Atl.	E.S.Cen.
2,078	6,227	2,496	699	2,837	433
W.S.Cen.	Mtn.St.	Pac.St.	Canada	Foreign	Other
817	666	3,702	100	...	45

Non-qualified paid subscriptions and or non-paid requests 222

BUSINESS ANALYSIS OF CIRCULATION
1 —Independent gourmet; specialty food store.
2 —Supermaket gourmet dept., gourmet; specialty food store chain.
3 —Department store gourmet dept.
4 —Gourmet cookware shop, gourmet gift shop.
5 —Gourmet distributor, gourmet broker, gourmet wholesaler, gourmet importer.
6 —Others allied to the field.
—TL Qual—Total Qualified
7 —Non-qualified paid subscriptions and or non-paid requests
TL —Total.

TL. Total. A. Owner, President. B. Vice President; General Manager. C. Division; Store Manager. D. Buyer; Assistant Buyer. E. Other Titled & Non-Titled Pers. incl. Co. Copies.

	TL	A	B	C	D	E
1—	9,243	5,222	955	934	948	1,184
2—	2,328	481	244	414	516	673
3—	935	157	118	128	316	216
4—	3,843	2,619	307	267	313	337
5—	3,595	1,691	558	138	321	887
6—	156	59	17	14	27	39
TL Qual—	20,100	10,229	2,199	1,895	2,441	3,336
7—	222	—	—	—	—	—
TL—	20,322	—	—	—	—	—

Gourmet Retailer, The

ABC ABP

Location ID: 7 BLST 61 Mid [illegible]
Published monthly by Specialty Media Inc, 3301 Ponce de Leon Blvd., Ste. 300, Coral Gables, FL 33134. Phone 305-446-3388. Fax 305-446-2868
For shipping info., see Print Media Production Source.

PUBLISHER'S EDITORIAL PROFILE

THE GOURMET RETAILER covers the upmarket food & housewares industries today, including cookware, specialty food, confections, perishables, bakeware, small electrics, cookbooks, cutlery and dairy-deli bakery operations, and coffee. Reporting on new products, shop merchandising, tabletop, stock and display, market reports, news analysis, editorials and product knowledge. Rec'd 7/29/92.

1. PERSONNEL
Pub—Edward R. Loeb.
Exec Editor—Nancy Moore.

2. REPRESENTATIVES and/or BRANCH OFFICES
Lloyd Neck, NY 11743—The LBS Sales Group Ltd., 5 Oakwood Dr. West. Phone 516-673-4848. FAX: 516-673-4870.
Los Angeles, CA 90048—Shari Wainberg, 6399 Wilshire Blvd., #906. Phone 213-653-5757.
Coral Gables, FL 33134—David Loeb, 3301 Ponce de Leon Blvd., Ste. 300. Phone 305-446-3388. FAX: 305-446-2868.
Arlington Heights, IL 60005—Arnie Bennett, 505 Cleveland St. #306. Phone 708-590-1332. FAX: 708-590-1729.

3. COMMISSION AND CASH DISCOUNT
15% to recognized agencies if paid within 30 days from date of invoice.
No cash discounts.

4. GENERAL RATE POLICY
Rates based on total number of insertions or issues used. Advertising must be inserted within 1 year of the first insertion to earn frequency discounts. Multiple units of space in 1 issue may be used to earn frequency discounts. 2-page spreads are counted as 2 units for purpose of determining frequency. Unfilled contracts will be short rated to next higher general frequency rate.
No cancellations accepted after closing date.

ADVERTISING RATES
Effective January 1, 1995. (Issue/Card 16)
Rates received October 14, 1994.

5. BLACK/WHITE RATES

	1 ti	3 ti	6 ti	12 ti	16 ti	24 ti
1 page	3553.	3153.	2857.	2738.	2619.	2500.
2/3 page	2738.	2619.	2262.	2023.	1905.	1785.
1/2 pg isl	2321.	2143.	1844.	1726.	1667.	1606.
1/2 page	2143.	2023.	1726.	1547.	1488.	1428.
1/3 page	1547.	1428.	1309.	1131.	1071.	1012.
1/4 page	1250.	1131.	952.	893.	863.	833.
1/6 page	833.	773.	714.	655.	625.	594.

Frequency Contract Rates must be contracted for prior to the 1st insertion with exact months and sizes of ads. Not subject to changes. Unfilled contracts will be short-rated to next higher general frequency rate.

5a. COMBINATION RATES
Advertisers running ROP ads in both Gourmet Retailer and Spice will earn frequency discount in each, based on combined number of insertions.

6. COLOR RATES

	1 ti	3 ti	6 ti	12 ti	16 ti	24 ti
2-Color:						
1 page	4086.	3626.	3286.	3149.	3012.	2875.
2/3 page	3149.	3012.	2601.	2327.	2191.	2053.
1/2 pg isl	2669.	2464.	2121.	1985.	1917.	1928.
1/2 page	2464.	2327.	1985.	1779.	1785.	1714.
1/3 page	1779.	1643.	1505.	1357.	1285.	1215.
1/4 page	1437.	1301.	1143.	1072.	1035.	999.
1/6 page	999.	928.	857.	786.	750.	713.

	1 ti	3 ti	6 ti	12 ti	16 ti	24 ti
4-Color:						
1 page	4667.	4416.	4000.	3834.	3668.	3499.
2/3 page	3834.	3668.	3166.	2834.	2667.	2501.
1/2 pg isl	3598.	3322.	2862.	2676.	2583.	2492.
1/2 page	3322.	3137.	2676.	2400.	2308.	2215.
1/3 page	2631.	2429.	2226.	1924.	1822.	1721.
1/4 page	2125.	1924.	1560.	1517.	1468.	1417.
1/6 page	1300.	1183.	958.	929.	901.	874.

7. COVERS

	1 ti	3 ti	6 ti	12 ti	16 ti	24 ti
4-Color:						
2nd cover	6301.	6067.	5834.	5601.	5410.	5160.
3rd cover	6301.	6067.	5834.	5601.	5410.	5160.
4th cover	7467.	7234.	7001.	6767.	6538.	6236.

Non-cancellable.

8. INSERTS
Supplied inserts are invoiced at black-and-white rates per page.
All normal binding charges included. Specialized binding will be billed separately.

9. BLEED
Extra 10%

10. SPECIAL POSITION
Guaranteed extra 10%

11. CLASSIFIED/MAIL ORDER
See Business Publication Advertising Source Classified section.

15. GENERAL REQUIREMENTS
Also see SRDS Print Media Production Source.
Printing Process: Offset Full Run Cover
Trim Size: 8-1/8 x 10-7/8; No./Cols. 3.
Binding Method: Perfect.
Colors Available: 4-color process; Matched; GAA/SWOP.
Covers: 4-color process.

AD PAGE DIMENSIONS

1 pg	7-1/4 x 10	1/3 v	2-1/4 x 10
2/3 v	4-3/4 x 10	1/3 sq	4-3/4 x 4-7/8
1/2 isl	4-3/4 x 7-3/8	1/4 sq	3-1/2 x 4-7/8
1/2 v	3-1/2 x 10	1/6 v	2-1/4 x 4-7/8
1/2 h	7-1/4 x 4-7/8	1/6 h	4-3/4 x 2-3/8

16. ISSUE AND CLOSING DATES
Published monthly.

Issue:	Closing (+)	Closing (†)	Closing (**)	Issue:	Closing (+)	Closing (†)	Closing (**)
Jan	11/11	11/18	11/25	Jul	5/12	5/19	5/26
Feb	12/12	12/19	12/26	Aug	6/11	6/18	6/25
Mar	1/11	1/18	1/25	Sep	7/11	7/18	7/25
Apr	2/13	2/20	2/27	Oct	8/11	8/18	8/25
May	3/13	3/20	3/27	Nov	9/11	9/18	9/25
Jun	4/11	4/18	4/25	Dec	10/11	10/18	10/25

(+) Space
(†) Camera ready
(**) Final film

18. CIRCULATION
Established 1979. Single copy 2.50; per year 24.00.
Summary data—for detail see Publisher's Statement.
A.B.C. 6-30-94 (6 mos. aver. qualified)

Total	Non-Pd	Paid	(Subs)	(Single)	(Assoc)
20,762	20,754	8	8	—	...

Average Non-Qualified (not incl. above):
Total 6,442
TERRITORIAL DISTRIBUTION 5/94—21,009

N.Eng.	Mid.Atl.	E.N.Cen.	W.N.Cen.	S.Atl.	E.S.Cen.
1,723	4,562	3,118	971	3,225	564
W.S.Cen.	Mtn.St.	Pac.St.	Canada	Foreign	Other
1,062	997	4,568	86	64	69

BUSINESS ANALYSIS OF CIRCULATION

Specialty Food Shops.	5,586
Dept. Store Gourmet Depts. Div. Mgrs. and Buyers (Specialty Food and Confection, Small Electrical Appliances, Housewares, Tabletop).	642
Ind. Supermarkets & Chains (Specialty Foods & Housewares Buyers).	1,335
Cookware, Gift Gourmet Shops, Cooking Schools	5,210
Confection Shops	691
Gourmet Coffee & Tea Shops.	1,518
Food Wholesalers, Distributors & Importers	2,626
Mail Order	936
Specialty Food Brokers & Manufacturer's Rep	1,770
Food & Housewares Writers	212
Others Allied to the Field	483
Total.	21,009

3. What is the closing date for the first national ad? ______________
   a. What is the closing date for the first regional ad if it is scheduled to run in June? ______________
4. If the full-page, four-color national ads were to be run on the back (fourth) cover, what would be the cost for the January ad? ______________

Newspapers

You are planning a series of 13 weekly newspaper ads in Denver, Colorado. The ad size will be four columns by 10.5 inches. The ads are to be scheduled on the best food day in the newspaper that provides the lowest CPM for its total circulation.

5. How many total inches will this schedule of ads use? ______________
   (Note: [Number of columns] × [Number of inches per column] × [Number of ads] = Total inches for schedule)
6. Using the lowest earned-per-inch rate, compute the CPM for one ad in each newspaper. (Refer to Assignment 12 on CPM computations, if necessary.)
   a. What is the CPM for an ad in the *Denver Post*? ______________
   b. What is the CPM for an ad in the *Rocky Mountain News*? ______________
7. What would be the cost of the entire schedule of ads in the most cost-efficient newspaper? ______________
8. On what day would you run the ads? ______________

Trade Magazines

You are planning a schedule of five 7 × 10 inch black-and-white ads in each of the trade magazines shown in Exhibit 8–3.

9. What is the cost in each publication for a black-and-white page?
   a. *Gourmet News* ______________
   b. *The Gourmet Retailer* ______________
10. Indicate the cost for the trade ad schedule:
    a. Five ads in *Gourmet News*: ______________
    b. Five ads in *The Gourmet Retailer*: ______________
    c. Total cost of the trade ad schedule: ______________
11. What would the cost be for the schedule if you ran an additional one-sixth page, black-and-white ad (called a *rate holder*) in each publication in order to earn the six-time rate for the entire schedule? ______________

Assignment 9

Market Selections Based on Sales Data

Objective: To help you understand how to use sales data as a guide to selecting markets that are to receive special marketing/advertising emphasis. Sales data, when available market by market, are a critical basis for selecting markets in which to place advertising.

Discussion

Often media plans call for special market emphasis in markets that represent high potential or sales. The media planner is sometimes required to select markets to receive added weight based on available sales information.

The amount of information available varies from client to client, but the more you have available, the more sophisticated the selection process can be. Some basic types of sales data include sales in dollars, sales change over previous years, brand development index (BDI), and category development index (CDI).

Brand development index (BDI) is a measure of the brand's sales strength. Although there are several ways to compute BDI, a common method is to compare brand sales to population. For example, if a market accounts for 5 percent of the total population, it is reasonable to assume that it should also account for 5 percent of the brand's sales. If the sales and population percentages are the same, the BDI would be 100. BDI figures below 100 indicate that sales are not as high as would be expected if they kept pace with the population. BDI figures above 100 indicate that sales are better than might be expected based on the population.

CDI, or category development index, indicates how well the category (or industry) does compared to population. For example, if a market accounts for 5 percent of the population, it should also account for 5 percent of industry sales in a product category (e.g., cake mixes).

When the BDI is higher than the CDI, it indicates that the brand is doing better than the industry in that market. A BDI lower than the CDI indicates that the brand is not performing as well as the industry. Although a low BDI indicates room for growth, it does not always call for additional advertising weight, because factors other than a lack of advertising could be inhibiting growth (e.g., a lack of distribution or inadequate sales force emphasis). When a BDI is much lower than a CDI for the same market, special research should be done to find the reason for the discrepancy.

When more than one type of information is available, it is a good idea to establish criteria for each type of information. For example, if you know dollar sales, percentage of change over the previous year, and BDI, you might set up the following criteria that a market would have to meet to receive extra advertising weight:

- Sales of more than $200,000 per year
- Sales increase of 5 percent or more
- BDI of 130 or more

In order to accommodate markets with low sales and good potential or markets of high development but recent sales declines, you might decide that to qualify, a market must meet two out of three criteria. The development of criteria involves personal judgment based on an understanding of sales data.

Refer to *Advertising Media Planning*, 5th ed., by Sissors and Bumba, Chapter 8.

Problem

Assume that you have developed a media plan that calls for extra advertising weight in markets with sales strength or good potential for sales growth. Keep in mind that all markets will receive the national advertising effort. You are interested in selecting markets that will receive *extra* advertising weight.

To begin this assignment, you should develop a set of criteria that a market must meet in order to qualify for extra advertising weight. Here are some guidelines to help you establish the criteria.

Annual sales volume of $________________ or more

Sales increase of at least ________________ percent over previous year

Current year BDI of ________________ or more

Current BDI level ________________ points or more above CDI

Now, using the four criteria, select the ten markets that are to get the extra advertising weight from the 25 markets shown on the following page. If a market does not meet all four criteria, tell why you selected it.

DMA	Current year sales (000)	Previous year sales (000)	% change	Current BDI	Previous year BDI	Current CDI
New York	$ 464	$ 483	− 3.9%	62	68	90
Los Angeles	561	498	+12.7	129	123	110
Chicago	580	481	+20.6	179	158	120
Philadelphia	281	250	+12.4	104	98	98
Boston	276	278	− 0.7	134	143	145
San Francisco	328	300	+ 9.3	164	159	155
Detroit	188	170	+10.6	101	97	92
Cleveland	239	236	+ 1.3	141	140	155
Washington, D.C.	107	84	+27.4	70	58	102
Pittsburgh	72	96	−25.0	54	77	115
St. Louis	112	125	−10.4	103	104	110
Dallas/Ft. Worth	145	121	+19.8	118	104	110
Minneapolis/St. Paul	153	163	− 6.1	146	165	160
Seattle/Tacoma	119	95	+25.3	124	105	105
Baltimore	38	50	−24.0	44	61	122
Indianapolis	109	95	+15.8	119	110	109
Houston	102	126	−19.0	118	122	129
Hartford/New Haven	98	94	+ 4.3	128	130	132
Atlanta	73	82	−10.9	74	87	110
Buffalo	72	57	+26.3	98	83	105
Cincinnati	64	70	− 8.6	86	100	107
Miami	63	70	−10.0	65	76	118
Milwaukee	51	58	−12.1	69	83	102
Memphis	109	66	+65.2	152	107	108
Kansas City	81	75	+ 8.0	111	109	101
25-market total	$4,485	$4,223	+ 6.2%			

Assignment 10

Weighting BDI and CDI Data

More Considerations on the Use of Sales Indices

Objective: To consider the importance of projecting sales and sales indices where such projections are believed to be appropriate. This assignment asks you to consider other ways to use category (CDI) and brand (BDI) indexes for market selection, beyond those considerations discussed in Assignment 9.

Refer to *Advertising Media Planning*, 5th ed., by Sissors and Bumba, Chapter 8.

Discussion

How do you determine which markets will most likely and profitably respond to advertising investment? This is an important question when you select markets to receive additional or heavy-up media support. Factors such as per-capita rate and growth of industry and brand sales, distribution, competitive activity, and results from past promotional activities help the experienced planner determine which are the best markets for additional support.

Media planners often invest considerable research and analysis to discover just which factors will best predict those markets that will be most responsive to advertising. Correlation analysis and other computer programming techniques are used to isolate the more important factors and the weighting these factors should receive in the sales forecast analysis.

Weighting of CDI and BDI Data

Media and marketing planners frequently work with CDI and BDI data (see Assignment 9) in selecting markets for additional spot spending. Often, markets are selected against sets of criteria such as the following:

(a) High category and brand sales

(b) High category but low brand sales

(c) High brand sales, despite only average or below-average category development

Use of criteria set (a) assumes that sales will respond where both industry and brand sales have been relatively high (something must be working right). Under criteria set (b), strong industry sales suggest the opportunity to promote your brand to achieve a larger share of sales. If you use set (c), you might wish to support current sales strength, even if industry sales are relatively low in these markets.

For each group of markets (based on criteria sets such as the three just mentioned), a relative weighting can be assigned to CDI and BDI. The result is a combined CDI/BDI number that presumably will predict, with reasonable accuracy, which markets are best for additional advertising investment. When no additional weighting is given to either the CDI or to the BDI, then, in effect, equal weights have been assigned.

The following shows calculation of market indices under three weighting assumptions for a market with a CDI of 165 and a BDI of 130.

		CDI/BDI weighted index
Assumption (a):	CDI and BDI are equal in weighting (CDI 50%; BDI 50%) (.5 × 165) + (.5 × 130) = 82.5 + 65.0 =	148
Assumption (b):	CDI is four times as important as BDI (CDI 80%; BDI 20%) (.8 × 165) + (.2 × 130) =132.0 + 26.0 =	158
Assumption (c):	BDI is twice as important as CDI (CDI 33%; BDI 67%) (.33 × 165) + (.67 × 130) = 54.45 + 87.1 =	142

The decision on how to weight CDI and BDI is especially important when some markets have a CDI considerably higher or lower than BDI and when differences between CDI and BDI vary greatly from one market to another. Obviously, if CDI is emphasized, then markets with strong category sales will receive extra consideration. Conversely, when greater emphasis is placed on BDI, markets with high brand sales will receive more emphasis than markets strong in category sales, but weak in brand sales.

Projection of CDI and BDI

CDI and BDI numbers are usually calculated on recent sales periods. However, the sophisticated marketer will consider previous sales trends and then project expected CDI and BDI numbers for each market for the upcoming period.

Two approaches are used to project CDI and BDI numbers for the next sales period. The most common approach is to compute sales growth (category sales for CDI and brand sales for BDI) for each market, as shown. For market A, the rate of sales growth is as follows:

Market A	Volume previous period	Volume current period	% change
Category sales	850,000	980,000	+15.3
Brand sales	250,000	267,000	+ 6.8

Then project the market volume for the future period and compute the percentage of total U.S. projected volume obtained from the specific market.

Category	Projected volume for future period (see Table 10–1)		% of U.S. volume
Market A	980,000 + (980,000 × 15.3%) =	1,129,940	2.15
		52,640,000	100.00
Brand			
Market A	267,000 + (267,000 × 6.8%) =	285,156	1.69
		16,870,000	100.00

To compute the CDI and BDI, divide percentage of U.S. category or brand sales obtained in the market by the percentage of U.S. population in the market.

Market A	(1.3% of U.S. TV HHs)	Index
CDI	(2.15% ÷ 1.3%) × 100	165
BDI	(1.69% ÷ 1.3%) × 100	130

An alternative way to compute the market index for a future sales period is to calculate the rate of change in previous indices and use it to project to the future period. When you use this approach, it is usually best to carry out computations beyond the decimal point (usually to thousandths of an index).

The following table projects market indices for category and brand sales to a future sales period. (Note: Index numbers for the future period are the same as those computed with the more common sales projection method previously mentioned.)

Market A	Previous period	Current period	Future period	Next future period
CDI	128	145	164	?
BDI	137	134	131	?

You can also project indices for additional future periods. Using any one of the methods discussed previously, calculate the CDI and BDI for the next future period. Be sure that you understand how to make these calculations.

Obviously, there are other criteria for market selection beyond those of category and brand sales (CDI and BDI). Each marketer must determine what other factors (if any) should be used to determine each market's potential. For example, the marketer could use weightings for distribution levels, media costs, rate of volume change, or an important competitor's sales volume or promotional activity—all of which vary on a market-by-market basis.

Indices can be computed for each variable or market factor considered and then combined with the market's CDI and BDI. If the assumptions used are correct, this index should represent the market's relative potential compared to all other markets. It should be remembered, however, that as more variables are included, index numbers will tend to "flatten out" and show only small differences between markets. Therefore, it is usually best to limit consideration to only those key variables that are most likely to predict market potential.

Table 10–1 Category and Brand Sales Projections for Five Markets

CDI

Markets	U.S. TV HHs (%)	Previous period sales (000)	Current period sales (000)	% change	Future period sales (000)	Previous period CDI	Current period CDI	Future period CDI
A	1.3%	$ 850	$ 980	+15.3%	$ 1,130	128	145	164
B	2.7	1,410	1,650	+17.0	1,931	102	118	137
C	1.8	1,030	1,100	+ 6.8	1,175	112	118	124
D	2.3	1,460	1,330	− 8.9	1,212	124	112	101
E	3.5	1,550	1,720	+11.0	1,909	87	95	104
Five-market total	11.6%	$ 6,300	$ 6,780	+ 7.6%	$ 7,357	106	113	120
Remainder of U.S.	88.4%	$44,700	$45,020	+ 0.7%	$45,290	99	98	97
Total U.S.	100.0%	$51,000	$51,800	+ 1.6%	$52,647	100	100	100

BDI

Markets	U.S. TV HHs (%)	Previous period sales (000)	Current period sales (000)	% change	Future period sales (000)	Previous period BDI	Current period BDI	Future period BDI
A	1.3%	$ 250	$ 267	+ 6.8%	$ 285	137	134	131
B	2.7	425	510	+20.0	612	112	123	135
C	1.8	260	275	+ 5.8	291	103	99	95
D	2.3	240	235	− 2.1	230	74	66	59
E	3.5	445	505	+13.5	573	91	94	97
Five-market total	11.6%	$ 1,620	$ 1,792	+10.6%	$ 1,991	100	100	100
Remainder of U.S.	88.4%	$12,410	$13,590	+ 9.5%	$14,880	100	100	100
Total U.S.	100.0%	$14,030	$15,382	+ 9.6%	$16,870	100	100	100

Problems

1. Compute the weighted CDI/BDI index for each of the five markets for which data are given in this assignment. You should review computations shown in the previous discussion and assume that research and judgment indicate the following:

   (a) BDI should be weighted three times the importance of CDI (CDI = 25%; BDI = 75%).

   (b) Use the CDI and BDI numbers projected for the future period shown in the following data chart (see columns 2, 3, and 4).

   (c) Assume no other factors or considerations are of importance.

2. Using the weighted CDI/BDI numbers computed in (1) above, allocate a media heavy-up budget of $300,000 to the five markets presented in this assignment. Specifically, follow these steps:

   (a) Adjust the percentage of U.S. TV households by weighted CDI/BDI for each market (see column 5).

   (b) Determine the percentage of media budget to be allocated to each market (see column 6).

   (c) Determine the heavy-up media dollars allocated to each market (see column 7).

		Future period indices				Five-market media allocation	
Market	U.S. TV HHs (%)	CDI	BDI	Weighted CDI/BDI	Column 1 × Column 4	(%)	($)
Column:	(1)	(2)	(3)	(4)	(5)	(6)	(7)
A	1.3%	165	130	______	______	______	______
B	2.7	136	134	______	______	______	______
C	1.8	124	96	______	______	______	______
D	2.3	100	59	______	______	______	______
E	3.5	104	97	______	______	______	______
Five-market total	11.6	120	101	______	______	100.0%	$300,000
Total U.S.	100.0%	100	100	100	–	–	–

3. Using the data provided in Table 10–1 (BDI), explain *how* you would allocate media on a "percentage-of-sales" basis for *your* brand (e.g., a market with 10 percent of the brand's sales would receive 10 percent of advertising dollars).

4. Explain for each market how budget allocation would be affected if trends continued and budget was allocated on indices computed for an additional period in the future (e.g., market A would have a CDI of 186 and a BDI of 128 in the next projected year). You will need to review trends shown in Table 10-1.

Section Two

Media Analysis Problems

Assignment 11

Understanding Coverage

Objective: To help you better understand the different meanings of the word *coverage* by asking you to define it in terms of the various media and media situations.

Discussion

Coverage is one of the most misunderstood terms in media planning because the term has different meanings for different media. The confusion began early in the history of advertising, after coverage was applied first to newspapers. When newer media developed, such as magazines, radio, and television, the term began to have different meanings.

Refer to *Advertising Media Planning*, 5th ed., by Sissors and Bumba, Chapter 4.

Problems

1. A network television program had a coverage of 98.5 percent (TV households). From this coverage figure, can we know how many households tuned in? Briefly explain in a way that demonstrates that you understand the meaning of the coverage figure.

2. Suppose that a target audience for product *X* consists of 63,000,000 men aged 21–54 in the United States. Magazine A reached 14,500,000 of the 63,000,000 with an average issue. What is the percentage of coverage for magazine A?

3. What is the minimum requirement for you, as a radio listener, to be counted in a coverage measurement of a radio station in a given market?

4. If there are 210,000 households and 640,000 adults in a given market, what is the percentage of coverage of newspaper A, if its circulation is 128,000 daily? Show how you arrived at the answer.

5. Suppose that in newspaper A from problem 4, a readership study found that 422,000 adults read it daily. What is the percentage coverage of newspaper A?

6. A product is selling nationally, and you devise a spot TV media plan with 75 markets in it. Those 75 markets have a coverage of 79 percent of U.S. TV households. Precisely explain what the 79 percent coverage means.

7. How many TV households can we expect to cover in each of the 75 markets in problem 6? Explain.

8. Is outdoor coverage different from television coverage? Explain briefly.

Assignment 12

Use of Cost-per-Thousand (CPM) Concepts

Objective: To help you understand the calculation and use of cost-per-thousand prospects (especially primary targets) as a means of determining media cost efficiency.

Discussion

Occasionally, media are selected on the basis of total cost (e.g., "We just can't afford network television or large-size newspaper ads to reach all markets"). More often, the media planner is concerned with the cost per thousand (CPM) of audience (especially prospects) delivered by the media.

Although it is important to reach as many target audience members as possible, it is also just as important to reach them at an efficient cost. The most efficient cost is the lowest CPM. There will be times when CPM can be ignored in planning because some other selection criterion has a higher priority—but not often.

To calculate a CPM, you need to know the cost of a specific media unit[1] and the audience size delivered:

$$\text{CPM} = \frac{\text{Cost of a media unit} \times 1{,}000}{\text{Audience delivered}}$$

An alternative formula for CPM, and one that is easier to use with small pocket calculators, is:

$$\text{CPM} = \frac{\text{Cost of a media unit}}{\text{Audience (000)}}$$

Both formulas will deliver the same answer, but the second one does not require multiplying the cost by 1,000, which sometimes results in a number too large for small calculators to handle. Also, because audience figures are usually reported in thousands (000), the second version is convenient to use. You must remember, however, that if the audience figure is not reported in thousands, you will have to divide the audience by 1,000 or "strike three zeros" from the audience figure.

[1]A media unit is the form in which advertising runs, such as a black-and-white page, a 30-second commercial, a four-color bleed ad, etc.

Example: If you reached 5 million viewers for $20,000, then CPM viewers would be $4.00:

$$\text{CPM} = \frac{\$20{,}000 \times 1{,}000}{5{,}000{,}000} = \frac{\$20{,}000{,}000}{5{,}000{,}000} = \$4.00$$

or,

$$\text{CPM} = \frac{\$20{,}000}{5{,}000} = \$4.00$$

The most difficult task is determining which audience base should be used for CPM computations. Obviously, all CPM numbers used to evaluate media should relate to comparable audience definitions. Since CPM numbers can be computed on circulation, total audience, homemakers, women aged 18–24, all product users, heavy users, etc., you must always identify which audience relates to CPM numbers. A lesser problem is to be sure costs are accurate, to include all discounts, and to compute costs for comparable ad units.

The steps are as follows:

1. Identify the proper audience.
2. Obtain accurate media costs.
3. Correctly compute CPM.
4. Consider the best way to present those CPM numbers that support your media recommendations.

Refer to *Advertising Media Planning*, 5th ed., by Sissors and Bumba, Chapter 4.

How to Use CPM to Compare Media Alternatives

CPM numbers are used mainly for intramedia comparisons. CPM numbers are used as input for comparing one vehicle with another, but other media considerations—such as reach and frequency of audience—become important. How can you meaningfully compare CPM for a radio spot and a full-page ad when the media are so different?

Virtually all media decisions are made with the CPM in mind. As one media planner states, "I may not decide solely on cheapest CPM, but I like to know how much extra it costs to reach audiences in the less efficient, but perhaps more effective, media."

Even when comparing similar media, you should avoid overemphasis of CPM to the exclusion of all other considerations. If the differences in CPM are slight, you should use some other basis for comparison.

Another note: Audience data are not precise. They are merely estimates based on samples and are subject to sampling and research error. CPM comparisons should be reviewed to reflect changes in costs, discounts earned, etc.

Problems

1. You are given the following circulation and audience data for two magazines. (All circulation and audience data are in thousands.)

Magazine	Total circulation	Total adult audience	Women aged 18+	Women HH 3+	Women aged 35–49
A	5,000	12,500	8,100	3,300	3,000
B	7,500	15,000	9,000	4,000	4,000

Costs for the magazines are:

Magazine A: $21,000
Magazine B: $23,500

What is the CPM for women aged 18+ for each magazine?

Magazine A: ______________
Magazine B: ______________

2. Assume that men do not purchase your product and that women in households of 3 or more people and aged 35–49 are twice as likely to purchase your product as other women. Using the data above, which magazine would you select? ______________
Explain why.

3. Newspapers sell advertising space by the column inch. For example, an ad three columns wide and 13 inches high would equal 39 column inches ($3 \times 13 = 39$). If a newspaper had an open inch rate of $12.00, the total cost for a 39-inch ad would be $468 ($39 \times \$12 = \$468$).
Assume that you are planning to run a four-column, 13-inch ad in a newspaper with an open inch rate of $16 and a circulation of 125,000. What would the CPM circulation be for this ad? ______________

4. If in addition to the information in problem 3, you received a 12 percent discount on the cost of the ad, what would be the total cost and the CPM circulation?

Total cost: ______________

CPM circulation: ______________

5. Which television program shown below is the most efficient in delivering women aged 18+? (Assume there are 96,760,000 women aged 18+ in U.S. TV households.)

Network program	Average audience rating of women aged 18+	Program cost	Cost efficiency (CPM women 18+)
Program A	14%	$ 90,000	________
Program B	16	97,000	________
Program C	19	102,000	________

Assignment 13

Understanding Television Ratings

Objective: To help you understand both network and local television rating reports, the relationship between the pieces of information, and how to extract specific pieces of information from the reports.

Discussion

Ratings of broadcast programs are a vital kind of statistic used by media planners in selecting media. It should be understood that a TV rating is an estimate of the audience size for a program. The estimates are taken from probability samples of the universe of TV households. There is no measurement of the audience size of a commercial within a program. Program ratings are made of national and local audiences. Because television viewing and program popularity vary from market to market, the rating of a program measured in any specific market will differ from the national rating of that program. National ratings tend to average local market differences. Sample pages from the Nielsen Television Index (national) and Nielsen Station Index (local) are reproduced as Exhibits 13–1 through 13–3.

You should be familiar with the following terms before proceeding with this assignment:

Household (HHLD) audience/average audience (AVG. AUD.). Households tuned to a program during the average minute reported both as a percentage of total U.S. TV households and in terms of the projected number of households reached.

Total Audience (TA%). Percentage of households tuning to all or any portion of a program for 5 minutes or more. For programs of less than 10 minutes duration, households tuned in for one minute or more are included. Total audience figures tend to be higher than average audience figures for a program because households watching any 5-minute portion of a program are included in the total audience, whereas average audience figures show the actual viewing per minute. The longer the program, the greater the difference between the program's total audience and average audience figures. This is because the longer the program, the more opportunities there are to tune in for 5 minutes and thereby increase the total audience percentage.

The TA% figures are reported on the same line as AVG. AUD. 1/2 HR % figures. However, the TA% figures are printed in italics and are always the first listed for a program (Exhibit 13–1).

Share of audience (SH)(SHR). Household audience of a program as a percentage of the households using television at the time the program was

Exhibit 13–1 Nielsen National TV Audience Estimates

Nielsen NATIONAL TV AUDIENCE ESTIMATES — EVE.MON. NOV.7

TIME	7:00	7:15	7:30	7:45	8:00	8:15	8:30	8:45	9:00	9:15	9:30	9:45	10:00	10:15	10:30	10:45
HUT	58.7	60.2	60.7	62.3	65.3	66.6	67.1	68.2	68.4	69.1	69.0	67.9	65.2	63.4	60.7	58.5
ABC TV					COACH		COACH 2 (R)(PAE)		←NFL MONDAY NIGHT FOOTBALL NY GIANTS AT DALLAS (9.00-11.39)(PAE)→							
HHLD AUDIENCE% & (000)					**10.0**	9,540	**8.7**	8,300	**18.8**	17,940						
TA%, AVG. AUD. 1/2 HR %					*11.9*		*10.3*		*37.1*	19.3*		21.3*		21.7*		18.4*
SHARE AUDIENCE %					15		13		30	29*		32*		33*		30*
AVG. AUD. BY 1/4 HR %					9.8	10.1	8.4	9.0	17.9	20.6	21.0	21.6	22.4	20.9	18.3	18.5
CBS TV					NANNY		DAVE'S WORLD		MURPHY BROWN		LOVE & WAR		←NORTHERN EXPOSURE→			
HHLD AUDIENCE% & (000)					**13.8**	13,170	**13.6**	12,970	**14.7**	14,020	**12.7**	12,120	**13.2**	12,590		
TA%, AVG. AUD. 1/2 HR %					*15.9*		*15.2*		*17.0*		*14.6*		*16.9*	13.0*		13.5*
SHARE AUDIENCE %					21		20		21		19		21	20*		23*
AVG. AUD. BY 1/4 HR %					13.4	14.3	13.4	13.9	14.5	14.9	12.6	12.9	12.7	13.2	13.5	13.5
NBC TV					FRESH PRINCE OF BEL AIR		BLOSSOM		←NBC MONDAY NIGHT MOVIES A BURNING PASSION→							
HHLD AUDIENCE% & (000)					**10.6**	10,110	**10.8**	10,300	**12.3**	11,730						
TA%, AVG. AUD. 1/2 HR %					*12.8*		*12.5*		*20.1*	12.2*		12.7*		12.3*		12.0*
SHARE AUDIENCE %					16		16		19	18*		19*		19*		20*
AVG. AUD. BY 1/4 HR %					10.2	10.9	10.6	11.1	12.1	12.2	12.8	12.6	12.6	12.0	11.9	12.1
FOX TV					←MELROSE PLACE (PAE)→				←PARTY OF FIVE→							
HHLD AUDIENCE% & (000)					**9.5**	9,060			**5.7**	5,440						
TA%, AVG. AUD. 1/2 HR %					*12.4*	9.1*		10.0*	*8.3*	5.8*		5.6*				
SHARE AUDIENCE %					14	14*		15*	8	8*		8*				
AVG. AUD. BY 1/4 HR %					8.9	9.3	10.0	10.0	6.2	5.3	5.7	5.6				
INDEPENDENTS (INCLUDING SUPERSTATIONS EXCEPT TBS)																
AVERAGE AUDIENCE	15.3 (+F)		16.0 (+F)		8.9		10.0		9.1		8.7		11.7 (+F)		9.5 (+F)	
SHARE AUDIENCE %	26		26		14		15		13		13		18		16	
PBS																
AVERAGE AUDIENCE	1.9		2.3		2.2		2.1		3.0		3.4		3.2		3.1	
SHARE AUDIENCE %	3		4		3		3		4		5		5		5	
CABLE ORIG. (INCLUDING TBS)																
AVERAGE AUDIENCE	10.7 (+F)		12.0 (+F)		14.2		15.7		14.0		14.2		11.9 (+F)		11.4 (+F)	
SHARE AUDIENCE %	18		20		22		23		20		21		19		19	
PAY SERVICES																
AVERAGE AUDIENCE	1.6		1.7		2.3		2.5		2.6		2.2		2.3		2.4	
SHARE AUDIENCE %	3		3		4		4		4		3		4		4	

U.S. TV Households: 95,400,000

Exhibit 13–2 Nielsen Program Audience Estimates

PROGRAM AUDIENCE ESTIMATES (Alpha) NOV.7-13

PROGRAM NAME DAY TIME DUR NET #STNS CVG% TYPE	NO. OF T/C	KEY	HOUSEHOLD AUDIENCE AVG. AUD. %	VCR CNTRB %	SH %	AVG. AUD. 0,000	LOH 18-49 W/CH <3	WORKING WOMEN 18+	WORKING WOMEN 18-49	WOMEN 15-24	WOMEN TOTAL	WOMEN 18-34	WOMEN 18-49	WOMEN 25-49	WOMEN 25-54	WOMEN 35-64	WOMEN 55+	MEN TOTAL	MEN 18-49	TEENS MALE 12-17	TEENS FEM. 12-17	TEENS TOT. 15-17	CHILDREN MALE 2-11	CHILDREN FEM 2-11	CHILDREN TOT. 2-5	CHILDREN TOT. 6-11
MONDAY-FRIDAY DAYTIME																										
ALL MY CHILDREN		A	6.1	1.0	21	582	122	241	210	112	876	298	554	458	493	391	287	228	148	9^	30	22^	32	41	46	28
MON-FRI 1.00P 60 ABC	30	B	6.0	1.0	21	575	140	245	216	112	873	306	570	477	517	400	264	212	140	10^	28	24	31	38	47	22
223 99 DD	30	C	6.0	1.0	21	575	140	245	216	112	873	306	570	477	517	400	264	212	140	10^	28	24	31	38	47	22
1.00 - 1.30		A	5.9	1.0	20	561	117	234	199	112	873	289	547	450	487	398	289	230	150	9^	28	22^	36	41	48	29
1.30 - 2.00		A	6.4	1.0	22	609	125	246	217	111	871	303	555	461	494	380	283	225	144	9^	31	22^	29	41	44	26
ANIMANIACS M-F		A	4.0	.0	11	385	34^	72	62	89	231	127	189	139	157	92	25^	187	173	149	105	96	421	336	333	424
MON-FRI 4.00P 30 FOX	40	B	3.9	.0	11	372	48	79	69	96	242	140	200	144	158	91	27^	176	159	143	88	87	427	335	328	434
180 96 CA	45	C	3.9	.0	11	372	48	81	70	97	244	142	201	143	158	92	28^	179	160	144	89	88	423	332	322	433
ANOTHER WORLD		A	2.9	.3	11	273	98	201	157	170	812	293	489	348	380	330	290	287	171	7v	51^	33^	42^	31^	40^	34^
MON-FRI 2.00P 60 NBC	40	B	2.9	.4	11	274	102	197	167	151	814	294	506	374	408	344	275	276	164	9v	27^	25^	32^	23^	38^	17^
212 97 DD	40	C	2.9	.4	11	274	102	197	167	151	814	294	506	374	408	344	275	276	164	9v	27^	25^	32^	23^	38^	17^
2.00 - 2.30		A	2.9	.3	11	273	93	202	159	183	825	300	499	346	377	337	295	292	174	6v	52^	34^	47^	34^	48^	33^
2.30 - 3.00		A	2.8	.3	10	271	105	202	156	158	804	288	483	352	387	325	287	285	170	8v	52^	32^	38^	28^	32^	34^
AS THE WORLD TURNS		A	5.0	.7	18	475	57	218	178	97	904	222	394	310	354	360	467	186	73	15^	22^	24^	17^	27^	31	13^
MON-FRI 2.00P 60 CBS	40	B	4.9	.6	19	467	66	197	161	85	898	225	385	311	362	351	462	208	84	11^	17^	18^	24^	28	37	15^
214 99 DD	40	C	4.9	.6	19	467	66	197	161	85	898	225	385	311	362	351	462	208	84	11^	17^	18^	24^	28	37	15^
2.00 - 2.30		A	5.0	.7	19	481	53	215	176	91	906	217	388	309	352	361	475	194	78	14^	21^	23^	14^	26^	28^	11^
2.30 - 3.00		A	4.9	.7	18	467	62	221	180	103	908	227	402	314	358	362	463	181	69	15^	22^	26^	19^	29^	33	15^
BOLD AND THE BEAUTIFUL		A	5.5	.6	19	523	56	180	141	74	871	186	325	258	305	327	499	224	91	19^	18^	16^	25^	36	46	15^
MON-FRI 1.30P 30 CBS	40	B	5.6	.6	20	530	66	170	131	72	877	197	333	267	322	327	490	234	90	8^	13^	10^	29	39	52	16^
205 96 DD	40	C	5.6	.6	20	530	66	170	131	72	877	197	333	267	322	327	490	234	90	8^	13^	10^	29	39	52	16^
DAYS OF OUR LIVES		A	5.0	1.0	17	475	114	219	177	190	804	320	492	349	386	314	275	253	145	19^	72	54	56	26^	51	30^
MON-FRI 1.00P 60 NBC	40	B	5.0	1.1	18	477	113	223	186	174	833	331	524	381	423	339	267	246	141	13^	45	36	30	22^	38	14^
217 99 DD	40	C	5.0	1.1	18	477	113	223	186	174	833	331	524	381	423	339	267	246	141	13^	45	36	30	22^	38	14^
1.00 - 1.30		A	4.8	1.0	16	460	114	215	175	182	805	318	488	349	388	312	278	257	140	17^	65	48	56	23^	50	29^
1.30 - 2.00		A	5.1	1.0	18	490	114	222	179	197	802	323	496	350	385	317	271	249	150	20^	78	59	56	27^	53	31
GENERAL HOSPITAL		A	6.1	.9	21	586	119	208	175	137	869	271	483	375	416	382	344	188	110	9^	40	33	31	32	41	22^
MON-FRI 3.00P 60 ABC	30	B	6.0	.8	21	576	129	213	179	134	877	274	504	396	439	399	331	196	118	10^	33	34	24	32	39	17^
221 99 DD	30	C	6.0	.8	21	576	129	213	179	134	877	274	504	396	439	399	331	196	118	10^	33	34	24	32	39	17^
3.00 - 3.30		A	6.1	.9	21	578	120	208	176	139	865	283	491	382	421	373	335	191	113	9^	40	33	29	36	44	21^
3.30 - 4.00		A	6.3	.9	20	596	117	208	173	136	873	257	475	368	411	392	356	185	107	9^	41	34	33	27^	37	23^
GUIDING LIGHT		A	4.6	.7	16	441	62	223	180	121	904	227	425	338	391	387	426	162	71	19^	43	43	25^	32^	38	19^
MON-FRI 3.00P 60 CBS	40	B	4.5	.7	16	433	72	195	159	111	892	225	414	325	382	381	421	190	84	13^	33	27	25^	30	40	15^
213 99 DD	40	C	4.5	.7	16	433	72	195	159	111	892	225	414	325	382	381	421	190	84	13^	33	27	25^	30	40	15^
3.00 - 3.30		A	4.6	.7	16	439	61	218	176	115	900	222	425	339	388	391	426	157	71	22^	38	40	26^	31^	39	17^
3.30 - 4.00		A	4.7	.7	15	446	61	228	184	127	905	231	423	335	393	380	424	168	71	16^	49	45	24^	33	36	21^
ONE LIFE TO LIVE		A	5.3	.5	19	504	114	215	186	130	865	287	521	421	450	370	314	203	126	11^	38	33	30	47	54	23^
MON-FRI 2.00P 60 ABC	30	B	5.0	.5	19	478	131	230	200	127	887	295	552	448	481	395	302	193	121	9^	29	28	28	36	49	16^
220 99 DD	30	C	5.0	.5	19	478	131	230	200	127	887	295	552	448	481	395	302	193	121	9^	29	28	28	36	49	16^
2.00 - 2.30		A	5.2	.6	19	495	109	218	190	124	864	283	520	422	450	371	315	204	127	8^	35	28^	30	47	56	21^
2.30 - 3.00		A	5.4	.6	20	515	117	210	181	133	860	289	518	417	447	366	311	200	124	13^	40	38	31	46	51	25^
PRICE IS RIGHT 1		A	4.7	.0	20	450	73	135	97	76	761	140	257	199	238	278	465	374	152	13^	25^	24^	54	64	75	42
MON-FRI 11.00A 30 CBS	40	B	4.4	.0	20	416	65	143	103	71	733	142	267	209	252	294	423	387	153	13^	18^	18^	45	50	70	25^
214 98 AP	40	C	4.4	.0	20	416	65	143	103	71	733	142	267	209	252	294	423	387	153	13^	18^	18^	45	50	70	25^
PRICE IS RIGHT 2		A	5.8	.1	24	551	73	130	93	85	774	137	253	186	226	278	481	379	144	17^	24^	24^	54	64	79	39
MON-FRI 11.30A 30 CBS	40	B	5.4	.1	24	519	63	137	97	72	742	137	260	201	244	295	439	388	147	14^	19^	19^	46	53	72	26
214 99 AP	40	C	5.4	.1	24	519	63	137	97	72	742	137	260	201	244	295	439	388	147	14^	19^	19^	46	53	72	26
YOUNG AND THE RESTLESS		A	7.5	1.0	28	716	81	202	158	99	897	211	394	312	366	364	449	238	99	15^	29	25	29	52	58	24
MON-FRI 12.30P 60 CBS	40	B	7.4	.9	29	703	82	199	160	95	884	223	400	318	372	356	430	235	102	9^	21	17	29	48	59	17
214 99 DD	40	C	7.4	.9	29	703	82	199	160	95	884	223	400	318	372	356	430	235	102	9^	21	17	29	48	59	17
12.30 - 1.00		A	7.3	1.0	28	696	84	201	156	98	891	209	389	309	363	359	448	238	98	15^	29	26	33	57	63	26
1.00 - 1.30		A	7.7	1.0	28	736	77	202	158	99	900	211	397	314	368	367	449	238	100	15^	30	24	26	48	53	21

A=CURRENT REPORT B=QUARTER-TO DATE AVERAGE C=PREMIERE-TO DATE AVERAGE

Exhibit 13–3 Nielsen Local Program Ratings (NSI)

MILWAUKEE, WI — MONDAY 6:30PM - 9:00PM

WK1 11/03-11/09 WK2 11/10-11/16 WK3 11/17-11/23 WK4 11/24-11/30

METRO HH RTG	METRO HH SHR	STATION	PROGRAM	DMA HH RATINGS WEEKS 1	2	3	4	MULTI-WEEK AVG RTG	MULTI-WEEK AVG SHR	SHARE TREND MAY 94	FEB 94	NOV 93	PERSONS 2+	18+	12-24	12-34	18-34	18-49	21-49	25-54	35+	35-64	50+	WOMEN 18+	12-24	18-34	18-49	25-49	25-54	WKG	MEN 18+	18-34	18-49	21-49	25-49	25-54	TNS 12-17	CHILD 2-11	6-11
1	2			3	4	5	6	7	8	11	12	13	15	16	17	18	19	20	21	22	23	24	25	26	27	28	29	31	32	34	35	36	37	38	39	40	41	42	43
3			R.S.E. THRESHOLDS 25+%	4	4	4	4	2					2	2	6	4	4	3	3	2	2	3	3	2	11	8	4	4	3	4	2	7	4	4	4	4	11	8	12
1			(1 S.E.) 4 WK AVG 50+%	1	1	1	1	LT					LT	LT	2	1	1	1	1	1	1	1	1	1	3	2	1	1	1	1	1	2	1	1	1	1	3	2	3
		6:30PM																																					
10	16	WCGV	AVG. ALL WKS	7	6	7	10	8	12	8	6	9	5	4	11	9	9	6	6	4	2	3	1	4	10	9	6	6	5	7	4	8	6	6	4	4	9	8	11
9	14		MARRIED-CHLDRN	7				7	11				2	3	7	6	8	4	4	1				3	8	10	5	3	3	5	2	5	3	3				2	
10	16		SIMPSONS		6	7	10	8	13				6	5	12	10	9	7	7	5	3	3	1	4	10	8	7	6	6	7	5	10	7	6	5	5	13	11	14
2	4	WDJT	NORTHRN EXPSRE	2	2	1	2	2	3		2	3		1						1	1	1	1	1			1	1	1	1									
11	18	WISN	INSIDE EDITION	11	11	9	10	10	16	15X	14	15	6	7	2	4	5	6	6	7	8	7	10	8	3	5	6	7	8	8	6	4	5	5	6	6	3	1	1
10	16	WITI	REAL-HWY PATRL	9	10	9	8	9	15	19	20	18	5	6	2	4	4	5	5	6	7	6	8	6	2	3	4	5	5	6	6	5	5	6	6	6	3	2	3
2	4	WMVS	MACNEIL&LEHRER	2	1	2	3	2	3	2	3	3	1	1			1	1	1	1	2	1	2	1		1	1	1	1	1	1	1				1			
1	1	WMVT	AVG. ALL WKS	<<	1	1	1	1	1																														
<<			COMPUTRS-WORK	<<				<<																															
1	1		NEW EXPLORERS		1			1	1																														
2	3		SCIENTFC-FRNTR			1		1	2																														
1	1		OUR FMLY-FUTRE				1	1	1																														
15	25	WTMJ	WHEEL-FORTNE	15	16	15	16	16	25	23X	29	27	8	10	2	3	3	4	4	5	14	9	22	13	3	3	4	5	6	9	8	2	3	3	4	4	4	2	3
9	14	WVTV	FULL HOUSE	9	7	8	6	7	12	17	17	15	5	2	6	6	5	3	3	3	1	1	1	3	11	5	4	3	3	3	2	5	3	3	3	3	11	15	17
61			HUT/PUT/TOTALS*	62	61	59	63	61		52	65	64	37	39	29	31	30	30	31	32	43	35	54	42	34	30	32	34	35	40	35	29	27	29	29	29	35	33	39
		7:00PM																																					
8	13	WCGV	MELROSE PL-FOX	9	6	6	6	7	11	9	11	10	5	6	9	10	12	8	8	6	2	3	1	6	11	13	9	7	6	7	5	11	7	7	6	5	4	1	2
3	5	WDJT	AVG. ALL WKS	2	3	1	3	2	3		2	2	1	1							2	1	3	2				1	1	1	1								
2	3		GAMBLER PT 1	2				2	3				1	2							3	2	5	2							2								
3	5		MYSTERY MOVIE		3	1	3	2	4				1	1					1	1	2	1	3	2		1	1	1	1	1	1								
15	24	WISN	COACH-ABC MON	14	13	11	13	13	21	16	15	17	8	9	4	6	7	8	8	9	10	10	12	8	3	4	6	7	8	9	11	9	10	10	11	11	6	5	8
10	15	WITI	NANNY-CBS	13	11	10	9	11	17	21	30	21	6	7	4	4	4	5	5	6	9	7	11	10	7	7	8	7	8	7	5	1	3	3	3	3	2	3	3
2	3	WMVS	MILWAUKEE TONT	1	1	2	1	1	2	2	2	3											1																
1	1	WMVT	TODAYS JAPAN	<<	<<	1	1	<<		X		1																											
12	20	WTMJ	FRESH PRNC-NBC	11	11	11	11	11	18	21X	21	23	7	6	12	12	10	6	7	6	4	4	4	6	15	12	7	7	7	8	5	8	5	6	5	4	18	10	12
5	8	WVTV	STAR TK-GENRTN	5	4	5	4	5	7	12	10	9	3	3	3	3	2	3	4	4	3	4	2	2	4	1	3	3	3	3	4	4	4	4	5	5	5	3	4
62			HUT/PUT/TOTALS*	64	60	61	63	62		55	66	63	41	42	40	41	40	38	40	38	44	39	50	45	50	43	40	39	40	44	40	38	36	38	38	37	43	30	37
		7:30PM																																					
10	15	WCGV	MELROSE PL-FOX	9	7	9	7	8	12	11	12	12	6	7	11	12	14	10	10	7	3	4	2	7	14	16	11	8	7	8	6	12	8	9	7	6	5	2	3
3	5	WDJT	AVG. ALL WKS	2	3	2	3	2	4	2	3	3	1	2				1	1	1	2	2	4	2		1	1	1	1	2	1								
3	4		GAMBLER PT 1	2				2	3				1	2							3	2	5	2							2								
4	6		MYSTERY MOVIE		3	2	3	3	4				1	2				1	1	1	2	2	3	2		1	1	1	1	2	1				1	1			
12	18	WISN	AVG. ALL WKS	13	11	7	11	11	16	17	14	17	7	7	4	5	4	6	6	7	9	9	10	7	3	3	5	6	7	9	8	6	7	7	7	8	6	4	5
12	18		COACH 2-ABC	13	11	7		10	16				7	7	5	5	4	5	6	7	9	9	12	7	4	3	5	6	7	8	8	5	6	6	6	7	7	4	5
13	20		MURDER-DAHMER				11	11	16				6	7	2	5	6	8	8	9	8	7	5	6		5	7	9	8	10	8	7	8	9	11	9	4	4	
17	26	WITI	DAVES WRLD-CBS	17	17	15	15	16	25	20	32	28	10	10	6	6	7	9	9	9	12	10	14	14	9	11	11	11	11	10	7	2	6	6	7	7	4	10	11
2	3	WMVS	AVG. ALL WKS	1	1	1	2	1	2	2	1	3									1		1	1				1	1	1									
1	1		VOTERS GUIDE	1				1	1																														
1	2		MEDIA MAYHEM		1			1	2																														
2	3		VIVA WISCONSIN			1		1	2					1							1		2	1							1								
3	5		YANNI-CONCERT				2	2	4				1	1				1	1	1	2	1	1	2			2	2	2	2									
1	1	WMVT	JOURNAL	1	<<	<<	1	<<			1												1																
9	13	WTMJ	MIKE HOLMGREN	9	11	7	7	9	13	17	17	16	5	5	4	5	5	4	4	5	5	5	7	5	5	4	4	4	4	6	6	6	5	5	6	6	5	3	4
5	7	WVTV	STAR TK-GENRTN	5	5	6	4	5	7	12	9	8	3	3	3	3	2	4	4	4	4	4	2	2	4		3	3	3	4	4	3	4	5	5	5	5	4	4
65			HUT/PUT/TOTALS*	66	65	62	65	65		59	69	67	43	46	36	39	40	41	43	42	49	44	56	49	46	44	44	42	43	48	42	36	38	41	42	41	37	31	39
		8:00PM																																					
6	9	WCGV	PARTY-FIVE-FOX	6	5	7	5	6	8	11	11	10	4	5	9	8	10	6	7	5	2	2	1	6	13	12	8	6	6	8	3	7	4	4	3	3	5	1	1
3	4	WDJT	AVG. ALL WKS	2	3	2	3	2	3	1	3	1	1	2				1	1	1	2	2	4	2		1	1	1	1	2	1								
2	3		GAMBLER PT 1	2				2	2				1	1							2	1	4	1							2								
4	5		MYSTERY MOVIE		3	2	3	3	4				1	2				1	1	1	2	2	3	3		1	1	2	1	2	1				1				
16	23	WISN	ABC MON-FTBL	16	15	15	14	15	22	20	16	32	9	10	6	8	9	9	10	10	10	10	11	7	3	6	6	7	7	7	14	13	13	13	14	13	7	4	4
19	27	WITI	MURPHY BRN-CBS	18	18	19	18	18	26	21	33	27	12	13	10	10	10	14	15	14	15	15	13	15	13	13	16	16	15	14	11	6	12	13	14	13	11	8	9
3	5	WMVS	AVG. ALL WKS	4	5	2	1	3	4	3	3	3	2	2		1	1	1	1	2	3	2	4	3		1	2	2	2	3	1	1	1	1	1	1			
4	6		WINDSORS	4	5			4	6				2	3	1	1	2	1	2	2	4	3	6	4	1	2	2	2	2	4	2	1	1	1	1	2			
3	4		NOMADS-WIND			2		2	4				1	1						1	2	2	3	2			1	1	1	1	1					1			
2	3		YANNI-CONCERT				1	1	2				1	1				1	1	1	1	1	1	1		1	2	2	2	2	1		1	1	1	1		1	
<<		WMVT	MACNEIL&LEHRER	<<	<<	<<	1	<<		1X	1	1																											
12	17	WTMJ	NBC MON-MOV	10	12	8	12	11	15	18X	18	18	6	7	4	5	5	5	5	6	8	7	11	9	5	7	7	8	8	8	4	3	3	3	3	3	5	5	6
6	9	WVTV	SUPER MOV	5	5	5	6	5	8	11	8	5	3	4	2	4	4	4	4	4	3	3	4	4	4	5	4	3	4	3	3	4	4	4	4	4	1		
70			HUT/PUT/TOTALS*	71	69	67	71	70		65	72	73	46	52	39	43	46	47	49	49	55	51	61	56	48	53	51	50	51	56	47	38	43	45	46	46	36	26	31
		8:30PM																																					
6	9	WCGV	PARTY-FIVE-FOX	6	5	8	5	6	8	9	11	10	4	5	8	8	9	6	7	5	2	3	1	6	12	12	8	7	6	9	3	7	4	4	4	3	5	1	1
3	5	WDJT	AVG. ALL WKS	2	3	2	3	2	3	2	3	2	1	2				1	1	1	2	2	4	2		1	1	1	1	1	1				1				
3	3		GAMBLER PT 1	2				2	3				1	2							3	2	5	2							2								
4	5		MYSTERY MOVIE		3	2	3	3	4				1	2			1	1	1	1	2	1	3	2		1	1	2	1	2	1		1	1	1	1			
19	27	WISN	ABC MON-FTBL	18	18	17	16	17	25	21	15	34	10	11	7	9	9	10	11	11	12	12	13	8	4	6	7	8	8	9	15	12	13	14	15	15	7	4	6
16	22	WITI	AVG. ALL WKS	16	15	14	16	15	22	19	32	21	10	11	8	9	10	12	13	12	12	12	9	13	10	12	14	15	14	12	9	7	10	11	11	11	9	5	6
16	22		LOVE & WAR-CBS	16	15		16	15	22				10	11	8	9	10	12	13	13	12	13	10	13	11	15	15	15	14	11	9	5	9	10	11	10	7	6	8
16	23		NANNY-MON			14		14	22				9	10	10	9	8	12	13	12	11	12	6	11	7	3	12	14	13	14	9	12	12	13	12	11	15	2	
4	6	WMVS	AVG. ALL WKS	4	6	4	2	4	6	3	3	2	2	2		1	1	1	2	2	3	3	4	3		1	2	2	2	4	2	1	1	1	1	2			
5	7		WINDSORS	4	6			5	7				2	3	1	2	2	2	2	3	4	4	6	4	1	2	2	2	3	5	2	3	2	2	2	2			
4	6		NOMADS-WIND			4		4	6				2	2				1	1	2	3	3	4	2			1	1	2	2	2		1	1	1	2			
2	3		YANNI-CONCERT				2	2	2				1	1				1	1	1	2	2	1	2			2	2	2	2	1		1	1	1	1			
<<		WMVT	MACNEIL&LEHRER	<<	<<	<<	1	<<		1X	1	1																											
14	19	WTMJ	NBC MON-MOV	9	14	10	13	12	17	19X	18	19	7	8	4	5	5	5	5	6	9	8	12	10	5	6	7	8	9	9	5	3	3	3	3	3	6	6	6
6	8	WVTV	SUPER MOV	4	4	5	6	5	7	11	8	5	3	3	2	3	4	3	4	4	3	3	3	3	3	4	4	3	4	2	3	3	3	4	4	4	1		
71			HUT/PUT/TOTALS*	71	69	67	73	70		70	73	74	46	53	38	43	45	47	50	50	56	53	62	56	45	52	51	52	53	56	48	39	43	46	46	47	36	23	29

TIME PERIOD

MONDAY 6:30PM - 9:00PM

NOVEMBER

telecast. Share of audience makes it possible to compare programs telecast when TV usage levels are different (e.g., different times of the day or different seasons of the year).

Households using TV (HUT). Number of U.S. TV households using their television sets during each 15-minute period, reported as a percentage of total U.S. TV households.

VCR CNTRB. Percentage of households recording the program with the TV set(s) off or tuned to a different program during the average minute. This rating is a portion of the average audience rating, not an addition to it.

Program coverage (CVG %). The percentage of total U.S. TV households that *can* receive the program over one or more stations. This is a potential audience size figure. It does not mean that they actually do watch the program, but only that they could receive it on their sets.

Metro area. A specific county or group of counties that comprise the central core of a market, often the same as the government definition of a Metropolitan Statistical Area.

Designated Market Area (DMA). DMA is a Nielsen term for the metro area plus those surrounding counties in which the metro-area TV stations have a plurality of the counties' share of TV viewing or the largest quarter-hour audience.

Peoplemeter. This is an electronic device that Nielsen has installed in NTI sample homes and on which family members and visitors can record their viewing.

Refer to *Advertising Media Planning*, 5th ed., by Sissors and Bumba, Chapter 4.

Problems

1. List the household audience and total audience (TA%) ratings for the programs indicated (Exhibit 13–1).

Program	HHLD Audience	Total Audience
NBC Monday Night Movies	____%	____%
Love & War	____%	____%

Given that "Love & War" has a slightly higher HHLD audience figure, how do you explain the much larger TA% figure for "NBC Monday Night Movies"?

2. List the household audience rating and share of audience for the programs indicated (Exhibit 13–1).

Program	HHLD Audience	Share
Nanny	________%	________%
Murphy Brown	________%	________%

Given that the share figures are the same for each program, how do you explain the difference in HHLD audience?

3. Audience composition data in the Nielsen Audience Estimates are used to determine a program's audience for a particular demographic segment. Because the audience composition data report the number of viewers per thousand viewing households, it is necessary to know the number of viewing households in order to compute the demographic audience size.

These data are reported in the program audience estimates under the heading "Household Audiences—Avg. Aud. (0,000)." The C, or premiere-to-date average, listing is usually the one used in computing demographic audience estimates. In the case of programs longer than 30 minutes, the total program data are usually used rather than data for a specific half-hour segment of the program (see Exhibit 13–2). The following form will help you understand how to compute program audience size for a particular demographic group.

Program	Average Audience HHs (000)		Women aged 25–54 per 1,000 viewing HHs		Total women aged 25–54
Another World	2,740*	×	408	=	1,117,920
As the World Turns	________	×	________	=	________
General Hospital	________	×	________	=	________
Guiding Light	________	×	________	=	________

*Because household audience data are reported in tens of thousands (0,000), it is necessary to add a zero to convert these figures to thousands.

4. Using the local and national Nielsen data provided in Exhibits 13–1 and 13–3, complete the following table. For hour-long programs, indicate data for the first half-hour.

	(From Exhibit 13–3)				(From Exhibit 13–1)	
	Metro areas		DMA (Multi-week average)		National	
Program	Rating	Share	Rating	Share	HHLD Aud.	Share
Nanny	____%	____	____%	____	________%	____
Dave's World	____%	____	____%	____	________%	____
Fresh Prince of Bel Air	____%	____	____%	____	________%	____

How do you explain the differences in ratings and shares for the Milwaukee metro area compared to the national ratings and shares for the same programs?

Assignment 14

Estimating Future Television Ratings/Audiences

Objective: To show you a relatively simple method of developing rough estimates of a program's future performance. Television ratings and audience estimates are reports of a program's *past* performance. As a media planner, you are interested in the program's future performance. Therefore, it is important to have some means of estimating future ratings and audiences for a program.

Discussion

Suppose you are getting ready to make a spot TV buy to run during July and August. The market you are planning to buy is surveyed by the rating service on an infrequent basis (many small markets are rated only twice a year), and the latest information you have are the February ratings. You must estimate the rating a program will receive in July based on the available data.

The following rating information is available from the February rating book for the program, which is telecast weekday afternoons in Baltimore.

Households				Total women				Women aged 18–49			
Rating	Share	HUT	(000)	Rating	Share	PVT*	(000)	Rating	Share	PVT*	(000)
11	35	32	86	9	39	23	71	7	34	21	42

*Persons viewing television.

Before you begin to estimate, you need one more piece of information: a means of estimating the HUT level you can expect during the season in which you will be buying the program. Exhibit 14–1 is an example of seasonal variation index data.

Going back to our original problem, we will develop estimated ratings for the program when it is telecast in July. Follow these steps:

1. Using Exhibit 14–1, select the proper HUT for Baltimore in July. You will note it is 26.
2. Using the February (latest available) share, multiply it by the July HUT to develop the estimated July rating ($35 \times .26 = 9.1$ or 9). Ratings should be rounded to the nearest whole percent, which is the way they are reported by Nielsen in the NSI reports.
3. To adjust the number of households reached, divide the number reached in February by the February rating (to find the number representing 1 percent) and multiply that number by the estimated July rating ($86 \div 11 \times 9 = 70.36$, or 70).

Exhibit 14–1 Seasonal Variation Indices

MONDAY - FRIDAY

NOON - 4.30PM

	TV HOUSEHOLDS								TOTAL WOMEN								WOMEN 18 49							
	HUT LEVELS				INDICES				PVT LEVELS				INDICES				PVT LEVELS				INDICES			
	NOV	FEB	MAY	JUL	NOV	FEB	MAY	JUL	NOV	FEB	MAY	JUL	NOV	FEB	MAY	JUL	NOV	FEB	MAY	JUL	NOV	FEB	MAY	JUL
ABILENE-SWTWATER	29	29	30	36	100	100	103	124	26	24	24	27	100	92	92	104	20	19	20	24	100	95	100	120
ALBANY, GA	26	33	29	40	100	127	112	154	21	26	26	33	100	124	124	157	18	22	23	30	100	122	128	167
ALBNY-SCHDY-TROY	23	28	20	21	100	122	87	91	18	21	14	16	100	117	78	89	15	19	12	15	100	127	80	100
ALBUQUERQUE	22	24	22	25	100	109	100	114	17	15	16	17	100	88	94	100	15	14	15	16	100	93	100	107
ALEXANDRIA, LA	34	38	37	44	100	112	109	129	29	30	34	36	100	103	117	124	22	26	31	34	100	118	141	155
ALEXANDRIA, MN	25	32	22	26	100	128	88	104	20	26	20	21	100	130	100	105	18	24	19	18	100	133	106	100
ALPENA	24	31	22	26	100	129	92	108	18	24	17	21	100	133	94	117	18	21	16	20	100	117	89	111
AMARILLO	29	29	30	31	100	97	103	107	25	24	25	27	100	96	100	109	21	21	22	27	100	100	105	129
ANCHORAGE	22	24	18	20	100	109	82	91	15	16	11	15	100	107	73	100	13	15	10	14	100	115	77	108
ANNISTON	26	33	31	32	100	127	119	123	18	26	26	24	100	144	144	133	16	23	24	23	100	144	150	144
ARDMORE-ADA	30	36	29	32	100	120	97	107	27	33	27	26	100	122	100	96	24	33	23	25	100	138	96	104
ATLANTA	26	28	23	30	100	108	88	115	19	21	17	22	100	111	89	116	18	18	14	19	100	100	78	106
AUGUSTA	26	33	25	36	100	127	96	138	20	26	21	26	100	130	105	130	17	23	18	26	100	135	106	153
AUSTIN, TX	21	19	18	23	100	90	86	110	18	17	16	21	100	94	89	117	15	14	12	19	100	93	80	127
BAKERSFIELD	24	24	23	29	100	100	96	121	20	18	17	20	100	90	85	100	17	17	14	20	100	100	82	118
BALTIMORE	22	32	20	26	100	145	91	118	17	23	15	20	100	135	88	118	15	21	13	18	100	140	87	120
BANGOR	27	31	28	27	100	115	104	100	20	24	22	21	100	120	110	105	19	25	18	21	100	132	95	111
BATON ROUGE	28	36	33	35	100	129	118	125	23	30	27	27	100	130	117	117	20	28	25	24	100	140	125	120
BEAUMNT-PT ARTHR	30	38	34	45	100	127	113	150	25	31	28	38	100	124	112	152	23	30	25	34	100	130	109	148
BELLINGHAM	17	20	17	15	100	118	100	88	13	14	13	11	100	108	100	85	12	13	14	8	100	108	117	67
BILLINGS	21	26	19	23	100	124	90	110	17	20	14	19	100	118	82	112	15	15	13	19	100	100	87	127
BLOXI-GLFRT-PGLA	26	35	30	37	100	135	115	142	20	30	24	27	100	150	120	135	19	29	22	26	100	153	116	137
BINGHAMTON	22	30	24	25	100	136	109	114	17	23	18	18	100	135	106	106	14	20	16	15	100	143	114	107
BIRMINGHAM	25	33	29	37	100	132	116	148	21	26	25	30	100	124	119	143	19	23	21	30	100	121	111	158
BLFLD-BKLY-OAK H	33	41	30	34	100	124	91	103	25	31	24	29	100	124	96	116	24	31	22	28	100	129	92	117
BOISE	22	23	19	22	100	105	86	100	15	19	15	17	100	120	100	113	13	18	13	15	100	138	100	115
BOSTON	22	26	20	22	100	118	91	100	15	19	15	16	100	127	100	107	12	15	12	14	100	125	100	117
BOWLING GREEN	25	32	29	31	100	128	116	124	19	26	20	25	100	137	105	132	18	27	18	24	100	150	100	133
BRSTL-KPT-JHN CY	27	38	28	29	100	141	104	107	20	30	23	23	100	150	115	115	17	27	20	20	100	159	118	118
BUFFALO	27	32	24	26	100	119	89	96	19	23	18	17	100	121	95	89	17	20	15	16	100	118	88	94
BRLNGTN-PLTSBRGH	23	29	24	24	100	126	104	104	17	22	20	17	100	129	118	100	15	19	18	17	100	127	120	113
CASPER RIVERTON	18	26	18	21	100	144	100	117	15	20	14	16	100	133	93	107	13	18	13	15	100	138	100	115
CEDR RPDS-WTRLOO	22	28	25	28	100	127	114	127	19	24	22	22	100	126	116	116	16	21	21	20	100	131	131	125
CHARLESTON, SC	33	35	29	34	100	106	88	103	26	26	22	24	100	100	85	92	23	24	19	20	100	104	83	87
CHRLSTN-HNTNGTON	31	39	30	33	100	126	97	106	24	30	24	25	100	125	100	104	22	29	23	24	100	132	105	109
CHARLOTTE	23	31	25	27	100	135	109	117	18	24	19	20	100	133	106	111	15	22	16	17	100	147	107	113
CHATTANOOGA	26	35	26	33	100	135	100	127	21	30	22	25	100	143	105	119	18	28	19	25	100	156	106	139
CHEYENNE	22	26	24	25	100	118	109	114	18	20	19	18	100	111	106	100	17	13	16	14	100	76	94	82
CHICAGO	27	28	24	26	100	104	89	96	20	20	19	19	100	100	95	95	17	18	16	18	100	106	94	106
CHICO REDDING	20	26	19	24	100	130	95	120	16	21	15	20	100	131	94	125	14	20	13	18	100	143	93	129
CINCINNATI	28	33	26	29	100	118	93	104	20	24	20	20	100	120	100	100	17	21	17	18	100	124	100	106
CLARKSBRG-WESTON	29	35	27	26	100	121	93	90	22	29	22	20	100	132	100	91	21	25	21	19	100	119	100	90
CLEVELAND	24	31	22	24	100	129	92	100	17	23	17	17	100	135	100	100	15	21	15	16	100	140	100	107
COLO SPGS-PUEBLO	24	23	21	27	100	96	88	113	19	17	17	21	100	89	89	111	19	16	15	19	100	84	79	100
COLUMBIA, SC	26	32	26	32	100	123	100	123	20	25	21	24	100	125	105	120	15	22	17	22	100	147	113	147

Repeat steps 1–3 to estimate ratings for total women and women aged 18–49. Be sure to use the appropriate PVT number for each demographic group. The new data as estimated for the July buy in Baltimore would look like this:

Households				Total women				Women aged 18–49			
Rating	Share	HUT	(000)	Rating	Share	PVT	(000)	Rating	Share	PVT	(000)
9	35	26	70	8	39	20	63	6	34	18	36

Note: The method described here for estimating ratings assumes that programming in the time period has been consistent and that shares will remain the same. If the program you are estimating has just moved to a new time, or if competition for the program has changed, you must make an estimate of the share the program will achieve. These estimates are based on share performance of the time period and share history of competitive programs. If the rating estimates are being made for a new program, also consider the share performance of similar program types.

Problems

1. Assume that you are planning to buy an afternoon program in Atlanta during May. The February rating and audience data follow. Using the method previously described, estimate the ratings and audiences and enter your estimates in the spaces provided.

	Households				Total women				Women aged 18–49			
	Rating	Share	HUT	(000)	Rating	Share	PVT	(000)	Rating	Share	PVT	(000)
Feb.	9	33	28	126	7	31	21	59	6	34	18	27
May	______	33	____	____	______	31	____	____	______	34	____	____

2. Assume that you are planning to buy an afternoon program in Burlington–Plattsburgh during February. The November rating and audience data are shown below. Using the method previously described, estimate the ratings and audience and enter your estimates in the spaces provided.

	Households				Total women				Women aged 18–49			
	Rating	Share	HUT	(000)	Rating	Share	PVT	(000)	Rating	Share	PVT	(000)
Nov.	9	38	23	21	6	35	17	12	5	32	15	8
Feb.	______	38	____	____	______	35	____	____	______	32	____	____

3. Assume that you are planning to buy an afternoon program in Charlotte during May. The February rating and audience data are shown. Using the method described previously, estimate the ratings and audiences for May and enter your estimates in the spaces provided.

	Households				Total women				Women aged 18–49			
	Rating	Share	HUT	(000)	Rating	Share	PVT	(000)	Rating	Share	PVT	(000)
Feb.	8	27	31	57	7	29	24	40	6	28	22	21
May	______	27	____	____	______	29	____	____	______	28	____	____

Assignment 15

Broadcast Program Selection

Objective: To help you use your knowledge of broadcast ratings, audience composition, and cost per thousand to make simple program selection decisions from among a group of television programs.

Discussion

Often media planners and buyers must make decisions about which TV shows to buy based on their knowledge of the program's audience delivery and cost efficiency. Sometimes the objective is to deliver the largest possible number of impressions with relatively little concern for cost efficiency. At other times, cost efficiency is the primary objective. In most cases, however, planners think in terms of the audience delivery of a specific demographic segment (e.g., women aged 25–54 or men aged 18–34).

The Nielsen network ratings and audience composition data you used in Assignment 13 will be needed to give you the necessary information on audience delivery. In addition, you will need to know the costs of commercials within the programs in order to calculate cost per thousand. These costs are given in Table 15–1.

Table 15–1 Selected Program Costs: 30-Second Commercials

Program	Network	30-second commercial cost
All My Children	ABC	$16,500
Another World	NBC	8,500
As the World Turns	CBS	12,500
Bold and the Beautiful	CBS	13,000
Days of Our Lives	NBC	13,800
General Hospital	ABC	16,000
Guiding Light	CBS	19,000
One Life to Live	ABC	14,100
Young and the Restless	CBS	15,500

Refer to *Advertising Media Planning*, 5th ed., by Sissors and Bumba, Chapter 0.

Problems

Assume that a large national advertiser has purchased the programs in Table 15–1 as part of a corporate buy. Your job, as a media planner, is to select those programs that would be the best vehicles for the brand that your agency handles.

The media objectives for your brand include the following:

- Target audience: Women aged 25–54
- Cost efficiency: Because of a modest budget, cost efficiency of reaching the target audience is more important than any other consideration.

1. Select three programs from Table 15–1 that will best fulfill the objective of your brand. Use Exhibit 13–2 as a source of data for your target audience. Justify your selections in terms of cost efficiency for reaching the target audience. Be sure to show cost per thousand for all programs.

2. You are trying to reach women aged 18–49 for your brand and have been offered the following packages of network programs:

1. All My Children, Another World, Young and the Restless
2. General Hospital, Guiding Light, One Life to Live
3. As the World Turns, Bold and the Beautiful, Days of Our Lives

Evaluate each of the program packages in terms of their cost efficiencies in reaching your target audience, then select the best package for your brand.

To calculate the cost per thousand for the package, first determine the total number of women aged 18–49 delivered by each program from Exhibit 13–2. Next, add these numbers to arrive at the total impressions for women aged 18–49. Then divide the *total cost for the package* by the total impressions for women aged 18–49 to get the cost per thousand for the package. Show your calculations. (See Assignment 12 on CPM and also see Assignment 22 for a further discussion of the meaning of impressions.)

Assignment 16

Estimating Reach and Frequency

Objective: To learn how to determine the reach and frequency of a given vehicle or combination of vehicles. Tables 16–1 through 16–6 will enable you to make rough estimates.

Refer to *Advertising Media Planning,* 5th ed., by Sissors and Bumba, Chapter 6.

Discussion

The tables shown in this assignment are called "reach tables" because they show the estimated four-week reach of media vehicles. They do not indicate the average frequency generated. However, this is not a problem because you can easily compute frequency if you know the number of gross rating points and the reach generated by your schedule.

Reach and frequency are components of gross rating points (GRPs) as expressed in the following formula:

$$\text{GRPs} = \text{Reach} \times \text{Frequency}$$

Therefore, if you know the GRP level and the reach developed by your schedule, you can restructure the formula to find the average frequency as follows:

$$\text{Frequency} = \frac{\text{GRPs}}{\text{Reach}}$$

In some cases you will have to interpolate to find reach if the number of GRPs you are planning to use falls between two GRP levels in the table. In other cases, you will have to extrapolate if the number of GRPs in your schedule is higher than the maximum number shown in the table.

Why four-week reach? Why not two-week or thirteen-week reach? Reach can be figured for any time frame; however, the industry standard is to use four-week intervals. This is the interval that Nielsen uses in its reports, and it is a handy time frame to use when computing monthly reach and frequency for use in a media plan.

How to Use Reach Tables

Table 16–1 Network TV Four-Week Reach (Scatter Plan Scheduling)

Households Reached in Four Weeks (%)				
GRPs Four weeks	Day	Early news	Prime	Late night
100	43	46	61	42
200	55	57	72	53
300	61	63	80	60
400	65	68	85	64
500	68	71	88	66
600	70	73	90	67

Television (Network and Spot).

1. First determine the amount of reach that is wanted and the daypart in which the advertising will be shown. Example: Suppose you want a four-week reach of 60 percent and want to use daytime network TV.
2. Using the network TV reach table, Table 16–1, look under the Day column to find out how many GRPs will be needed to achieve 50 percent reach. Answer: About 300.
3. To figure frequency, divide the GRPs by reach: 300 ÷ 61 = 4.9.
4. Most reach tables list household reach, so you might want to convert the figures to target audience reach. To do this, look up the conversion factor in the appendix at the end of this workbook. A conversion factor represents the percentage of a demographic group that will be found in the universe of all TV households. For example, a conversion factor of 64 for women 25–54 viewing network daytime TV means that you will find a woman between the ages of 25–54 in 64 percent of the households viewing daytime network TV. Conversion factors are percentages and should be converted to their decimal equivalents when multiplying (e.g., 64 percent becomes .64).
5. Multiply the GRPs by the conversion factor: 300 × .64 = 192.
6. Looking up 192 GRPs in the network TV reach table, you find that the target audience reach for women 25–54 is about 53%. The frequency would be: 192 ÷ 53 = 3.6.
7. To determine the number of household GRPs needed to achieve a specific target audience GRP level, divide the household GRPs by the conversion factor and multiply the result by 100. Example: To achieve a reach of 50 percent in late night, about 190 GRPs are needed. If the target audience is women 18–49, the conversion factor is 62. Therefore, 306 household GRPs would be needed to generate 190 GRPs against women 18–49 in late night ((190 ÷ 62) × 100 = 306).
8. Reach and frequency for spot television are found in the same way, except you must use the reach tables and conversion factors for spot TV. (See Table 16–2 and the appendix.)

Table 16–2 Spot TV Four-Week Reach (Scatter Plan Scheduling)

GRPs (Four weeks)	Day	Prime	Fringe
100	39	55	44
200	50	65	53
300	55	72	59
400	59	77	63
500	61	79	67
600	63	81	70

Radio.

1. Network and spot radio reach and frequency can be estimated by using Tables 16–3 and 16–4. First determine the number of GRPs and the number of radio networks or spot radio stations you plan to use. Then look up the estimated four-week reach. To determine the estimated four-week frequency, divide the GRPs by the estimated four-week reach. Assume you are planning to use 200 GRPs in four weeks on four different radio networks. The estimated reach would be 41 percent and the frequency 4.9 (200 ÷ 41 = 4.878 or 4.9).
2. Assignment 19 shows you how to compute reach and frequency for spot radio when you know the stations you plan to use and have rating information for each station.

Table 16–3 Network Radio Four-Week Reach

	% reach by number of networks						
Four-week adult GRP	1	2	3	4	5	6	7
25	9	12	17	—	—	—	—
50	12	17	20	24	27	—	—
100	15	23	30	31	35	36	40
200	18	28	34	41	46	49	51
400	—	33	43	47	52	57	58
MAX	—	—	47	57	62	65	70

Table 16–4 Spot Radio Four-Week Reach

	% reach by number of stations						
Four-week adult GRP	1	2	3	4	5	6	7
50	19	—	—	—	—	—	—
100	21	32	—	—	—	—	—
200	26	38	47	55	62	—	—
400	30	47	54	63	67	71	73
MAX	—	—	60	70	75	80	85

Newspapers:

1. To use Table 16–5 to estimate newspaper reach, first figure the newspaper's ADI gross circulation coverage. This is done by dividing the newspaper's circulation by the number of households in the ADI. Both of these figures can be found in SRDS.

2. Assume that the newspaper you are planning to use has a circulation of 150,000 in an ADI in which there are 350,000 households. The gross circulation coverage would be 43 percent (150,000 ÷ 350,000 = .4285 or 43 percent).
3. Next, look up the reach opposite the appropriate gross circulation coverage figure and under the number of insertions you plan to run. You will have to interpolate if the coverage figure falls between the coverage figures listed in the table. If you are planning to run four insertions, the reach would be approximately 55 percent.
4. To figure frequency, first determine GRPs. To do this, multiply the reach for one insertion (column 1) by the number of insertions. In our example above, the GRPs would be 152 (38 × 4 = 152), and the frequency would be 2.8 (152 ÷ 55 = 2.76 or 2.8).

Table 16–5 Metro Daily Newspaper Four-Week Reach

% gross circulation coverage	% adult reach by number of insertions in four weeks						
	1	2	3	4	8	10	MAX
30	27	35	40	43	49	51	53
40	36	44	49	52	56	59	61
50	42	51	56	62	64	66	68
60	48	57	62	65	70	71	72
70	56	66	72	75	80	81	82
80	65	75	81	84	87	88	89

How to Estimate Newspaper Audience Sizes

Newspaper audience size data are not always easy to find. Some newspapers are not measured, and others are measured infrequently. However, it is often desirable to calculate the demographic audience size for newspapers. The steps below show how to do it.

1. Find the circulation of the newspaper from SRDS (see Assignment 8).

2. Use Table 16–6 to find the readers-per-copy conversion factor and multiply the circulation by the conversion factor. Example: If a newspaper's circulation is 100,000 and the target audience is men aged 18–24, then:

   .168 × 100,000 = 16,800 readers (men aged 18–24)

Table 16–6 National Average Newspaper Readers per Copy

Age	Men	Women	Adults
18–24	.168	.152	.320
25–34	.242	.210	.452
35–44	.182	.181	.363
45–54	.172	.181	.353
55–64	.157	.181	.338
65+	.146	.185	.331

Source: National Newspaper Advertising Bureau & Simmons Market Research Bureau.

3. If your target audience consists of several different age groups, then add the conversion factors. For example, if the audience is women aged 18–34, the conversion factor would be .362. (.152 + .210 = .362.)

4. In step 3 above, if the newspaper had a circulation of 75,000, then multiply the circulation by .362 to arrive at an audience of 27,150 (.362 × 75,000 = 27,150).

Problems

1. What household reach and frequency will be developed by the following group of late-night, network television programs, each of which will be purchased once per week for four weeks?

   Program A: Average rating per telecast, 7
   Program B: Average rating per telecast, 6
   Program C: Average rating per telecast, 5
   Program D: Average rating per telecast, 6

2. You have a target market of women aged 18–49 and want to develop a reach of 50 percent in daytime, network TV. How many GRPs do you need to buy? (Use the conversion factors found in the appendix.)

   What frequency will be developed?

3. You have purchased 300 household GRPs in late fringe time spot TV. What reach and frequency will you develop against a target audience of men aged 18–34?

4. You are planning to buy 300 adult GRPs using four radio networks. How much reach and frequency will be developed?

5. How much reach and frequency would 400 adult GRPs generate in spot radio if five different stations were used?

6. You are planning to buy one insertion a week for four weeks in a metropolitan daily newspaper with a circulation of 345,000. There are 575,000 households in the newspaper's coverage area.
   a. What is the gross circulation coverage?

   b. How many adult GRPs will this schedule generate?

   c. What will be the four-week reach and frequency?

7. You are planning to buy ads in a newspaper with a circulation of 165,000, and your target audience is women aged 25–54. How many target audience members will you reach?

   If there are 235,000 women aged 25–54 in the newspaper's coverage area, what percentage reach will you develop?

Assignment 17

Estimating the Reach and Frequency of a Combination of Media Vehicles (Sainsbury Formula)

Objective: To help you learn a relatively simple method of estimating the reach and frequency of a combination of media vehicles, and to show you how this method can be used to solve media selection problems. It may be used for print or broadcast vehicles.

Discussion

Nielsen provides four-week reach figures for individual network programs. Frequency can easily be computed once reach is known. (Gross rating points divided by reach equals frequency.) However, it is often useful to know the reach and frequency developed by several TV programs, several magazines, or combinations of other media.

Most media plans have reach and frequency objectives. If your plan calls for the use of several network TV programs, then you need some method of determining the reach and frequency developed by the programs to find out how close they come to meeting the goals established in the reach and frequency objective of your plan.

As a media planning tool, the formula covered in this assignment can be used to determine what will happen to reach and frequency when an additional vehicle is added to the schedule. It can be used to help select media that will best fit your reach and frequency objectives from those that are available.

In using the formula in this assignment, remember that you are making a rough estimate of the reach (and, therefore, the frequency) that the combination develops. *By no means is this formula the most precise.* As the number of vehicles used increases, the formula tends to overestimate reach. Therefore, the formula is recommended only for practice planning and study. Its main virtue is simplicity; it can be calculated by hand.

Refer to *Advertising Media Planning,* 5th ed., by Sissors and Bumba, Chapter 5.

The Sainsbury Method of Estimating Net Reach

The Sainsbury method of estimating the net reach of a number of vehicles has been widely used in the United States and England for many years. It can be used for TV vehicles or combinations of TV, magazines, and other media vehicles. The creator of the formula was E. J. Sainsbury of the London Press Exchange.

There are two versions of the Sainsbury formula for estimating net reach.[1] Both provide identical answers. The original version, however, takes a bit less

[1] J. M. Caffyn and M. Sagorsky, "Net Audiences of British Newspapers: A Comparison of the Agostini and Sainsbury Methods," *Journal of Advertising Research*, March 1963, pp. 21–25.

time to calculate than the second version. Exhibit 17–1 compares examples for each version. Additional vehicles can be added easily, using either version of the Sainsbury formula. However, when the net reaches of each combination are known, then version 1 is easier to use.

Exhibit 17–1 Two Versions of the Sainsbury Formula

Example: Assume that we know the reaches of three vehicles: A = 40 percent, B = 30 percent, and C = 20 percent. What is the net reach of A, B, and C?

Version 1 (Original)

The formula (RV1 = Reach of vehicle 1):

1.00–[(1.00–RV1) × (1.00–RV2)], etc.

Step 1: Subtract each reach from 100 percent (which equals nonreach).[2]

	Reach	Nonreach
A	40%	60%
B	30	70
C	20	80

Step 2: Multiply the nonreach percentages by each other as follows:

.60 × .70 × .80 = 33.6% nonreach

Step 3: Subtract 33.6 percent from 100 percent:

100%–33.6% = 66.4% or 66% net reach of ABC

Version 2

The formula (RV1 = Reach of vehicle 1):

(RV1 + RV2)–(RV1 × RV2) = RV1,2

To add a third vehicle, use the same method once the reach of vehicles 1 and 2 has been calculated (RV1,2):

(RV1,2 + RV3)–(RV1,2 × RV3) = RV1,2,3

Step 1: Add: .40 + .30 = .70

Step 2: Multiply: .40 × .30 = .12

Step 3: Subtract: .70–.12 = .58 reach of vehicles A and B

Step 4: Add: .58 + .20 = .78

Step 5: Multiply: .58 × .20 = .116

Step 6: Subtract: .78–.116 = .664 or 66% net reach of ABC

Because this formula tends to overestimate reach, it is recommended that the results be reduced up to 10 percent, depending on the number of vehicles used:

Number of vehicles	Percentage of reduction
1–2	0%
3	5
4	7
5+	10

In the foregoing example the 66 percent combined reach of ABC should be lowered by 5 percent because three vehicles are being combined. It would then become 63 percent (66 × .95 = 62.7 or 63).

---

[2]The Sainsbury formula refers to nonreach as "non-cover."

The reductions indicated do make the Sainsbury formula more realistic, but it is still not perfect. However, it does provide a method to quickly calculate preliminary estimates of reach for a combination of media vehicles. In order to figure combined frequency, first determine the gross rating points delivered by each group of vehicles (reach × frequency = GRPs). Then divide the combined GRPs by the net reach for the combination. Be sure to reduce the combined net reach figure by the appropriate percentage before dividing it into the combined GRPs. (Combined GRPs ÷ combined net reach = combined frequency.) Refer to Assignment 16 for a discussion of estimating reach and frequency.

Problems

As you work on the following problems, remember to reduce the combined reach figure by the appropriate percentage if you are combining three or more vehicles. You should reduce the reach figure *before* you compute combined frequency.

1. Assume that you have developed a media plan and have calculated the monthly reach and frequency figures for the individual media being used, as shown. Now you are to compute the combined national and spot market reach and frequency. Remember that the spot markets receive the national reach and frequency in addition to the reach and frequency developed by the spot market media.

	January		February		March	
	Reach	Frequency	Reach	Frequency	Reach	Frequency
Network TV	41	2.1	52	2.0	55	2.2
National magazines	30	1.2	32	1.3	34	1.3
Spot TV	—	—	55	2.7	58	2.2
National reach/frequency	_____	_____	_____	_____	_____	_____
Spot market reach/frequency	_____	_____	_____	_____	_____	_____

2. Assume that you have developed a media plan that calls for the use of network TV and that also has a media objective calling for a minimum four-week frequency of 3.5 with maximum affordable reach. Your budget will permit the purchase of three network shows. In reviewing the availabilities, you have reduced the list of programs to four:

   Program A: Reach 42, frequency 2.2
   Program B: Reach 47, frequency 1.9
   Program C: Reach 28, frequency 2.9
   Program D: Reach 25, frequency 3.3

To help you keep track of your calculations, record the reach and frequency figures here:

Combination ABC: Reach_______________%, frequency_______________
Combination ABD: Reach_______________%, frequency_______________
Combination ACD: Reach_______________%, frequency_______________
Combination BCD: Reach_______________%, frequency_______________

List the combination that best fulfills the media objective of a minimum four-week frequency of 3.5 plus maximum reach.

What combination of programs would you select if the primary media objective was maximum frequency, regardless of reach?

Assignment 18

Converting Television Household Data to Target Audience Reach and Frequency

Objective: To show how you can convert household reach and frequency to target audience reach and frequency. The four-week reach of network television programs is readily available on a household basis; however, in planning media you will be most interested in the four-week reach and frequency of a specific target audience.

Discussion

In media planning for television, you can usually learn the four-week household reach and frequency of a given program by checking Nielsen data. If a scatter plan is being used, it is also relatively easy to find the four-week household reach and frequency by consulting various formulas available for that purpose.

But usually it is more important to know target audience reach and frequency, because most media plans are targeted to specific demographic groups, such as men aged 18–49 or women aged 35–64. And you cannot assume that there is one target audience member in each household that tunes in to a program.

For Network Television

Suppose you want to know the four-week reach and frequency of the network program "Coach" for a target audience of men aged 18–34. How could you develop this information?

Assume that you have a four-week household reach report such as that shown in Table 18–1. From this you can determine that the four-week household reach is 18.6 percent for "Coach."

Next, you can look up demographic audience data for the program in Nielsen's *National Audience Demographics* report as shown in Exhibit 18–1. From this report you find that "Coach" had a 4.7 rating among men aged 18–34.

You now have two pieces of data: household reach and target audience rating. You can synthesize these data into four-week reach and frequency figures for men aged 18–34 if you are willing to make an assumption about the data, namely that the four-week turnover rate for men aged 18–34 is the same as the turnover rate for households. *Turnover* means the number of times a program gets a new audience.

Exhibit 18–1 A Portion of NTI *National Audience Demographics* Report

NTI NATIONAL AUDIENCE DEMOGRAPHICS REPORT
NOVEMBER
TABLE 3A -- ESTIMATES OF INDIVIDUAL NETWORK PROGRAMS (TOTAL DURATION)
EVENING

PROGRAM NAME DAY	START TIME	DUR	NTWK	TYPE	WEEKS MINS	KEY	HOUSE-HOLDS	WORKING WOMEN	WOMEN 15-24	WOMEN 18+	WOMEN 18-24	WOMEN 18-34	WOMEN 18-49	WOMEN 21+	WOMEN 21-49	WOMEN 21-54	WOMEN 25-49	WOMEN 25-54	WOMEN 35-64	WOMEN 55+	TEENS TOTAL 12-17	TEENS FEMALE 12-17	TEENS TOTAL 12-14	TEENS TOTAL 15-17	CHILDREN 6-8	CHILDREN 9-11
BEVERLY HILLS,90210						A	11.2	9.1	15.6	7.4	14.3	14.2	10.3	7.2	10.3	9.5	9.4	8.6	4.8	2.3	11.8	15.5	10.6	13.1	5.2	7.3
WED	8.00PM	60	FOX	GD	1234	B	10.68	4.00	2.67	7.24	1.73	4.57	6.40	6.71	5.87	6.06	4.67	4.86	2.28	.66	2.51	1.61	1.15	1.36	.59	.80
					240	C		374	250	678	162	428	599	628	550	567	437	455	214	61	235	151	108	127	55	75
						D	18	22	44	16	42	37	26	15	26	23	23	21	11	4	34	42	29	40	16	19
BLOSSOM						A	10.2	6.5	7.8	6.6	6.1	6.9	7.2	6.7	7.4	7.3	7.4	7.3	6.9	5.4	11.3	12.9	12.6	10.0	6.2	11.4
MON	8.30PM	30	NBC	CS	1234	B	9.71	2.88	1.34	6.46	.73	2.23	4.44	6.24	4.21	4.66	3.71	4.15	3.27	1.58	2.40	1.35	1.37	1.03	.69	1.26
					120	C		297	138	666	75	230	457	642	434	480	382	428	337	162	247	139	141	106	71	130
						D	15	14	22	13	17	17	17	13	17	16	17	16	14	9	33	38	37	29	22	33
CBS SUNDAY MOVIE						A	18.6	14.1	4.5	16.6	4.4	7.8	10.8	17.3	11.5	12.6	12.4	13.5	17.8	27.6	3.4	4.3	3.2	3.6	2.1	3.1
SUN	9.00PM	120	CBS	FF	1234	B	17.70	6.20	.77	16.21	.53	2.50	6.72	16.05	6.56	8.04	6.19	7.67	8.47	8.01	.73	.45	.35	.38	.23	.34
VARIOUS					480	C		350	43	916	30	142	379	907	371	454	350	433	479	453	41	26	20	21	13	19
						D	28	29	13	33	13	18	24	34	25	26	26	28	34	47	11	15	10	11	12	12
COACH						A	9.8	6.2	3.2	6.7	3.3	4.6	5.3	6.9	5.6	6.0	5.8	6.2	7.2	9.0	2.7	2.4	2.5	3.0	2.1	3.7
MON	8.00PM	30	ABC	CS	1234	B	9.35	2.71	.54	6.54	.40	1.49	3.31	6.43	3.20	3.83	2.92	3.55	3.43	2.60	.58	.25	.27	.32	.23	.41
					120	C		290	58	700	42	160	354	688	343	410	312	379	367	278	62	27	29	34	25	44
						D	15	15	10	15	10	12	14	15	14	15	14	15	16	15	9	8	8	10	8	12

PROGRAM NAME DAY	START TIME	DUR	NTWK	TYPE	WEEKS MINS	KEY	TOTAL PERSONS (2+)	MEN 15-24	MEN 18+	MEN 18-24	MEN 18-34	MEN 18-49	MEN 21+	MEN 21-49	MEN 21-54	MEN 25-49	MEN 25-54	MEN 35-64	MEN 55+	CHILDREN TOTAL 2-11	CHILDREN MALE 2-11	CHILDREN FEMALE 2-11	CHILDREN TOTAL 2-5	CHILDREN TOTAL 6-11	CHILDREN MALE 6-11	CHILDREN FEMALE 6-11
BEVERLY HILLS,90210						A	6.8	10.8	5.1	12.0	9.3	6.7	4.8	6.4	6.0	5.4	5.1	3.2	1.5	6.2	6.5	6.0	6.2	6.2	6.1	6.4
WED	8.00PM	60	FOX	GD	1234	B	16.69	1.85	4.56	1.44	2.95	4.03	4.07	3.54	3.74	2.59	2.79	1.43	.34	2.37	1.26	1.11	.99	1.39	.70	.69
					240	C	1562	174	427	134	276	377	381	331	350	242	261	134	32	222	118	104	92	130	65	65
						D	17	38	13	42	29	20	12	19	17	15	14	8	3	18	19	18	20	17	17	18
BLOSSOM						A	6.3	5.7	4.2	4.6	4.7	4.6	4.2	4.6	4.6	4.6	4.6	4.3	3.2	7.6	7.2	8.0	6.0	8.8	7.4	10.2
MON	8.30PM	30	NBC	CS	1234	B	15.54	.97	3.77	.55	1.49	2.78	3.56	2.57	2.84	2.23	2.50	1.92	.71	2.90	1.41	1.49	.96	1.95	.85	1.10
					120	C	1601	100	388	57	154	287	366	265	293	230	258	198	74	299	145	154	98	201	87	114
						D	15	18	10	16	13	12	9	12	11	12	11	10	6	26	25	28	24	28	23	33
CBS SUNDAY MOVIE						A	10.6	2.8	9.1	2.9	3.8	5.5	9.6	5.9	6.6	6.2	7.0	9.9	17.7	2.5	1.7	3.3	2.3	2.6	1.8	3.4
SUN	9.00PM	120	CBS	FF	1234	B	26.03	.49	8.15	.35	1.19	3.33	8.08	3.26	4.08	2.99	3.81	4.42	4.00	.94	.33	.61	.37	.57	.20	.37
VARIOUS					480	C	1471	28	461	20	67	188	457	184	231	169	215	250	226	53	18	35	21	32	12	21
						D	24	8	19	9	9	13	20	13	14	13	15	20	32	12	9	16	13	12	9	15
COACH						A	5.6	3.4	6.3	3.5	4.7	5.5	6.5	5.7	5.9	6.0	6.2	6.8	8.2	2.8	3.0	2.5	2.6	2.9	3.3	2.5
MON	8.00PM	30	ABC	CS	1234	B	13.86	.59	5.66	.42	1.48	3.29	5.53	3.16	3.68	2.87	3.39	3.04	1.85	1.07	.59	.47	.42	.65	.37	.27
					120	C	1482	63	606	45	159	352	592	338	393	307	363	326	198	114	64	51	45	69	40	29
						D	14	12	16	13	15	16	16	16	17	17	17	17	15	10	11	9	11	10	11	9

KEY:
- A Ratings %.
- B Projections (millions).
- C Viewers per 1000 viewing households.
- D Households and persons program shares.

Table 18–1 Four-Week Household Reach for Selected Programs

Program	Per Telecast Rating	Four-Week Reach
Beverly Hills, 90210	11.2	22.6
Blossom	10.2	22.4
CBS Sunday Movie	18.6	42.8
Coach	9.8	18.6

One formula to estimate target audience reach and frequency requires you to figure household program turnover as detailed in the following steps:

1. Calculate household program turnover by dividing four-week household reach by the one-week household rating for the program (data from Exhibit 18–1).

$$\frac{\text{TV HH four-week reach}}{\text{TV HH one-telecast rating}} = \frac{18.6}{9.8} = 1.9 \text{ program turnover}$$

2. Calculate the percentage of men 18–34 reached in four weeks by multiplying the one-time audience rating (from Exhibit 18–1) by the program turnover.

$$4.7 \times 1.9 = 8.93 \text{ or } 8.9 \text{ four-week reach of men 18–34}$$

3. To calculate frequency, multiply the one-week target audience rating by the number of telecasts (this would be four in the case of a program telecast once a week) to develop target audience gross rating points, and then divide the gross rating points by the four-week target audience reach.

$$(4.7 \times 4) \div 8.9 = 2.112 \text{ or } 2.1 \text{ frequency}$$

Please note that reach and frequency found in this manner can be considered rough estimates only. They assume that the turnover of a target audience for a program is similar to the household turnover for a program. Although this is a reasonable assumption, there is no assurance that it holds true in every case.

For Spot Television

Spot television costs are often shown in the form of "cost per rating point" for various dayparts (see Exhibit 32–1, for example). These costs are often based on households rather than target audience rating points, so it is sometimes necessary to convert household ratings to target audience ratings.

To make this conversion, multiply the household ratings by a conversion factor. In the appendix you will find conversion factors for both network and spot television (Tables 1 and 2). For example, suppose you want to buy 200 GRPs in prime-time spot television and your target audience is women 18–49.

1. Look up the conversion factor for prime-time spot television for women 18–49. It is 71.

2. Multiply the household GRPs by the conversion factor.

$$200 \times .71 = 142 \text{ women 18–49 GRPs}$$

3. Using a reach table for spot television (see Assignment 16, Table 16–2), convert the target audience GRPs to an estimated reach figure: 142 GRPs in prime-time spot television would generate about 59–60 percent reach.

4. To figure target audience frequency, divide the target audience GRPs by the estimated target audience reach.

$$\frac{148}{60} = 2.46 \text{ or } 2.5 \text{ frequency}$$

Refer to *Advertising Media Planning,* 5th ed., by Sissors and Bumba, Chapter 6.

Problems

Using the data in Table 18–1 and Exhibit 18–1, calculate the requested data for the following programs. Show your work.

1. Estimate the four-week target reach and frequency of women aged 25–54 for the program "CBS Sunday Movie."

2. Estimate the four-week target reach and frequency of working women for the program "Beverly Hills, 90210."

3. Estimate the four-week target reach and frequency of men aged 55 and older for the program "Coach."

4. Compare the estimated four-week reach and frequency against teenagers (Total Teens 12–17) for "Blossom" and "Beverly Hills, 90210."

5. Assume that you want to buy 500 GRPs a month in daytime spot TV to reach women 25–54. Using the conversion factors in the appendix, how many target GRPs will the 500 household GRPs translate to? Using the reach tables in Assignment 16, what reach and frequency will you develop in daytime spot TV against the target audience of women 25–54?

Assignment 19

Estimating Reach and Frequency for Radio

Objective: To learn one method of estimating radio reach and frequency based on audience data available from syndicated research services. This assignment also will show you the relationship between the number of stations and commercials used per week and reach and frequency. The method described in this assignment is only one of several procedures that could be used.

Discussion

There are several ways to develop reach and frequency estimates for a radio schedule. Some of them involve the use of special computer programs. This assignment covers the use of a relatively simple method of figuring these estimates, using the audience data supplied by Arbitron in that firm's radio audience listening estimates.

The problem posed here is to develop the four-week reach and frequency for a specific schedule. The method also can be used as an aid in planning by showing the planner how many stations or commercials to use to reach a specified reach and frequency goal. When using this method as a planning aid, remember these guidelines:

- To increase reach, add more stations to the schedule; to reduce reach, subtract stations.
- To increase frequency, add more commercials per week; to reduce frequency, decrease the number of commercials per week.

Exhibit 19–1 illustrates the procedure for estimating the four-week reach and frequency delivered by a group of radio stations. In this example, the target audience is men aged 25–44. The schedule calls for 12 spots per week (48 spots in four weeks) on stations KFDI-FM, KICT, KRZZ, and KZSN-FM in Wichita, KS. Here is the method:

Column A. List stations in desired order.

Column B. Enter the number of persons in the target group delivered by each station. Data are contained in the row titled "MET CUME PERSONS" under each station listing. In some cases you will have to add together the cume persons from two or more age groups. For example, adding cume persons data for men 18–24 and men 25–34 will give you cume persons for the demographic group of men 18–34. Also, you must remember to add two zeros to the cume persons numbers, because the data are reported in hundreds (00).

Column C. Enter the total number of persons in the target group. In this example there are 84,500 men aged 25–44 in the Wichita metro area.

Column D. Obtained by dividing each entry in column B by the entry in column C. Round to the nearest whole number.

Column E. Total of entries in column D.

Column F. Enter appropriate factor for number of stations being used.

Column R. Obtained by multiplying column E × column F.

Column G. Enter the number of persons in the target group delivered by each station per average quarter hour. These data are contained in the row titled "MET AQH PERSONS" under each station listed in Exhibit 19–2. Again, you might have to combine age groups to match your target audience, and you must add two zeros to the AQH Persons numbers.

Column H. Same entry as column C.

Column I. Obtained by dividing each entry in column G by the entry in column H. Round to the nearest tenth.

Column J. Enter the number of spots to be run on each station in *four* weeks.

Column K. Obtained by multiplying column I by column J.

Column L. Total of entries in column K.

The entry in column R is the estimated four-week reach. To compute the estimated four-week frequency, divide the total GRPs (column L) by the reach (column R) (480 ÷ 52 = 9.2 frequency).

Exhibit 19–1 Radio Four-Week Reach and Frequency

Target Group M 25-44
Population 84,500

Reach 52
Frequency 9.2

A Stations	B Cumes	C Population	D Cume Ratings (B ÷ C)	E Total Cume Ratings	F Duplication & Lack of Potential Factor	R Reach (E x F)	G Avg. Qtr. Hr.	H Population	I Qtr. Hr. Ratings (G ÷ H)	J # of Spots Over 4 Weeks	K GRP (I x J)	L Total GRPs
KFDI-FM	13700		16				1400		1.7	48	82	
KICT	14500		17				1500		1.8	48	86	
KRZZ	23400		28				3400		4.0	48	192	
KZSN-FM	17900		21				2100		2.5	48	120	
		84500 Population		Add ratings for stations needed & give total. 82 Total	× .64 (2 stations use .72; 3 stations use .68; 4 stations use .64; 5 or more use .62)	= 52		84500 Population				Add GRPs for stations needed & give total. 480 Total

Exhibit 19–2 Arbitron Listening Estimates—Wichita, KS

Specific Audience
MONDAY - SUNDAY 6AM-MID

	Persons 12+	Persons 18+	Men 18+	Men 18-24	Men 25-34	Men 35-44	Men 45-54	Men 55-64	Women 18+	Women 18-24	Women 25-34	Women 35-44	Women 45-54	Women 55-64	Teens 12-17
KDLE															
MET AQH PERSONS	6	5	1		1				4	1	1	1	1		1
MET AQH RATING	.1	.1	.1		.2				.2	.4	.2	.3	.4		.2
MET AQH SHARE	.9	.8	.3		1.0				1.3	2.7	1.3	1.4	2.4		2.1
MET CUME PERSONS	150	127	58	5	35		10	4	69	21	22	15	7		23
MET CUME RATING	3.7	3.5	3.3	2.2	8.0		3.8	2.0	3.6	9.3	5.2	3.8	2.5		5.4
TSA AQH PERSONS	8	5	1		1				4	1	1	1	1		3
TSA CUME PERSONS	180	136	62	9	35		10	4	74	21	22	15	12		44
KFDI															
MET AQH PERSONS	37	37	17		1	1	1	4	20		2		2	4	
MET AQH RATING	.9	1.0	1.0		.2	.2	.4	2.0	1.1		.5		.7	1.9	
MET AQH SHARE	5.5	5.9	5.3		1.0	1.4	2.3	11.8	6.7		2.7		4.9	14.3	
MET CUME PERSONS	433	433	214	11	23	22	26	47	219	9	9	26	40	35	
MET CUME RATING	10.5	11.8	12.0	4.8	5.3	5.4	9.8	23.7	11.5	4.0	2.1	6.5	14.3	16.7	
TSA AQH PERSONS	59	59	29		1	3	4	5	30		2	1	2	5	
TSA CUME PERSONS	688	684	346	11	27	46	48	80	338	9	9	36	56	67	4
KFDI-FM															
MET AQH PERSONS	68	68	37		9	5	4	9	31	2	3	5	6	6	
MET AQH RATING	1.7	1.8	2.1		2.1	1.2	1.5	4.5	1.6	.9	.7	1.3	2.2	2.9	
MET AQH SHARE	10.2	10.9	11.5		9.4	6.9	9.3	26.5	10.4	5.4	4.0	7.0	14.6	21.4	
MET CUME PERSONS	816	809	343	17	64	73	60	59	466	39	79	81	73	72	7
MET CUME RATING	19.9	22.0	19.3	7.4	14.7	17.8	22.7	29.8	24.5	17.2	18.7	20.3	26.2	34.3	1.6
TSA AQH PERSONS	86	86	47	2	11	6	5	11	39	2	5	6	9	7	
TSA CUME PERSONS	1129	1115	492	47	87	89	96	75	623	45	106	101	112	103	14
KFH															
MET AQH PERSONS	11	11	8		1	3	1	2	3				1	1	
MET AQH RATING	.3	.3	.4		.2	.7	.4	1.0	.2				.4	.5	
MET AQH SHARE	1.6	1.8	2.5		1.0	4.2	2.3	5.9	1.0				2.4	3.6	
MET CUME PERSONS	251	247	159	5	17	44	32	34	88		22	11	14	14	4
MET CUME RATING	6.1	6.7	8.9	2.2	3.9	10.7	12.1	17.2	4.6		5.2	2.8	5.0	6.7	.9
TSA AQH PERSONS	20	19	12		2	3	4	2	7			2	1	2	1
TSA CUME PERSONS	326	314	183	5	25	50	40	34	131		22	15	19	26	12
KICT															
MET AQH PERSONS	49	43	31	15	12	3	1		12	7	3	2			6
MET AQH RATING	1.2	1.2	1.7	6.6	2.8	.7	.4		.6	3.1	.7	.5			1.4
MET AQH SHARE	7.3	6.9	9.6	36.6	12.5	4.2	2.3		4.0	18.9	4.0	2.8			12.8
MET CUME PERSONS	575	480	265	98	98	47	14	4	215	94	66	48	7		95
MET CUME RATING	14.0	13.1	14.9	42.8	22.5	11.5	5.3	2.0	11.3	41.4	15.6	12.0	2.5		22.2
TSA AQH PERSONS	84	68	50	20	22	7	1		18	9	6	3			16
TSA CUME PERSONS	960	778	455	148	195	90	14	4	323	136	108	67	12		182
KKRD															
MET AQH PERSONS	63	43	18	9	6	3			25	9	9	5	1		20
MET AQH RATING	1.5	1.2	1.0	3.9	1.4	.7			1.3	4.0	2.1	1.3	.4		4.7
MET AQH SHARE	9.4	6.9	5.6	22.0	6.3	4.2			8.4	24.3	12.0	7.0	2.4		42.6
MET CUME PERSONS	1086	797	356	126	123	95	12		441	133	156	100	33	7	289
MET CUME RATING	26.5	21.7	20.0	55.0	28.3	23.2	4.5		23.2	58.6	37.0	25.0	11.8	3.3	67.5
TSA AQH PERSONS	73	47	20	10	6	3	1		27	9	9	7	1		26
TSA CUME PERSONS	1294	914	404	137	126	110	28	3	510	139	176	135	41	7	380
KLLS															
MET AQH PERSONS	4	4							4	2	2				
MET AQH RATING	.1	.1							.2	.9	.5				
MET AQH SHARE	.6	.6							1.3	5.4	2.7				
MET CUME PERSONS	102	87	34	11	17		6		53	17	18	11		7	15
MET CUME RATING	2.5	2.4	1.9	4.8	3.9		2.3		2.8	7.5	4.3	2.8		3.3	3.5
TSA AQH PERSONS	5	5	1		1				4	2	2				
TSA CUME PERSONS	106	90	37	11	20		6		53	17	18	11		7	16
KNSS															
MET AQH PERSONS	29	29	19	1	3	7	3	3	10		2	2	1	2	
MET AQH RATING	.7	.8	1.1	.4	.7	1.7	1.1	1.5	.5		.5	.5	.4	1.0	
MET AQH SHARE	4.3	4.7	5.9	2.4	3.1	9.7	7.0	8.8	3.3		2.7	2.8	2.4	7.1	
MET CUME PERSONS	473	441	277	22	40	84	42	47	164	4	18	41	28	34	32
MET CUME RATING	11.5	12.0	15.6	9.6	9.2	20.5	15.9	23.7	8.6	1.8	4.3	10.3	10.0	16.2	7.5
TSA AQH PERSONS	31	31	21	1	3	8	3	4	10		2	2	1	2	
TSA CUME PERSONS	509	477	302	22	40	92	50	52	175	4	21	45	30	34	32
KOEZ															
MET AQH PERSONS	37	37	16		2	2	3	2	21	1	1	4	5	2	
MET AQH RATING	.9	1.0	.9		.5	.5	1.1	1.0	1.1	.4	.2	1.0	1.8	1.0	
MET AQH SHARE	5.5	5.9	5.0		2.1	2.8	7.0	5.9	7.0	2.7	1.3	5.6	12.2	7.1	
MET CUME PERSONS	441	437	197		17	21	40	50	240	17	10	22	57	38	4
MET CUME RATING	10.7	11.9	11.1		3.9	5.1	15.2	25.3	12.6	7.5	2.4	5.5	20.4	18.1	.9
TSA AQH PERSONS	49	49	20		2	2	5	4	29	1	1	5	5	5	
TSA CUME PERSONS	692	686	272		17	21	72	78	414	17	26	48	81	74	6
KQAM															
MET AQH PERSONS	5	5	5	1	1	1	1	1							
MET AQH RATING	.1	.1	.3	.4	.2	.2	.4	.5							
MET AQH SHARE	.7	.8	1.5	2.4	1.0	1.4	2.3	2.9							
MET CUME PERSONS	127	123	97	5	29	29	18	8	26			15	3		4
MET CUME RATING	3.1	3.3	5.5	2.2	6.7	7.1	6.8	4.0	1.4			3.8	1.1		.9
TSA AQH PERSONS	7	7	7	1	2	1	1	1							
TSA CUME PERSONS	151	147	113	5	43	29	18	8	34	6		15	3		4

Footnote Symbols: * Audience estimates adjusted for actual broadcast schedule. + Station(s) changed call letters since the prior survey - see Page 5B.
& Both of the previous footnotes apply.

ARBITRON

WICHITA SPRING

Exhibit 19–2 (continued)

Specific Audience

MONDAY - SUNDAY 6AM-MID

	Persons 12+	Persons 18+	Men 18+	Men 18-24	Men 25-34	Men 35-44	Men 45-54	Men 55-64	Women 18+	Women 18-24	Women 25-34	Women 35-44	Women 45-54	Women 55-64	Teens 12-17
KEYN															
MET AQH PERSONS	47	44	24	1	3	9	9	2	20		3	11	4	2	3
MET AQH RATING	1.1	1.2	1.3	.4	.7	2.2	3.4	1.0	1.1		.7	2.8	1.4	1.0	.7
MET AQH SHARE	7.0	7.1	7.4	2.4	3.1	12.5	20.9	5.9	6.7		4.0	15.5	9.8	7.1	6.4
MET CUME PERSONS	637	564	274	16	35	115	79	21	290	13	49	138	61	17	73
MET CUME RATING	15.5	15.3	15.4	7.0	8.0	28.0	29.9	10.6	15.3	5.7	11.6	34.5	21.9	8.1	17.1
TSA AQH PERSONS	61	58	35	3	3	14	13	2	23		4	13	4	2	3
TSA CUME PERSONS	846	744	375	28	46	174	95	23	369	13	64	173	87	19	102
KRBB															
MET AQH PERSONS	44	44	15	1	6	5	2	1	29	2	10	8	4	3	
MET AQH RATING	1.1	1.2	.8	.4	1.4	1.2	.8	.5	1.5	.9	2.4	2.0	1.4	1.4	
MET AQH SHARE	6.6	7.1	4.6	2.4	6.3	6.9	4.7	2.9	9.7	5.4	13.3	11.3	9.8	10.7	
MET CUME PERSONS	591	556	229	16	87	78	35	9	327	30	102	100	58	25	35
MET CUME RATING	14.4	15.1	12.9	7.0	20.0	19.0	13.3	4.5	17.2	13.2	24.2	25.0	20.8	11.9	8.2
TSA AQH PERSONS	62	62	17	1	7	6	2	1	45	2	11	17	10	3	
TSA CUME PERSONS	805	758	271	22	104	88	35	18	487	62	133	164	89	27	47
KRZZ															
MET AQH PERSONS	51	49	39	4	23	11	1		10	2	5	2	1		2
MET AQH RATING	1.2	1.3	2.2	1.7	5.3	2.7	.4		.5	.9	1.2	.5	.4		.5
MET AQH SHARE	7.6	7.9	12.1	9.8	24.0	15.3	2.3		3.3	5.4	6.7	2.8	2.4		4.3
MET CUME PERSONS	532	478	286	32	150	84	16	4	192	61	84	26	14	3	54
MET CUME RATING	13.0	13.0	16.1	14.0	34.5	20.5	6.1	2.0	10.1	26.9	19.9	6.5	5.0	1.4	12.6
TSA AQH PERSONS	56	54	42	4	24	13	1		12	2	6	3	1		2
TSA CUME PERSONS	662	601	348	36	182	110	16	4	253	61	123	44	18	3	61
KSGL															
MET AQH PERSONS	5	5	2		1		1		3			1	1		
MET AQH RATING	.1	.1	.1		.2		.4		.2			.3	.4		
MET AQH SHARE	.7	.8	.6		1.0		2.3		1.0			1.4	2.4		
MET CUME PERSONS	124	120	41		6	4	14	17	79	4	10	22	16	7	4
MET CUME RATING	3.0	3.3	2.3		1.4	1.0	5.3	8.6	4.2	1.8	2.4	5.5	5.7	3.3	.9
TSA AQH PERSONS	7	7	4		1		1	1	3			1	1		
TSA CUME PERSONS	193	189	76		6	4	14	30	113	4	14	22	16	20	4
KTLI															
MET AQH PERSONS	14	13	3		2		1		10	1	4	3	1	1	1
MET AQH RATING	.3	.4	.2		.5		.4		.5	.4	.9	.8	.4	.5	.2
MET AQH SHARE	2.1	2.1	.9		2.1		2.3		3.3	2.7	5.3	4.2	2.4	3.6	2.1
MET CUME PERSONS	178	145	42	5	12	11	14		103	9	35	26	19	10	33
MET CUME RATING	4.3	3.9	2.4	2.2	2.8	2.7	5.3		5.4	4.0	8.3	6.5	6.8	4.8	7.7
TSA AQH PERSONS	17	16	5		3	1	1		11	1	5	3	1	1	1
TSA CUME PERSONS	203	167	55	9	17	15	14		112	11	42	26	19	10	36
KXLK															
MET AQH PERSONS	33	31	12	1	4	4	2	1	19	1	8	5	3	1	2
MET AQH RATING	.8	.8	.7	.4	.9	1.0	.8	.5	1.0	.4	1.9	1.3	1.1	.5	.5
MET AQH SHARE	4.9	5.0	3.7	2.4	4.2	5.6	4.7	2.9	6.4	2.7	10.7	7.0	7.3	3.6	4.3
MET CUME PERSONS	455	416	170	16	64	56	26	8	246	44	80	75	29	10	39
MET CUME RATING	11.1	11.3	9.6	7.0	14.7	13.7	9.8	4.0	13.0	19.4	19.0	18.8	10.4	4.8	9.1
TSA AQH PERSONS	41	38	15	1	5	5	3	1	23	1	9	8	3	1	3
TSA CUME PERSONS	603	531	212	18	89	63	34	8	319	65	97	87	31	16	72
KYQQ															
MET AQH PERSONS	20	17	8	2	4	1	1		9	2	3	3		1	3
MET AQH RATING	.5	.5	.4	.9	.9	.2	.4		.5	.9	.7	.8		.5	.7
MET AQH SHARE	3.0	2.7	2.5	4.9	4.2	1.4	2.3		3.0	5.4	4.0	4.2		3.6	6.4
MET CUME PERSONS	446	374	170	54	65	29	18		204	64	68	44	13	7	72
MET CUME RATING	10.9	10.2	9.6	23.6	14.9	7.1	6.8		10.7	28.2	16.1	11.0	4.7	3.3	16.8
TSA AQH PERSONS	39	35	17	3	6	4	2	2	18	4	4	6	1	2	4
TSA CUME PERSONS	746	624	292	72	89	64	44	19	332	86	92	87	34	20	122
KZSN															
MET AQH PERSONS	5	5	5	1		1	1	1							
MET AQH RATING	.1	.1	.3	.4		.2	.4	.5							
MET AQH SHARE	.7	.8	1.5	2.4		1.4	2.3	2.9							
MET CUME PERSONS	122	114	75	11	12	15	17	12	39		13	15	7		8
MET CUME RATING	3.0	3.1	4.2	4.8	2.8	3.7	6.4	6.1	2.1		3.1	3.8	2.5		1.9
TSA AQH PERSONS	5	5	5	1		1	1	1							
TSA CUME PERSONS	151	140	95	11	12	35	17	12	45		13	15	7	3	11
KZSN-FM															
MET AQH PERSONS	80	75	33	4	10	11	6	1	42	6	12	12	6	2	5
MET AQH RATING	1.9	2.0	1.9	1.7	2.3	2.7	2.3	.5	2.2	2.6	2.8	3.0	2.2	1.0	1.2
MET AQH SHARE	12.0	12.1	10.2	9.8	10.4	15.3	14.0	2.9	14.0	16.2	16.0	16.9	14.6	7.1	10.6
MET CUME PERSONS	914	828	381	81	99	80	76	34	447	82	134	114	55	30	86
MET CUME RATING	22.3	22.5	21.4	35.4	22.8	19.5	28.8	17.2	23.5	36.1	31.8	28.5	19.7	14.3	20.1
TSA AQH PERSONS	106	100	45	8	15	12	7	2	55	10	15	13	7	3	6
TSA CUME PERSONS	1293	1168	515	106	132	108	101	50	653	103	187	172	82	50	125
TOTALS															
MET AQH PERSONS	669	622	323	41	96	72	43	34	299	37	75	71	41	28	47
MET AQH RATING	16.3	16.9	18.2	17.9	22.1	17.6	16.3	17.2	15.7	16.3	17.8	17.8	14.7	13.3	11.0
MET CUME PERSONS	3894	3479	1684	213	417	384	257	194	1795	222	413	385	267	196	415
MET CUME RATING	94.9	94.6	94.7	93.0	95.9	93.7	97.3	98.0	94.5	97.8	97.9	96.3	95.7	93.3	97.0

Footnote Symbols: * Audience estimates adjusted for actual broadcast schedule. + Station(s) changed call letters since the prior survey - see Page 5B.
& Both of the previous footnotes apply.

Exhibit 19–2 shows data from the Arbitron Radio USA report. Before using this information you should understand the following terms:

Met. Metropolitan survey area. An area generally corresponding to the federal government's Metropolitan Statistical Areas.

AQH Persons. Average Quarter-Hour Persons. The estimated number of persons who listened to a station for a minimum of five minutes within a quarter hour. These data are reported in hundreds (00).

AQH Rating. The AQH Persons estimate shown as a percentage of the universe.

AQH Share. The Average Quarter-Hour Persons estimate for a given station expressed as a percentage of the total Metro Quarter-Hour Persons estimate. The total metro estimates are shown following the station listings at the bottom of the exhibit.

Cume Persons. The estimated number of *different* persons who listened to a station for a minimum of five minutes in a quarter hour within the reported daypart. In Exhibit 19–2, the reported daypart is Monday–Sunday, 6 a.m. to midnight. Cume estimates are also referred to as cumulative or unduplicated audience estimates. Like the AQH Persons data, cume persons data are reported in hundreds (00).

Cume Rating. The estimated number of cume persons expressed as a percentage of the metro universe.

TSA. Total Survey Area. A geographic area that includes the metro survey area and can include additional surrounding counties.

Problems

You are planning a radio buy in Wichita, KS, to reach a target audience of women aged 25–44. The plan calls for purchasing 12 commercials per week on each of the following stations: KKRD, KEYN, KRBB, and KZSN-FM. There are 82,200 women aged 25–44 in the Wichita metro survey area.

1. Based on this information, and using the Arbitron radio audience data, complete the blank worksheet provided and develop the four-week reach and frequency for the planned buy. Write your answers here, but also turn in the completed worksheet:

   Reach ____________%, frequency ____________

2. Using the same stations as in problem 1, determine the four-week reach and frequency if 15 spots per week are used on each station.

   Reach ____________%, frequency ____________

3. Assume that in addition to the stations listed, you add station KXLK, with all stations receiving 12 commercials per week. Determine the four-week reach and frequency.

   Reach ______________%, frequency ______________

Worksheet: Radio Four-Week Reach and Frequency

Target Group ______________
Population ______________

Reach ______________
Frequency ______________

A Stations	B Cumes	C Population	D Cume Ratings (B ÷ C)	E Total Cume Ratings	F Duplication & Lack of Potential Factor	R Reach (E x F)	G Avg. Qtr. Hr.	H Population	I Qtr. Hr. Ratings (G ÷ H)	J # of Spots Over 4 Weeks	K GRP (I x J)	L Total GRPs
		Population		Add ratings for stations needed & give total. Total	X 2 stations use .72 3 stations use .68 4 stations use .64 5 or more use .62	=		Population	X	=		Add GRPs for stations needed & give total. Total

Assignment 20

How to Estimate Reach and Frequency from Competitive Media Expenditure Data

Objective: To help you make a rough estimate of reach and frequency of competitors' advertising programs.

Discussion

In order to determine the level of reach and frequency in your plan, it would be valuable to know how much reach and frequency your competitors have achieved. It would be especially valuable to know the reach and frequency of one or more competitors from whom you expect to gain customers, or whom you must defend against to protect your brand share. Such estimates can be made if media expenditure data of competitors are known.

In order to make rough estimates of competitors' reach and frequency, you need to know at least two kinds of facts: (a) which media the competitor uses; and (b) how much money the competitor spends in that media. The more specific this information is, the better the estimate of reach and frequency. For example, if you knew precisely which network television programs the competitor used, you could estimate the reach and frequency for each program using Nielsen's Cumulative Audience Estimates. The net reach could be estimated by the Sainsbury formula discussed in Assignment 17.

Unfortunately, students and others who plan media often do not have that much information or many data sources at their disposal. The following example shows you how to make reach and frequency estimates given a minimum amount of information.

Example

Suppose that all you know is that competitor A spends $10 million per year for media advertising. About 50 percent of that amount is in prime-time network television; another 25 percent is spent in spot television; and 25 percent is spent in daytime network television. Spot TV was assumed to be daytime in the top 50 markets. Both of you have as targets women aged 18–49. How can reach and frequency be determined?

1. Estimate what percentage of sales for a product category occurs each month. Sometimes this is available, and other times only index figures per month are available. If index figures are available, they can be converted into percentages by adding them and dividing the total into the index for each month as follows:

Month	Index	Percent	Month	Index	Percent
January	65	5.4%	July	120	10.0%
February	79	6.6	August	132	11.0
March	87	7.3	September	126	10.5
April	105	8.8	October	100	8.3
May	111	9.3	November	86	7.2
June	116	9.7	December	72	6.0
			Total (12 months)	1,199	100.0%

If there are neither index nor percentage of sales per month, then the planner must make rough estimations about the peaks and valleys of sales, because most product categories have high and low monthly sales during the year.

2. In this example, August—with 11 percent of sales—is highest. To learn how many dollars are spent in various media, multiply 11 percent times the total spent times the percentage spent in each medium, as follows:

   Prime-time network expenditure (.11 × 10,000,000) × .50 = $550,000
   Daytime network expenditure (.11 × 10,000,000) × .25 = $275,000
   Daytime spot TV expenditure (.11 × 10,000,000) × .25 = $275,000

3. At this point, the procedure is summarized as follows:

   a. Find the cost per rating point (C/RP). This can be found in the appendix (Table 3). If you did not have the C/RP but did have the average cost and average rating per commercial, you could compute the C/RP by dividing the average cost by the average rating.

   b. Divide the media expenditure, such as daytime network ($275,000), by the C/RP. This gives you an estimate of the GRPs that the competitor probably bought.

   c. Multiply those GRPs by the appropriate demographic conversion factor to find target GRPs (TRPs). Conversion factors are included in the appendix (Tables 1 and 2).

   d. Use the appropriate reach table from Assignment 16 in this workbook to find out how much reach the TRPs provide.

   e. To find the frequency, divide the TRPs by the reach.

   f. Do this for each medium and then combine the reaches using the Sainsbury formula as discussed in Assignment 17.

The following are calculations for the problem presented earlier:

	1 Cost per rating point	2 HH GRPs	3 Conversion factor	4 TRPs (Target GRPs)	5 Estimated reach	6 Estimated frequency
Prime-time network	$14,000	39	.65	25	15	1.7

Col. No.
1. From appendix, Table 3
2. 550,000 ÷ 14,000 = 39
3. From appendix (Table 2): Network, Prime, W-18/49
4. Multiply HH GRPs by conversion factor
5. Look up reach table in Assignment 16. Because there is no reach for a GRP level of 25, use a ratio from table: 100 : 61 = 25 : *x*. *x* = 15
6. Divide TRPs by reach

	1	2	3	4	5	6
Daytime network	$3,168	87	.68	59	25	2.4

Col. No.
1. From appendix, Table 3
2. 275,000 ÷ 3,168 = 87
3. From appendix (Table 2): Daytime Network, W-18/49
4. Multiply HH GRPs by conversion factor
5. Look up reach table in Assignment 16 and use ratio: 100 : 43 = 59 : *x*. *x* = 25
6. Divide TRPs by reach

	1	2	3	4	5	6
Spot TV	$2,849	97	.64	62	24	2.6

Col. No.
1. From spot TV cost table for 50 markets (See Exhibit 32–1)
2. 275,000 ÷ 2,849 = 97
3. From Appendix (Table 1): Spot TV, Day, W-18/49
4. Multiply HH GRPs by conversion factor
5. Look up reach table in Assignment 16 and use ratio: 100 : 39 = 62 : *x*. *x* = 24
6. Divide TRPs by reach

Sainsbury for net reach (See Assignment 17)

Network TV (National Reach)

Prime time	15	= 36% net reach nationally
Daytime	25	

Network + Spot TV (Spot Market Reach)

Network Prime Time	15	= 49% reach in spot markets (reach reduced by 5 percent because three vehicles were combined)
Network Daytime	25	
Spot TV Daytime	24	

Frequency (TRPs ÷ Target Reach)

National

Network Prime Time TRPs	25	
Network Daytime TRPs	59	84 ÷ 36 = 2.3
	84	

Spot Markets

Network Prime Time TRPs	25	
Network Daytime TRPs	59	146 ÷ 49 = 3.0
Spot TV Daytime TRPs	62	
	146	

Note: National and spot market reach and frequency were developed separately since spot markets receive additional weight not received by other markets.

Often it is difficult to find the precise data you need to make your calculations. Then you must improvise. But when improvising, it is important not to underestimate the reach and frequency of competitors. Such underestimating could mislead you as you try to develop a media plan to counter competitive efforts.

Problem

Assume that you must estimate the reach and frequency of competitor *X*, who spends $8,500,000 a year. All that you know about *X* is that the company allocates 50 percent of budget in prime-time TV, 25 percent in daytime TV, and 25 percent in late fringe TV. All dollars are spent on network TV. You also estimate that the best sales month for the product category is August, in which 15 percent of the total budget is probably spent.

Your task is to estimate the net reach and frequency for August for competitor *X*. Your target market (and the competitor's) are women aged 18–49.

Assignment 21

Determining the Effective Frequency and Reach of a Media Plan

Objective: To present the opportunity for students to learn how to determine the effective frequency and reach of a media plan based on prevailing concepts.

Discussion

The Problem

It is important to remember when dealing with effective reach that effective frequency is also part of the same concept. You cannot discuss one without the other. So for every exposure to media, or to media plan vehicles, there is a different effective reach.

A media planner's work is not finished when the reach and frequency calculations of selected vehicles are complete. The question he or she should ask is, Are all the audience members reached in this plan of equal value? For example, suppose that the selected vehicles attain a 70 percent reach of a target market, such as women aged 18–34. Are all of the 70 percent reached of equal value to the advertiser?

The expert consensus about this question is, "no." Some of those reached are more valuable than others. Opinion is divided as to which are most valuable. In the past, the answer would have been that audiences who have been reached three or more times (during a four-week period) were most valuable. That was called the 3+ effective frequency level. Today, we are certain that is not correct.

The problem with the 3+ effective frequency level is that it is an oversimplification. Some audiences do indeed respond after they have been exposed to three ads, but some respond at the first exposure, and some do not respond after many exposures.

Joseph Ostrow, Executive Vice President and Director of Media for Foote, Cone & Belding advertising agency in New York, in his fine analysis of the situation, explained that there are many factors to be considered to arrive at an effective frequency level. One example illustrates the problem: If an agency is advertising a product like paper clips, it could take many repetitions of advertising to make an impression on audience members' minds. The reason is that paper clips are a rather dull product and are not considered very important in our lives most of the time. So consumers tend not to pay much attention to paper clip advertising. Therefore, the effective frequency level for paper clips could be as high as ten or more repetitions before consumers respond in some way.

On the other hand, new car models that come out every year are of keen importance to many people in the American economy. The public eagerly await the introductions of new cars, and advertising has an almost immediate effect on many of them with only one exposure. Some people, of course, do not pay attention to new-car ads immediately, but might do so later. So the effective frequency level for new cars could be as low as one for many buyers, but higher for others who do not buy immediately.

Some experts believe that there is an effective frequency range of exposures that are needed, such as 2–7 or 3–10, and so forth. We believe, however, that Ostrow is probably the most objective in answering the question. Therefore, his technique has been modified and discussed in our text. (See Exhibit 21–1). Essentially, the technique involves giving or taking weights away from the 3+ technique used so often in the past.

Method

The following is a step-by-step explanation of how to arrive at an effective frequency (and effective reach) level.

1. Circle pluses and minuses that apply to each effective frequency criterion. Note that some criteria are not pertinent to every brand or marketing situation.
2. Add all the pluses and minuses.
3. Take the result (from step 2) and add or subtract from the old 3+ effective frequency base. Ostrow's criteria are the source of these considerations, and the suggested points are the authors':

		Suggested additional points
1. He or she is introducing a new product.		+.2
2. The brand will be among those that are less well known.		+.2
3. The product has a short purchase cycle.		+.2
4. The product is used frequently, if not daily.		+.1
5. The introduction is in a highly competitive market.		+.2
6. Ad copy is somewhat complex.		+.2
7. Copy is more unusual than competitors'.		−.2
8. Copy will be in relatively large-size ad units.		−.1
9. There is high ad clutter in category media.		+.2
10. Media environment is compatible with product.		−.1
11. Advertising will be continuous.		−.2
12. Many media will be used.		+.2
13. There will be many opportunities for repetition.		−.2
Sum of Points		+.7
Effective frequency base	3.0	
Additional points	+ .7	
Modified effective frequency level	3.7	

It is important to note that there are times when there is no criterion that covers your particular marketing/copy or media situation. You might have to add your own. Examples include high or low involvement, either thinking or feeling, and degree of interest in the product category.

Refer to *Advertising Media Planning,* 5th ed., by Sissors and Bumba, Chapter 6.

Exhibit 21–1 Ostrow Technique for Setting Frequency Levels

Marketing Factors That Affect Effective Frequency

Established brands	−.2	−.1	+.1	+.2	New brands
High market share	−.2	−.1	+.1	+.2	Low market share
Dominant brand in market	−.2	−.1	+.1	+.2	Smaller, less well-known brands
High brand loyalty	−.2	−.1	+.1	+.2	Low brand loyalty
Long purchase cycle	−.2	−.1	+.1	+.2	Short purchase cycle (high volume segments)
Product used occasionally	−.2	−.1	+.1	+.2	Product used daily
			+.1	+.2	Needed to beat competition
			+.1	+.2	Advertising to older consumers, or children

Copy Factors That Affect Effective Frequency

Simple copy	−.2	−.1	+.1	+.2	Complex copy
Copy more unusual than competition	−.2	−.1	+.1	+.2	Copy less unusual than competition
Continuing campaign	−.2	−.1	+.1	+.2	New copy campaign
Product sell copy	−.2	−.1	+.1	+.2	Image type copy
Single kind of message	−.2	−.1	+.1	+.2	More different kinds of messages
To avoid wearout: New messages	−.2	−.1	+.1	+.2	Older messages
Larger ad units	−.2	−.1	+.1	+.2	Small ad units

Media Factors That Affect Effective Frequency

Lower ad clutter	−.2	−.1	+.1	+.2	High ad clutter
Compatible editorial environment	−.2	−.1	+.1	+.2	Incompatible environment
Attentiveness high	−.2	−.1	+.1	+.2	Attentiveness low
Continuous advertising	−.2	−.1	+.1	+.2	Pulsed or flighted advertising
Few media used	−.2	−.1	+.1	+.2	Many media used
Opportunities for media repetition	−.2	−.1	+.1	+.2	Fewer opportunities

Source: Joseph W. Ostrow, "Setting Frequency Levels," in *Effective Frequency: The State of the Art.* Copyright 1982. Reprinted by permission.

Problem

Assume that you are introducing a new floor wax with the following marketing, copy, and media considerations. You need to arrive at an effective frequency level that you can justify to the client. Here are the details:

1. It is a new product. Obviously, it has no market share.
2. It has no brand loyalty.
3. The brand will spend more money than the leading brands to make a strong entry into the marketplace.
4. The purchase cycle varies from one month to six months.
5. The product is used about once or twice a month.
6. There are few competitors in this market, but they are strong.
7. Advertising will be directed to older people.
8. Copy is complex, although not unique.
9. Copy represents some new ideas for an older age market.
10. The advertising will try to build a brand image.
11. There are different ads that will feature different messages.
12. The advertising will run in full-page size, and perhaps on billboards.
13. There is not too much clutter in the category.
14. Ads should appear in homemaking publications.
15. Vehicles should be those that generate high attentiveness levels, such as *Better Homes & Gardens.*
16. Advertising will be flighted to provide some continuity.
17. Only print and outdoor media may be used.
18. Outdoor may have much repetition, but print may not.

Using the above list of criteria, arrive at an effective frequency level. Show your work. If you add any additional criteria, explain why they were added.

Assignment 22

Use of Gross Impressions in Media Planning

Objective: To explain the concept of gross impressions and show how they can be used in media planning. Planners often use gross impressions for a variety of purposes, but most often in lieu of a net reach number (for a combination of different media vehicles).

Discussion

In media plans that utilize more than one medium, a problem often arises, namely, determining the net unduplicated audience size (or net reach)[1] of a combination of different media such as magazines, network television, radio, and outdoor.

There are formulas for calculating the net reach of combinations of two or more media vehicles, but media planners are always aware that the formulas produce rough estimates. Therefore, a planner might want to see another number to view delivery of a combination of either the same or different vehicles.

This "other" figure could be gross impressions for the combination. However, gross impressions are not unduplicated. They are duplicated, or gross, data. Although the gross impressions figure does not tell the planner as much as net reach would, it is often a useful number that provides some dimension to the data by which the planner can compare one set of media vehicles with other sets until the final selection stage of planning.

What Are Gross Impressions?

When an audience member is exposed to a medium, he or she has received one impression. If a person tunes in to the same TV news program once each day for five days a week, he or she has received five impressions. Carrying this idea one step further, suppose that you select a magazine that reaches six million targets with one issue. If you buy an ad once a week for four weeks in this magazine, you can find the gross impressions by multiplying your one-week reach times four, or 24 million gross impressions per month. Gross impressions are sometimes called the weight of a media plan because they are the sum of all impressions.

The term *gross* means duplicated impressions. In other words, with gross impressions you are not asking how many *different* target audience members you are reaching in four weeks, only how many duplicated members.

---

[1]Net reach means net unduplicated audience; also cumulative audience.

So you are sacrificing some knowledge when you use the concept of gross impressions. You would really like to know the "unduplicated audience size" for four weeks, but you are willing to settle for "duplicated" impressions.

Caution: Gross impressions, when calculated for all media used in a plan, tend to be very large, sometimes in the hundreds of millions. Such large numbers are often confusing because it seems as if advertisers are reaching more people than they really are. Furthermore, cost per thousand calculated on the base of gross impressions also tends to be low, again, tending to mislead planners if they are not careful to understand what measurement they are really using.

The best way to think about gross impressions is to remember that they are "duplicated impressions." If it were possible to calculate the net reach (and some formulas are available to do so), it would be much lower than gross impressions.

The Relationship of Gross Impressions to Gross Rating Points

Gross impressions are the projections of gross rating points (GRPs) into whole numbers. Whereas GRPs are percentages (ratings) added together to provide a duplicated percentage figure, gross impressions are gross rating points multiplied by the audience base.

	1 One-telecast HH rating	2 Four-week HH GRP	3 Total U.S. TV HHs (Audience base)	4* Monthly gross impressions
Network TV program A (Telecast once a week and four weeks a month)	20	80	95,400,000	76,320,000

*Column 4 = Column 2 × Column 3 (.80 × 95.4 million = 76,320,000)

Note that if the monthly GRPs had been 120, then the universe size (95.4 million) would have been multiplied by 1.20, and the gross impressions would have been 114,480,000.

Problem

Assume that you are faced with the following two media plans when you are relatively early in the decision-making process. These plans are titled A and B. According to gross impressions and cost efficiency for gross impressions, which is best? Obviously, other considerations might require that you eventually change your mind. But at this point assume that everything else between the two plans is equal, except gross impressions and cost efficiency.

Show your work and explain your decision.

Media selected	Kind of ad/ commercial	Cost per single ad/ commercial	Number of insertions	Targets reached per vehicle for one ad/commercial
Media Plan A:				
Magazine A	Full-page, four-color	$94,000	4	9,200,000
Network TV program B	30 sec., fringe	20,500	8	2,150,000
Spot TV (top 50 markets)	30 sec., daytime	4,600	18	1,875,000
Media Plan B:				
Magazine D	Full-page, four-color	$82,000	3	8,900,000
Network TV program E	30 sec., daytime	9,000	10	2,850,000
Network TV program F	30 sec., prime time	90,000	4	8,500,000

Section Three

Media Strategy Planning Problems

Assignment 23

Strategic Impressions in Media Planning

Objective: To help you understand a part of a media plan called strategic impressions. You should not only know what strategic impressions are, but also how they can be determined. They are very important when you have two or more important target groups.

Discussion

Media plans are created with at least one goal, which often is to reach individuals of different market segments of the same demographic class. For example, a media plan objective might require that you reach men and women, but in different proportions. If you were advertising refrigerators, you would probably want more women than men in the audience, but surely you would want both. Your proportions might be 70 percent women and 30 percent men.

In completing the plan you could possibly calculate the net reach of a combination of men and women. But it would not tell you what the proportions of men to women were, and this information might be necessary, especially if you were to select media vehicles that deliver targets in diametrically opposed proportions.

The answer to the problem lies in the calculations of strategic impressions (either in place of, or in addition to, net reach). A strategic impression tells you whether the media vehicles will deliver targets in the most advantageous proportions (or in the most strategic proportions). However, remember that these impressions are not cumulative measurements. They are duplicated measurements, which of course is the meaning of an impression. (See Assignment 22 for a discussion of gross impressions.)

To see how strategic impressions would look in a media plan, refer to Table 23–1. In this plan, you want to reach 70 percent women and 30 percent men. The vehicles you have selected are magazine A and television program B. The net reach of these vehicles was 22.3 percent. But strategic impressions are more important here. So you can prove your point as shown in the table.

Refer to *Advertising Media Planning,* 5th ed., by Sissors and Bumba, Chapter 9.

Table 23–1 Media Vehicles Selected for Your Plan

	Gross impressions of magazine A per month (000)	Four-week gross impressions of network TV program B (000)	Total (gross) impressions (000)	Strategic impressions (%)
Number of women reached (18+)	11,300	12,500	23,800	70%
Number of men reached (18+)	5,000	5,200	10,200	30
Total impressions			34,000	100%

How are these proportions determined? The answer can be found in two ways: (1) by judgment based on experience and (2) by looking at data in Simmons or MRI. Suppose that you were studying data for a certain kind of product class and you wanted to know what proportions of strategic impressions to use. You would turn to the product category listing in Simmons or MRI to find data such as:

	Total users of product	
Men users	7,602,000	30%
Women users	17,738,000	70
Total users	25,340,000	100%

These data are for all users, but you might be more interested in using data for heavy users only, or perhaps a combination of heavy and moderate users. Which group you use depends on a number of considerations:

1. Do you have enough money to reach all users?
2. What percentage reach level of all users is acceptable? And, again, do you have enough money?
3. Do you need frequency? If so, at what level, and with what reach level? Available money could mean that you select a smaller group of target audiences.
4. In terms of the marketing objectives, where have most sales occurred in the past? Will this group continue to purchase the product? Can we expect sales from some other group?
5. Most often, it is better to do a good advertising communication job with a smaller group than it is to do a mediocre job with a larger group. But there could be exceptions, such as when the brand in question is truly superior to all other brands, or where you have a unique selling proposition that is meaningful to consumers, or where your creative message is so intriguing that you get a great deal of word-of-mouth advertising free. But exceptions do not occur very often.
6. In order to combine user categories, it is a good idea to calculate new index numbers (using Simmons or MRI data). Here is an example:

	Total U.S. (000)	Heavy users A	Heavy users C	Heavy users D	Moderate users A	Moderate users C	Moderate users D
Total female homemakers	81,513	13,450	16.5	100	9,211	11.3	100
Aged 18–24	6,865	1,030	—	91	851	—	110
Aged 25–34	20,273	3,548	—	106	2,717	—	119

a. Add total heavy and moderate users (13,450 + 9,211 = 22,661).
b. Find percentage of all homemakers who are heavy/moderate users (22,661 ÷ 81,513 = 27.8%).
c. Add the total U.S. homemakers aged 18–24 + 25–34 (6,865 + 20,273 = 27,138).
d. Add heavy and moderate users aged 18–24 and 25–34 (1,030 + 3,548 + 851 + 2,717 = 8,146).
e. Find percentage of heavy/moderate users of total (8,146 ÷ 27,138 = 30.0%).
f. Calculate new combined-index number for heavy/moderate users aged 18–34 (30.0 ÷ 27.8 × 100 = 108 index number).
g. Convert new index numbers to percentages.

7. After all new index numbers have been calculated, the combined and new index numbers will look like this:

	New combined-index numbers	Strategic impressions (%)
18–34	108	33%
35–49	120	37
50+	100	30
	328	100%

Now the planner can allocate strategic impression goals on the proportional basis of the new index numbers.

One final thought about strategic impressions: They can be weighted according to the experience of a planner on behalf of the brand. In other words, if the data show that women aged 18–34 should constitute the largest number of strategic impressions, the experienced planner will argue that for *this* brand, there is evidence to suggest that women aged 35–49 would be better. Therefore, this planner will weight the impressions in a manner that is most meaningful to the client and the product.

Problem

How shall we divide strategic impressions for a media plan for the margarine market? The decision to buy margarine is made almost exclusively by women, so we may disregard males in this example. But women do not buy margarine in equal amounts. Some are heavy, others are moderate, and still others are light users. Different age groups also buy in varying amounts.

Exhibit 23–1 MRI: Margarine Usage

						Pounds/Last 30 Days											
		All				Heavy More than 4				Medium 3-4				Light Less than 3			
	Total	A	B	C	D	A	B	C	D	A	B	C	D	A	B	C	D
	U.S.		%	%			%	%			%	%			%	%	
Base: Female Homemakers	'000	'000	Down	Across	Index	'000	Down	Across	Index	'000	Down	Across	Index	'000	Down	Across	Index
All Female Homemakers	81513	73299	100.0	89.9	100	15269	100.0	18.7	100	19871	100.0	24.4	100	38159	100.0	46.8	100
18-24	6862	6172	8.4	89.9	100	1177	7.7	17.2	92	1557	7.8	22.7	93	3438	9.0	50.1	107
25-34	20273	18145	24.8	89.5	100	3861	25.3	19.0	102	4884	24.6	24.1	99	9400	24.6	46.4	99
35-44	16640	15023	20.5	90.3	100	3791	24.8	22.8	122	4511	22.7	27.1	111	6721	17.6	40.4	86
45-54	11752	10424	14.2	88.7	99	2523	16.5	21.5	115	2718	13.7	23.1	95	5184	13.6	44.1	94
55-64	11215	10120	13.8	90.2	100	2024	13.3	18.0	96	1910	14.6	25.9	106	5187	13.6	46.3	99
65 or over	14770	13415	18.3	90.8	101	1893	12.4	12.8	68	3294	16.6	22.3	91	8229	21.6	55.7	119
18-34	27135	24317	33.2	89.6	100	5038	33.0	18.6	99	6441	32.4	23.7	97	1838	33.6	47.3	101
18-49	49793	44643	60.9	89.7	100	10136	66.4	20.4	109	12213	61.5	24.5	101	22295	58.4	44.8	96
25-54	48666	43591	59.5	89.6	100	10175	66.6	20.9	112	12111	60.9	24.9	102	21305	55.8	43.8	94

1. Shown in Exhibit 23–1 are data from MRI on users of margarine. Decide how many strategic impressions are needed from a combination of heavy users and medium users.

2. Show your answers in the following spaces:

   For women aged 18–34, ____________%
   For women aged 35–54, ____________%
   For women aged 55+, ____________%

3. Briefly explain how you arrived at your decisions in problem 2.

4. Briefly explain whether, if given the opportunity, you would have preferred to use "All Users" instead of a combination of heavy and medium users.

Assignment 24

Quintile and Frequency Distributions in Media Planning

Objective: To explain the concept of quintile and frequency distributions as used in marketing and media analysis.

Discussion

Media data often are reported as a single number or statistic whose value is not always apparent. For example, "frequency" is a number that is often misinterpreted because the user forgets that it is an average. Both high and low numbers could have gone into making up the statistical average. But some averages have a narrow range of scores, and others have a wide range. To illustrate the problem, two identical averages are shown as follows, but with different ranges:

A: 5 + 5 + 5 + 5 = 20	Average = 5	Range = 0
B: 9 + 8 + 2 + 1 = 20	Average = 5	Range = 8

Alternative B is much different from alternative A, but no one would ever know simply by looking at an average score. That is where frequency and quintile distributions come into play; they show how data are distributed.

The Frequency Distribution

Anyone who has studied statistics in college should be familiar with a frequency distribution. It consists of a table showing the number of persons who responded any given number of times to a question, experimental treatment, or research variable. In media planning, a television reach statistic is the number of persons who tuned in to a television program at least once during a four-week period. But reach tells planners nothing about how many other times audience members saw the same program during the four-week period. The following frequency distribution (Exhibit 24–1) supplies the latter information.

Exhibit 24–1 Frequency Distribution of Commercial Messages Received

No. of MSGs Used	Avg MSG %	4-Wk Reach %	Avg No. MSGs	% Dist. of Total TV Hshlds by no. of CML MSGs received: 1	2	3	4	5	6	7	8	9–10	11–12
21	7.4	63.3	2.5	25.1	15.6	9.3	5.4	3.2	1.8	1.3	1.1	.4	.1

Source: *Brand Cumulative Audiences*, A. C. Nielsen Co.

In the exhibit, the brand used 21 commercials during this time period. The average rating for these commercials was 7.4. The four-week reach was 63.3 percent of U.S. TV households. The frequency was 2.5 average. The percentage of total TV households in the United States that received only one message was 25.1 percent, 15.6 percent received two messages, 9.3 percent received three messages, and so forth. Some households therefore saw the messages a different number of times than others.

A Quintile (or a Tercile) Distribution

A quintile distribution is used for the same reason as a frequency distribution, with two major exceptions. In a quintile distribution, the sample is divided into five approximately equal sections, but in a frequency distribution, the sample can be divided into any number of sections (or intervals). The number of persons within these sections is divided so that the top quintile represents the largest number of responses and the bottom quintile represents the smallest. In a frequency distribution, however, the largest frequency can be located almost anywhere, although it is usually near the midpoint of a set of intervals (as a clue to a measure of central tendency for the sample).

A tercile distribution divides the sample into thirds rather than fifths, with the first tercile representing the highest level of media viewing. The five quintile sections are shown later and labeled as follows:

Quintile I: The top 20 percent
Quintile II: The second largest 20 percent
Quintile III: The third largest 20 percent
Quintile IV: The fourth largest 20 percent
Quintile V: The smallest 20 percent

This arrangement has special value for media planners because it quickly allows them to see the top, the bottom, and a midpoint section (quintile III). The following shows the reach and frequency of a media plan in which the average frequency is 9.4. If an account executive tells a client that a plan will reach the audience 9.4 times a month, we can be sure that this is wrong, because frequency is an average. But how wrong? A quintile distribution will quickly show the answer:

Quintile I:	18.5 average frequency
Quintile II:	10.8 average frequency
Quintile III:	7.3 average frequency
Quintile IV:	6.8 average frequency
Quintile V:	3.5 average frequency
Sum	46.9 ÷ 5 = 9.4 average for plan

Quintile II comes closest to the 9.4. But the range of error is great. Quintile I is wasting impressions. If the client approved the 9.4 plan's average frequency, then advertising impressions are being overdelivered in quintile I (18.5−9.4 = 9.1 overdelivery). On the other hand, the plan is underdelivering targets in quintile V (9.4−3.5 = 5.9). So the quintile distribution quickly shows a planner a better picture of the plan's repetition delivery. As a result, the planner might opt for different media selections to reduce the range.

There are many other uses for quintile distributions. A planner might find quintiles shown in product categories of SMRB or MRI to be helpful in making media choices.

Quintile Analysis in SMRB or MRI

Simmons Market Research Bureau and Mediamark Research, Inc., report quintiles for heavy and light media exposure, cross-tabulated by user groups. Both SMRB and MRI present data for magazines, newspapers, outdoor, radio, and television. SMRB also includes exposure to the Yellow Pages and breakdowns by dayparts for broadcast media. These analyses are used to show how heavy users of one media class relate to heavy users of another media class.

Both SMRB and MRI use an asterisk to indicate data based on small samples of respondents. Such data are relatively unstable and should be used with caution.

Exhibit 24–2 shows quintiles for different media from SMRB for users of caffeinated instant and freeze-dried coffee. The data show not only users, but also index numbers (calculated the same way they were for demographics; see

Exhibit 24–2 Simmons Media Quintiles

CAFFEINATED INSTANT & FREEZE-DRIED COFFEE: USAGE ON AVERAGE DAY (FEMALE HOMEMAKERS) 0278 P-18

		TOTAL U.S.	ALL USERS				HEAVY USERS FOUR OR MORE				MEDIUM USERS TWO – THREE				LIGHT USERS ONE OR LESS			
			A	B	C	D	A	B	C	D	A	B	C	D	A	B	C	D
		'000	'000	% DOWN	% ACROSS	INDX	'000	% DOWN	% ACROSS	INDX	'000	% DOWN	% ACROSS	INDX	'000	% DOWN	% ACROSS	INDX
TOTAL FEMALE HOMEMAKERS		86361	21825	100.0	25.3	100	6829	100.0	7.9	100	8234	100.0	9.5	100	6762	100.0	7.8	100
MAGAZINES	QUINTILE 1	17469	4632	21.2	26.5	105	1443	21.1	8.3	104	1703	20.7	9.7	102	1486	22.0	8.5	109
	QUINTILE 2	20537	5281	24.2	25.7	102	1485	21.7	7.2	91	1803	21.9	8.8	92	1992	29.5	9.7	124
	QUINTILE 3	15763	4000	18.3	25.4	100	1377	20.2	8.7	110	1599	19.4	10.1	106	1025	15.2	6.5	83
	QUINTILE 4	17033	3983	18.2	23.4	93	1226	18.0	7.2	91	1513	18.4	8.9	93	1245	18.4	7.3	93
	QUINTILE 5	15559	3929	18.0	25.3	100	1299	19.0	8.3	106	1616	19.6	10.4	109	1014	15.0	6.5	83
NEWSPAPERS	QUINTILE 1	13180	3716	17.0	28.2	112	1244	18.2	9.4	119	1284	15.6	9.7	102	1188	17.6	9.0	115
	QUINTILE 2	22906	6179	28.3	27.0	107	2067	30.3	9.0	114	2115	25.7	9.2	97	1997	29.5	8.7	111
	QUINTILE 3	15554	3538	16.2	22.7	90	1015	14.9	6.5	83	1400	17.0	9.0	94	1123	16.6	7.2	92
	QUINTILE 4	14504	3614	16.6	24.9	99	993	14.5	6.8	87	1295	15.7	8.9	94	1326	19.6	9.1	117
	QUINTILE 5	20216	4778	21.9	23.6	94	1510	22.1	7.5	94	2140	26.0	10.6	111	1128	16.7	5.6	71
OUTDOOR	QUINTILE 1	17099	3644	16.7	21.3	84	1158	17.0	6.8	86	1401	17.0	8.2	86	1085	16.0	6.3	81
	QUINTILE 2	16543	4288	19.6	25.9	103	1234	18.1	7.5	94	1447	17.6	8.7	92	1607	23.8	9.7	124
	QUINTILE 3	16987	4631	21.2	27.3	108	1298	19.0	7.6	97	1941	23.6	11.4	120	1393	20.6	8.2	105
	QUINTILE 4	17324	4534	20.8	26.2	104	1681	24.6	9.7	123	1539	18.7	8.9	93	1314	19.4	7.6	97
	QUINTILE 5	18408	4729	21.7	25.7	102	1459	21.4	7.9	100	1906	23.1	10.4	109	1363	20.2	7.4	95
RADIO-DRIVE TIME	QUINTILE 1	17119	4272	19.6	25.0	99	1486	21.8	8.7	110	1474	17.9	8.6	90	1312	19.4	7.7	98
	QUINTILE 2	15857	3912	17.9	24.7	98	1022	15.0	6.4	82	1519	18.4	9.6	100	1372	20.3	8.7	111
	QUINTILE 3	15003	3615	16.6	24.1	95	967	14.2	6.4	82	1443	17.5	9.6	101	1205	17.8	8.0	103
	QUINTILE 4	16497	4276	19.6	25.9	103	1454	21.3	8.8	111	1643	20.0	10.0	104	1179	17.4	7.1	91
	QUINTILE 5	21885	5751	26.4	26.3	104	1900	27.8	8.7	110	2155	26.2	9.8	103	1695	25.1	7.7	99
RADIO-MID-DAY	TERCILE 1	21807	5143	23.6	23.6	93	1708	25.0	7.8	99	1929	23.4	8.8	93	1506	22.3	6.9	88
	TERCILE 2	22536	6133	28.1	27.2	108	1642	24.0	7.3	92	2442	29.7	10.8	114	2049	30.3	9.1	116
	TERCILE 3	42017	10548	48.3	25.1	99	3478	50.9	8.3	105	3863	46.9	9.2	96	3207	47.4	7.6	97
RADIO-TOTAL	QUINTILE 1	16661	3969	18.2	23.8	94	1248	18.3	7.5	95	1450	17.6	8.7	91	1271	18.8	7.6	97
	QUINTILE 2	17196	4515	20.7	26.3	104	1425	20.9	8.3	105	1735	21.1	10.1	106	1355	20.0	7.9	101
	QUINTILE 3	16469	4182	19.2	25.4	100	1305	19.1	7.9	100	1528	18.6	9.3	97	1349	19.9	8.2	105
	QUINTILE 4	18529	4519	20.7	24.4	97	1203	17.6	6.5	82	1774	21.5	9.6	100	1541	22.8	8.3	106
	QUINTILE 5	17505	4641	21.3	26.5	105	1648	24.1	9.4	119	1746	21.2	10.0	105	1247	18.4	7.1	91
TV-PRIME TIME	QUINTILE 1	17554	4930	22.6	28.1	111	1578	23.1	9.0	114	2152	26.1	12.3	129	1200	17.7	6.8	87
	QUINTILE 2	17199	4587	21.0	26.7	106	1395	20.4	8.1	103	1539	18.7	8.9	94	1652	24.4	9.6	123
	QUINTILE 3	18453	4562	20.9	24.7	98	1254	18.4	6.8	86	1670	20.3	9.1	95	1638	24.2	8.9	113
	QUINTILE 4	16826	3915	17.9	23.3	92	1210	17.7	7.2	91	1542	18.7	9.2	96	1163	17.2	6.9	88
	QUINTILE 5	16329	3831	17.6	23.5	93	1392	20.4	8.5	108	1330	16.2	8.1	85	1108	16.4	6.8	87
TV-DAYTIME	TERCILE 1	28166	7453	34.1	26.5	105	2612	38.2	9.3	117	2736	33.2	9.7	102	2105	31.1	7.5	95
	TERCILE 2	28146	7271	33.3	25.8	102	2175	31.8	7.7	98	2813	34.2	10.0	105	2283	33.8	8.1	104
	TERCILE 3	30049	7101	32.5	23.6	94	2042	29.9	6.8	86	2685	32.6	8.9	94	2374	35.1	7.9	101
TV-TOTAL	QUINTILE 1	17762	5018	23.0	28.3	112	1568	23.0	8.8	112	2146	26.1	12.1	127	1304	19.3	7.3	94
	QUINTILE 2	17351	4448	20.4	25.6	101	1604	23.5	9.2	117	1445	17.5	8.3	87	1399	20.7	8.1	103
	QUINTILE 3	16995	4121	18.9	24.2	96	1083	15.9	6.4	81	1590	19.3	9.4	98	1448	21.4	8.5	109
	QUINTILE 4	17185	4528	20.7	26.3	104	1207	17.7	7.0	89	1748	21.2	10.2	107	1573	23.3	9.2	117
	QUINTILE 5	17067	3709	17.0	21.7	86	1366	20.0	8.0	101	1306	15.9	7.7	80	1037	15.3	6.1	78
YELLOW PAGES	QUINTILE 1	18521	4295	19.7	23.2	92	1357	19.9	7.3	93	1340	16.3	7.2	76	1598	23.6	8.6	110
	QUINTILE 2	14842	3339	15.3	22.5	89	792	11.6	5.3	67	1472	17.9	9.9	104	1075	15.9	7.2	93
	QUINTILE 3	19444	5232	24.0	26.9	106	1446	21.2	7.4	94	1636	19.9	8.4	88	2149	31.8	11.1	141
	QUINTILE 4	12666	3533	16.2	27.9	110	1195	17.5	9.4	119	1555	18.9	12.3	129	783	11.6	6.2	79
	QUINTILE 5	20887	5427	24.9	26.0	103	2040	29.9	9.8	124	2230	27.1	10.7	112	1157	17.1	5.5	71

Chapter 1 in *Advertising Media Planning,* 5th ed., by Sissors and Bumba). So index numbers over 100 represent better than average exposures among the five quintiles. However, it is important to note that high index numbers in quintiles I and II represent a potentially good medium in which to advertise, other things being equal. But high index numbers in quintiles IV and V represent a poor choice of media. Quintile III can be considered a high or low quintile, depending on how it relates to upper or lower scores.

A planner presumably would *not* select those media whose quintile I and II index numbers are low. So by comparing all the media quintile alternatives, good evidence might now be available for choosing media classes.

Table 24–1 shows quintile data from SMRB for women only. The data show how many media exposures are needed to fall into each quintile.

Table 24–1 Simmons Selected Media Choices and Quintiles for Women

	Quintile I	Quintile II	Quintile III	Quintile IV	Quintile V
Magazines	10+	6–9	4–5	2–3	0–1
	(Number of magazines read from a total of 118)				
Newspapers	5+	4	3	2	0–1
	(Number of weekday papers read in two days studied, and weekend/Sunday papers read in two weeks studied)				
Radio (drive time)	22+	12–21	6–11	1–5	None
	(Based on number of quarter hours listened to on two weekdays, 6 a.m.–10 a.m., and 3 p.m.–7 p.m.)				
Outdoor	41+	21–40	10–20	3–9	0–2
	(Based on the estimated frequency of exposure to a 100 showing for 30 days)				
Television (all day)	157+	109–156	73–108	42–72	0–41
	(Based on the number of half-hours viewed in two weeks, Monday–Sunday, 8 a.m.–2 a.m.)				

Source: SMRB, 1990.

Problems

Using the quintile data from Simmons (Exhibit 24–2), answer the following questions:

1. In which media classes would you most likely place advertising for caffeinated instant and freeze-dried coffee if your targets were "All Users"? Explain why.

2. What media class, other than the Yellow Pages, would you be least likely to use?

3. Would you change your choice of media classes if your targets were "Heavy Users"? What changes would you make?

4. Based on your understanding of media classes and considering the type of product, why would you be unlikely to use the Yellow Pages even if that media class had high index numbers for quintiles I and II?

5. In column B of the "All Users" in Exhibit 24–2, you will notice that the percentages for each quintile are not 20 percent. Briefly explain why they are not equally divided into groups of 20 percent. (Note that the answer is not a "given," but can be explained by studying the requirements for being counted in a quintile as shown in Table 24–1.)

Assignment 25

Proving That a Media Plan Delivers the Planned Objectives

Objective: To help you understand how to prove that the objectives in a media plan can be achieved. The technique involves the use of gross and strategic impressions, primarily.

Discussion

It is one thing to create media plans with specific objectives, and another to prove that these objectives can be achieved. It is illogical to create plans with objectives that are not achievable.

It should be noted that the best way to know whether objectives have been met is to measure the effects in the marketplace *after* the plan has been executed. But if there are errors in planning, that may be too late to save the plan. It is better to discover errors in thinking *before* the plan has been executed. Then changes can be made if necessary.

The proof of delivery is primarily through the use of gross and strategic impressions. But other proofs are used, too, as the example will show.

An Example of Proof: Media Objectives of Plan 1

We will simulate a situation in which a planner has devised the following media objectives and strategies in the first of a number of alternative plans:

1. Reach target audiences, defined as follows: women 35 years or older, who live in A counties, with incomes over $40,000.
2. Spend at least 62 percent of the budget in key markets.
3. Have a reach of 75 and an average frequency of 5 for targets.
4. Spend the following per quarter:

First:	24% of budget
Second:	23
Third:	26
Fourth:	27
Total:	100%

5. Achieve maximum flexibility.
6. Provide as many weeks of advertising as possible after reach and frequency goals have been met.
7. Use media vehicles that are compatible with copy requirements to communicate taste appeal and brand image.

8. The delivery of media vehicles to all target groups is shown under the heading "Media Objectives." These objectives are in the form of percentages and are set on the basis of product usage, plus experience with the advertiser's brand.

Proof

The proof comes from a gross impression analysis showing strategic target delivery compared to nontarget delivery. The data come from Simmons or Nielsen.

The Plan

Media vehicles used	Total GRPs, first quarter (nine weeks)	Total GRPs, second quarter (nine weeks)	Total GRPs, third quarter (nine weeks)	Total GRPs, fourth quarter (nine weeks)
Day network	315	315	315	315
Late-night network	126	126	225	225
Fringe spot	486	486	585	585

A Sample of Gross Impression Analysis (by Age)

Age	Day network	Late network	Fringe spot	Total	%
18–24	156,150	86,573	108,438	351,161	16.1
25–34	177,528	104,631	137,354	419,513	19.2
35–49	198,905	142,872	170,608	512,385	23.5
50+	396,881	197,046	306,517	900,444	41.2
Totals	929,464	531,122	722,917	2,183,503	100.0

Media Objective Analysis (Age)

Age	Media objective		Targets delivered		Index
18–24	13.9%		16.1%		116*
25–34	17.9		19.2		107
35–49	21.3	68.2%	23.5	64.7%	110
50+	46.9		41.2		88

*(16.1 ÷ 13.9) x 100 = 116

You may ask, "Why is the planner interested in the delivery of targets aged 18–24 and 25–34, when the targets are women 35 years or older?" The answer is that although the planner has sales potential primarily in the 35+ age group, she also has sales potential in younger groups. Therefore, she would like to see how well each group was reached in the media plan.

Another reason, however, is that she wants to check that her distribution of impressions matches product usage (or sales) in the proper proportions. She erroneously might be delivering too many impressions to the younger women and not enough to the older ones.

This analysis shows that the percentage distribution is fairly good. The media objective was to deliver 68.2 percent (21.3% + 46.9% = 68.2%) of impressions to women over 35, and 64.7 percent was actually delivered. The index numbers are a bit low for the 50+ women (only 41.2 percent). At this point, the planner must decide whether she needs more impressions delivered to the women 50+. If so, she can select vehicles that will better reach the 50+ group, or she can add vehicles to her plan that will accomplish the task.

Media objective analysis for income

HH annual income	Media objective	Targets delivered	Index
Under $20,000	28.6%	41.5%	145*
$20,000–40,000	33.0	34.0	103
$40,000+	38.4	24.5	64

*(41.5 ÷ 28.6) x 100 = 145

This plan is not doing a good job of delivering households with incomes over $40,000 a year. Therefore, the plan should be changed.

Media objective analysis for county size

County size	Media objective	Targets delivered	Index
A	51.0%	47.0%	92*
B	24.1	26.7	111
C	17.3	15.5	90
D	7.6	10.8	142

*(47.0 ÷ 51.0) x 100 = 92

The plan is underdelivering A counties, although a 92 index is not bad. Again, the planner will have to defend her decision to go with plan 1 or devise alternative plans with better delivery.

Media objective for key market investment

	Sales	Ad budget	Index
Primary geographic markets	62.2%	69.1%	111
Rest of United States	37.8	30.9	82

Advertising spending is being concentrated in the correct part of the United States in proportions that are just about those that had been planned.

Reach and frequency objectives

	Delivered reach	Delivered frequency
Key markets	81	5.1
Rest of United States	57	3.4

The plan is fairly adequate here to meet the goals of 75 percent reach and 5 frequency.

Quarterly spending objectives

Goal		Actual
First quarter	24%	22%
Second quarter	23	21
Third quarter	26	30
Fourth quarter	27	27
Total	100%	100%

Spending by quarter follows goals fairly well. An increase in the third quarter can be justified by the concept of spending when the market is active.

Flexibility objective
The goal was to have flexible media that would allow the marketer to move money around to various geographic areas if opportunities or problems arise. The plan calls for 45 percent of the budget to go into spot TV, which is a very flexible medium.

Continuity and creative objectives
The plan called for as many weeks as affordable after reach and frequency goals have been achieved. This plan calls for 36 weeks of advertising with flighting of two-week hiatuses to spread the time span out.

Creative strategy called for a medium that would communicate taste appeal of the product and add to the brand image. Television was chosen to do that, and for the nature of this product, it was well suited.

Summary

In essence, then, although there were some problems in meeting objectives, most of them were fulfilled. Those that were not achieved will now have to be the subject of consultation with the marketing planners, brand managers, and others to see whether another plan is necessary, or whether the present one will do.

Problem

Assume that you are the planner who has created the following media objectives:

1. Targets:
Primary: Adults aged 55 and over
Secondary: Household incomes over $40,000
Geographic emphasis in A counties

2. Target goals:

Age		HH annual income		County size	
Adults 18–34	25.0%	Under $20,000	25.0%	A counties	37.0%
35–54	35.0	$20,000–40,000	35.0	B counties	33.0
55+	40.0	$40,000+	40.0	C and D counties	30.0
	100.0%		100.0%		100.0%

3. Reach and frequency goals (per four-week period):
Reach: 70 percent (Adults 55+) Frequency: 3 (Adults 55+)

4. All other goals have been met and proven.

Your problem is to prove from the following media selections that the goals have been met, using strategic impressions analysis and reach and frequency estimations. Use the guidelines in "How to Proceed."

Show all your work and explain how you arrived at your answers.

Target Delivery Data for One Ad in Each Vehicle (000)			
	Better Homes & Gardens	*Reader's Digest*	"60 Minutes"
Ages:			
18–34	11,207	14,243	5,260
35–54	12,226	16,425	9,460
55+	9,837	18,196	15,910
HH annual income:			
Under $20,000	8,681	14,248	7,553
$20,000–40,000	11,413	16,999	9,210
$40,000+	13,175	17,617	13,867
County size:			
A counties	11,221	16,537	12,030
B counties	10,885	16,402	9,620
C and D counties	11,163	15,925	8,980
Number of ads to be run per year	10	10	12

How to Proceed

1. Multiply each piece of demographic data by the number of ads to be run. Example: 18–34 *BH&G* = 11,207 × 10 ads = 112,070, or 112,070,000 total gross impressions. Do this for every audience demographic section. Note that "60 Minutes" is run 12 times, not 10.
2. Add each demographic category across to give you total gross impressions for the three vehicles:

   Total adults 18–34: *BH&G* + *Reader's Digest* + "60 Minutes"

3. Add the totals for each demographic group. You should have a total for age, a total for household income, and a total for county size.
4. Calculate the percentage of total gross impressions for each demographic segment. There should be a percentage for 18–34, another percentage for 35–54, and another for 55+. The same is true for each income and county size segment.
5. Calculate the index numbers for each segment by the following formula:

$$\text{Index} = \frac{\text{Percent distribution of gross impressions per segment}}{\text{Percent goal per demographic segment}}$$

6. Analyze gross impression index numbers and compare to goals. Have the goals been realized? Explain.
7. Calculate the reach and frequency of each vehicle for adults 55+. Use the one-ad delivery as a basis for reach. The total population of adults 55+ is 50,764,000. Example for *BH&G*:

$$\text{Coverage (Reach)} = \frac{\text{9,837,000 readers}}{\text{50,764,000 population base}} = 19.4\% \text{ coverage}$$

8. Using the Sainsbury formula for reach and frequency, calculate the net reach of *BH&G* + *Reader's Digest* + "60 Minutes."
9. Evaluate whether you reached your goals. If so, explain how you know.

Assignment 26

Writing Media Objectives

Objective: To help you understand the relationship between marketing and media objectives. The first step in planning media strategy is creating media objectives. Therefore, you should understand them, especially their relationships with marketing planning.

Discussion

The first part of an advertising plan is usually the marketing situation. This section contains the marketing background and marketing objectives that have been established for the brand. It is from this marketing review that media objectives are developed. The logic of this is apparent when you consider that the function of the media objectives is to help fulfill the marketing objectives—to help solve marketing problems—to help take advantage of marketing opportunities.

Media objectives form the starting point for media planning. They outline what the media plan is expected to accomplish. Because the media objectives tell what is to be accomplished, they do not mention specific media selection. Media selection is the *how;* the objectives deal only with *what* is to be done.

The following is an improperly written media objective: "Use network television to provide broad national coverage." Properly written, this objective would not mention a specific media choice. An example of a properly written media objective might be: "Use media that will provide broad national coverage to support national sales and distribution." Media objectives can take many forms and cover many different areas; however, the following objectives are basic to most media plans:

- **Target audience:** Whom are you trying to reach?
- **Geographic coverage:** Where should advertising be placed? Is there a need for geographic emphasis?
- **Continuity (or pattern of scheduling):** Do you need to cover the entire year and yet add weight to a particular season? Or is any other pattern of scheduling necessary?
- **Reach/frequency:** Do you want reach? Frequency? Which is more important?
- **Creative implications:** Does the copy platform or creative strategy have any implications for planning media? (Sometimes the creative strategy, by its nature, limits selection planning to a single medium.)
- **Budget limitation:** If known, budget parameters should be included.

- **Merchandisability:** This should be included, if appropriate, based on marketing data.
- **Flexibility:** Include if flexibility in scheduling or budget reallocation is required.
- **Promotion support:** Include if media will be needed to support promotion effort.

Refer to *Advertising Media Planning,* 5th ed., by Sissors and Bumba, Chapter 0.

Problem

Based on the following market information, you are to develop a set of media objectives. Write them down and explain why each was selected. In developing your objectives, remember that you are establishing the "what" of a media plan. Make sure that you write an objective for as many of the basic areas as you have marketing information.

Marketing Situation Review

Listed here are some of the details included in a marketing situation review for a line of packaged, frozen, prepared vegetables.

Distribution. National, although better in metro areas of 200,000 or more population than in small rural markets. The company does not maintain its own sales force, but sells through brokers and wholesalers. Nationally, distribution in food stores is about 70 percent, with stronger distribution in chains than in independent stores.

Sales status. The following table shows sales and ACV distribution by Nielsen territory. The brand is well established, having been introduced five years ago. This year a strong competitive brand was successfully test marketed in Columbus, Ohio, and Grand Rapids–Kalamazoo, Michigan, and is expected to expand into the entire East Central Nielsen territory next year.

Nielsen Territory	CDI	BDI	Brand ACV Distribution
New England	132	90	66
Mid-Atlantic	117	86	65
East Central	99	120	81
West Central	98	102	72
South East	85	80	52
South West	90	90	64
Pacific	99	110	75

Seasonality. Brand sales by Nielsen bimonthly reporting periods are as follows:

Period	Index	Period	Index
DJ	117	JJ	71
FM	120	AS	80
AM	103	ON	109

Consumers. Greatest volume can be expected from families of three or more members in middle- and upper-income groups living in urban areas. Primary purchasers are female heads of households.

Copy platform. The two basic appeals are ease of preparation and taste. Ease of preparation can be easily demonstrated. The product has enough visual appeal to encourage the use of appetizing illustrations.

Promotion plans. Plans call for a sweepstakes promotion in January and a national couponing effort in November.

Budget. The "working media" budget is $6,500,000. This is to cover all media costs, including media used to support promotions, but it does not include production or non–media promotion costs.

Marketing objectives.

1. Continue to support national distribution and sales with a sales goal of a 10 percent increase next year.
2. Consolidate sales position in the East Central territory to minimize competitive threats.
3. Hold present users and expand market by attracting new users.
4. Expand food store distribution in areas where it is below 70 percent and continue to maintain strong communication with food store managers and chain headquarters.

Assignment 27

Planning Media Strategy

Objective: To help you see the relationship between media objectives and media strategies.

Discussion

Strategies flow from media objectives. It is therefore important that one implements the other rather than being treated as isolated media activities.

Refer to *Advertising Media Planning*, 5th ed., by Sissors and Bumba, Chapter 12.

Problem

Following is a set of media objectives derived from a marketing case for a line of blue jeans for women. Write a set of media strategies and explain why you selected each strategy. Do not present a complete media plan, only a statement of strategies and a rationale for each.

The selection of a strategy is dependent in part on what you can afford to buy, so you will find it helpful to consult the media cost information in the appendix. It would be impractical to recommend year-long advertising in prime-time network television if there is no way the available budget could cover the expense of such a strategy. You can get a pretty good idea of the affordability of broadcast media by checking the cost per rating point data and then figuring how many rating points you could buy.

For example, if you wanted to buy 50 GRPs per week for 26 weeks in daytime TV, and the average cost per rating point is approximately $4,000, such a strategy would cost $5,200,000 ($50 \times 26 \times 4{,}000 = 5{,}200{,}000$). On the other hand, assuming a cost of $3,200 per rating point, network radio would cost $4,160,000 for a similar schedule. For magazines, you can look up the cost per four-color or black-and-white page for magazines that are typical of the type you plan to use, to determine how many pages you could afford. Your cost estimates do not have to be precise at this point. You just want approximate costs to see whether your proposed strategy is feasible.

Media Objectives

1. **Target audience.** Direct advertising messages to the primary target audience of women aged 14–24. Women aged 25–34 represent a secondary target market.

2. **Geographic coverage.** Use national media to support a national launch of the product.
3. **Seasonality.** Year-long advertising is desirable, but it is far more important to provide adequate advertising weight during the peak selling seasons: back-to-school (August–September) and holiday gift giving periods (December–January).
4. **Reach/frequency.** Provide maximum affordable reach while maintaining a minimum target audience frequency of 3.0 during the peak selling seasons.
5. **Creative implications.** Primary media selection must provide for visualization of the product.
6. **Trade communication.** Provide for strong communication with the retail trade in order to build awareness and encourage stocking of the brand.
7. **Budget.** The foregoing media objectives are to be accomplished within a working media budget of $7,000,000.

Background

The company has successfully produced and marketed blue jeans, primarily to males. The company enjoys a strong brand franchise with both men and with retailers. This new product, getting ready for a national launch, is directed specifically toward fashion-conscious young women. The company does not have much recognition by nor a strong brand franchise with young women. Also, retailers do not associate this company with fashion-oriented merchandise for women.

This new product is a tight-fitting jean that comes in a variety of colors. Because of the tight fit, women 14–24 are considered to be a more viable market than are older women.

The parent company has used a variety of media to advertise their other lines of jeans: television (network, spot, and cable), network radio, and magazines—both consumer and trade. Competitive jeans manufacturers have spent most (90 percent) of their media dollars in magazines.

Additional Marketing Information

Seasonality of Jeans Purchases

Month	Percentage of purchases	Index
January	31.0%	126
February	18.5	75
March	17.0	69
April	14.5	59
May	17.5	71
June	19.0	77
July	16.0	65
August	43.5	177
September	37.0	150
October	20.0	81
November	19.5	79
December	41.5	169

Brand Development Indices for Target Audience

Age Group	BDI
Women 14–17	400
Women 18–24	179
Women 25–34	153

Assignment 28

Media Plan Checklist

Objective: To provide a sample checklist of the minimum media planning requirements.

Discussion

In planning media, you must include many kinds of information that are necessary for the implementation of a plan. This checklist should serve as a reminder of minimum requirements for planning.

Checklist

I. **Media objectives** (see Assignment 26)
   A. Do media objectives relate to marketing data and plan objectives?
   B. Are objectives clearly stated *without* mentioning specific media choices?
   C. Do objectives cover the following basic areas?
      1. Target audience (consumer and trade)
      2. Geographic coverage requirements
      3. Reach/frequency goals (relative importance)
      4. Scheduling (seasonality and continuity requirements)
      5. Budget considerations (size, need for flexibility, efficiency)
   D. Are additional objectives needed?
      1. Creative implications
      2. Merchandisability
      3. Promotion support
      4. Flexibility

II. **Overall strategy**
   A. Media types selected and brief rationale
   B. Is each selection related to one or more media objective?
   C. Media types not selected and reasons for nonuse

III. **Plan recommendations and rationale**
   A. If TV is recommended, have you included the following?
      1. Daypart selected and rationale for selection (including CPRP/CPM comparisons and demographics)
      2. Program types selected and rationale (audience delivery/demographics)
      3. Length of commercial unit
      4. GRPs in each daypart and total GRPs per week/month/year
      5. Spot TV markets and rationale for selection
      6. Spot TV dayparts and rationale
      7. Spot TV GRP levels/number of weeks per market
   B. If magazines are recommended, have you included the following?

1. Type of magazines (e.g., women's service, news, etc.) and space unit and color
2. Specific magazines selected and rationale,including CPM comparisons and demographics *for all magazines considered*
3. Number of insertions in each magazine and rationale
4. Regional editions, if any, and rationale for selection

C. If newspapers are recommended, have you included the following?
1. Markets selected and rationale for selection
2. Coverage required in each market
3. Papers selected, coverage of each, and CPM comparisons where needed
4. Number of insertions and size of ads

D. If radio is recommended, have you included the following?
1. Network selection and rationale, including CPM and audience delivery comparisons
2. Length of commercials and GRPs per week/month/year
3. Spot radio markets and rationale for selection
4. Spot radio dayparts, types of programming, and rationale
5. Spot radio GRP levels/number of weeks per market

E. If outdoor is recommended, have you included the following?
1. Markets selected and rationale for selection
2. Number of showings, number of months per market, and rationale

F. Have you developed reach and frequency figures for both the national plan and heavy-up areas by month for all media combined?

IV. Media schedule

A. Have you included a flow chart showing specific schedules by week/month?

B. Have you included rationale for scheduling by season/flight?

V. Budget

A. Do you have a budget recap sheet showing totals spent in each media class and percentage of budget allocated to each class?

B. Do you have a cost summary table showing each vehicle, number of insertions (or GRPs), cost per insertion/GRP, and cost for year?

C. Have you included tables showing market-by-market costs for spot TV, spot radio, newspapers, and outdoor per week and for the year?

D. Have you included a cost-per-month or cost-per-quarter breakdown?

VI. General

A. Is the plan well organized and presented in a logical pattern?

B. Have you indicated sources of data used in support of recommendations?

C. Have long tables been put in the appendix section?

D. Have you carefully checked for misspelled words, poor grammar, proper headings on tables, typographical errors, etc.?

Assignment 29

Media Strategy Planning Problem
National Support of a Product on a Small Budget

Objective: To provide you with an opportunity to plan media strategy for a specialized marketing situation—in this case, the national support of a specialty product that has a relatively small budget. As with most media strategy plans, your recommended plan should consider both marketing and media implications.

Discussion

You are to develop complete media strategy recommendations only. Do not go beyond strategy statements and a rationale. Specifically, do the following.

1. Provide complete statements of media strategies.
2. Indicate an approximate monthly schedule of media vehicles.
3. Emphasize media strategy recommendations, rather than providing details of complete media plan tactics.
4. Be sure to consider the questions that appear in the "Problems" section.

You should determine when to start consumer advertising and how to best spend the available media budget of $3,500,000. Reasonable production and promotional dollars are covered outside the media budget.

Background

The product
Acme brand adhesive bandages are available in a variety of styles, package sizes, and assortments. Prices range from $.59 to $2.79. The bandage has a unique perforated plastic cover over the gauze pad that prevents the pad from adhering to healing sores. Otherwise, the product has the same properties as its primary competitor.

Sales status/competition
Acme is well established and has a 17 percent share of market. Over the past five years, the brand has increased its share of market from 12 percent to 17 percent. Last year Acme enjoyed an 8 percent sales increase. There is only one

major competitor, which owns a 75 percent share of market. The rest of the market is made up of small, private-label brands, none of which owns more than a 3 percent share of market. The major competitive brand spends about two and one-half times as much on advertising as does Acme.

Distribution

Acme brand is distributed nationally, although the brand does better in metropolitan markets than in small, rural areas. The brand does not maintain its own sales force, but sells through brokers and wholesalers. As with the major competitor, Acme bandages are sold in food, drug, and discount stores. Nationally, Acme has 70 percent all commodity volume (ACV) distribution; however, distribution varies by Nielsen territory, as shown in the table below.

Nielsen Territory	CDI	BDI	Acme ACV Distribution
New England	104	91	63
Middle Atlantic	101	85	60
East Central	104	98	71
West Central	104	121	78
South East	96	95	68
South West	99	97	70
Pacific	95	115	75

As shown, Acme brand has its greatest sales strength in the West Central and Pacific regions. Specific market-by-market sales data are not available, but it is safe to assume that sales are above average in metropolitan areas (top 50 markets) that are located in the Nielsen West Central and Pacific territories.

Consumer profile

Greatest volume can be expected from families with young children, middle- and upper-income groups, living in urban areas. The primary purchaser is the female head of household aged 18–49. Other family members have little influence on brand selection.

Seasonality

Bandage sales are highest during the summer months when children are playing outside more and are more likely to get minor cuts and scrapes. Sales by bimonthly reporting periods follow:

Period	Index
January–February	75
March–April	85
May–June	120
July–August	135
September–October	105
November–December	80

Copy platform/promotion plans

The basic copy appeal is Acme brand's unique gauze pad. The creative group has developed a jingle that tells the story in a cute and appealing way. Plans also call for a national coupon drop in May to kick off the summer sales period.

Marketing objectives

1. Continue to support national distribution and sales with a sales goal of a 10 percent increase next year.
2. Provide extra support in metro areas where sales are currently strong.
3. Hold present users and expand market by attracting new users to the brand.
4. Expand distribution in all classes of trade and maintain strong communication with buyers and managers of food, drug, and discount stores and chains.

Media objectives

1. Target Audience: Direct messages to women 18–49, with young children, living in urban areas.
2. Regionality: Use national media to support national distribution and sales, but also provide advertising heavy-up in the top 50 markets that are located in the West Central and Pacific Nielsen territories.
3. Seasonality: While year-long continuity would be desirable, it is much more important to provide adequate media weight during the peak summer selling season.
4. Reach/frequency: Emphasize reach nationally to attract new customers, but increase frequency in key markets to hold current users.
5. Creative implications: Primary media must be able to accommodate the commercial jingle.
6. Promotion support: Provide media support for the national couponing effort scheduled for May.
7. Trade communications: Provide media specifically to reach buyers and managers of food, drug, and discount stores.
8. As stated earlier, the foregoing objectives are to be accomplished within a working media budget of $3,500,000. Additional funds will be provided to cover production and coupon redemption costs.

Problems

Write a detailed media strategy based on the data given in this case. You are also to use the adhesive bandage data provided in Exhibit 29–1 to help you select viable media vehicles. You may use any consumer media class/vehicle for which cost data is provided in the appendix or in Exhibit 32–1. For costs of selected trade magazines, use the cost data in Table 29–1.

Answer the following questions before beginning your strategy statements.

1. Is year-long advertising possible? If not, during what periods of the year should the product be advertised? Should some periods get heavier weight than others?

2. Although national coverage is needed, are there some key markets that merit additional weight? What criteria would you establish for their selection?

3. Do the media objectives require the use of any specific media vehicles?

Table 29–1 Trade Magazine Cost Data

Magazine	Circulation	Cost (Black-and-white page)	Cost (Four-color page)
Progressive Grocer	63,686	$10,375	$13,860
Supermarket News	51,739	10,800	10,800*
Supermarket Business	70,387	11,000	14,595
American Druggist	92,135	6,400	8,400
Drug Topics	93,549	6,910	9,045
Discount Merchandiser	34,851	7,900	10,500
Discount Store News	33,392	8,344	10,839

*No charge for color.

Exhibit 29–1 MRI: Adhesive Bandages User Profile

BASE: WOMEN	TOTAL U.S. '000	ALL A '000	ALL B % DOWN	ALL C % ACROSS	ALL D INDEX	TIMES/LAST 30 DAYS: HEAVY MORE THAN 3 A '000	HEAVY B % DOWN	HEAVY C % ACROSS	HEAVY D INDEX	MEDIUM 2 - 3 A '000	MEDIUM B % DOWN	MEDIUM C % ACROSS	MEDIUM D INDEX	LIGHT LESS THAN 2 A '000	LIGHT B % DOWN	LIGHT C % ACROSS	LIGHT D INDEX
ALL WOMEN	91533	58192	100.0	63.6	100	15285	100.0	16.7	100	18434	100.0	20.1	100	24473	100.0	26.7	100
HOUSEHOLD HEADS	28637	17356	29.8	60.6	95	4795	31.4	16.7	100	5578	30.3	19.5	97	6982	28.5	24.4	91
HOMEMAKERS	79236	50395	86.6	63.6	100	13046	85.4	16.5	99	15931	86.4	20.1	100	21418	87.5	27.0	101
GRADUATED COLLEGE	13342	8364	14.4	62.7	99	1887	12.3	14.1	85	2624	14.2	19.7	98	3853	15.7	28.9	108
ATTENDED COLLEGE	16443	10751	18.5	65.4	103	2329	15.2	14.2	85	3658	19.8	22.2	110	4764	19.5	29.0	108
GRADUATED HIGH SCHOOL	38387	24293	41.7	63.3	100	6644	43.5	17.3	104	7453	40.4	19.4	96	10196	41.7	26.6	99
DID NOT GRADUATE HIGH SCHOOL	23360	14785	25.4	63.3	100	4425	28.9	18.9	113	4699	25.5	20.1	100	5660	23.1	24.2	91
18-24	13551	8420	14.5	62.1	98	1906	12.5	14.1	84	2908	15.8	21.5	107	3607	14.7	26.6	100
25-34	21489	13542	23.3	63.0	99	3225	21.1	15.0	90	4125	22.4	19.2	95	6192	25.3	28.8	108
35-44	16481	10596	18.2	64.3	101	2427	15.9	14.7	88	3351	18.2	20.3	101	4818	19.7	29.2	109
45-54	11755	7414	12.7	63.1	99	1911	12.5	16.3	97	2385	12.9	20.3	101	3117	12.7	26.5	99
55-64	12048	8005	13.8	66.4	105	2467	16.1	20.5	123	2532	13.7	21.0	104	3006	12.3	25.0	93
65 OR OVER	16208	10215	17.6	63.0	99	3348	21.9	20.7	124	3133	17.0	19.3	96	3734	15.3	23.0	86
18-34	35040	21962	37.7	62.7	99	5131	33.6	14.6	88	7033	38.2	20.1	100	9798	40.0	28.0	105
18-49	57551	36425	62.6	63.3	100	8520	55.7	14.8	89	11596	62.9	20.1	100	16309	66.6	28.3	106
25-54	49725	31551	54.2	63.5	100	7563	49.5	15.2	91	9861	53.5	19.8	98	14127	57.7	28.4	106
EMPLOYED FULL TIME	40464	25060	43.1	61.9	97	5967	39.0	14.7	88	8180	44.4	20.2	100	10913	44.6	27.0	101
PART-TIME	8408	5452	9.4	64.8	102	1145	7.5	13.6	82	1793	9.7	21.3	106	2514	10.3	29.9	112
NOT EMPLOYED	42661	27680	47.6	64.9	102	8173	53.5	19.2	115	8461	45.9	19.8	98	11046	45.1	25.9	97
PROFESSIONAL	7150	4495	7.7	62.9	99	779	5.1	10.9	65	1414	7.7	19.8	98	2303	9.4	32.2	120
EXECUTIVE/ADMIN./MANAGERIAL	5018	2993	5.1	59.6	94	642	4.2	12.8	77	830	4.5	16.5	82	1521	6.2	30.3	113
CLERICAL/SALES/TECHNICAL	21943	13122	22.5	59.8	94	3038	19.9	13.8	83	4546	24.7	20.7	103	5538	22.6	25.2	94
PRECISION/CRAFTS/REPAIR	1124	724	1.2	64.4	101	*233	1.5	20.7	124	*198	1.1	17.6	87	*293	1.2	26.1	97
OTHER EMPLOYED	13637	9178	15.8	67.3	106	2420	15.8	17.7	106	2986	16.2	21.9	109	3773	15.4	27.7	103
H/D INCOME $50,000 OR MORE	17575	10752	18.5	61.2	96	2334	15.3	13.3	80	3040	16.5	17.3	86	5378	22.0	30.6	114
$40,000 - 49,999	11717	7890	13.6	67.3	106	1962	12.8	16.7	100	2551	13.8	21.8	108	3377	13.8	28.8	108
$35,000 - 39,999	7326	4705	8.1	64.2	101	1238	8.1	16.9	101	1564	8.5	21.3	106	1905	7.8	26.0	97
$25,000 - 34,999	16193	11067	19.0	68.3	108	2405	15.7	14.9	89	4133	22.4	25.5	127	4529	18.5	28.0	105
$15,000 - 24,999	17660	11326	19.5	64.1	101	3288	21.5	18.6	111	3467	18.8	19.6	97	4571	18.7	25.9	97
LESS THAN $15,000	21061	12452	21.4	59.1	93	4060	26.6	19.3	115	3679	20.0	17.5	87	4714	19.3	22.4	84
CENSUS REGION: NORTH EAST	20010	12806	22.0	64.0	101	3649	23.9	18.2	109	4234	23.0	21.2	105	4922	20.1	24.6	92
NORTH CENTRAL	22638	14853	25.5	65.6	103	3873	25.3	17.1	102	4502	24.4	19.9	99	6478	26.5	28.6	107
SOUTH	31488	19888	34.2	63.2	99	5503	36.0	17.5	105	6561	35.6	20.8	103	7824	32.0	24.8	93
WEST	17397	10645	18.3	61.2	96	2260	14.8	13.0	78	3137	17.0	18.0	90	5249	21.4	30.2	113
MARKETING REG.: NEW ENGLAND	5192	3428	5.9	66.0	104	909	5.9	17.5	105	1071	5.8	20.6	102	1448	5.9	27.9	104
MIDDLE ATLANTIC	16530	10660	18.3	64.5	101	3141	20.5	19.0	114	3581	19.4	21.7	108	3938	16.1	23.8	89
EAST CENTRAL	12990	8596	14.8	66.2	104	2054	13.4	15.8	95	2915	15.8	22.4	111	3628	14.8	27.9	104
WEST CENTRAL	14361	9482	16.3	66.0	104	2594	17.0	18.1	108	2793	15.2	19.4	97	4094	16.7	28.5	107
SOUTH EAST	16688	10166	17.5	60.9	96	2663	17.4	16.0	96	3433	18.6	20.6	102	4070	16.6	24.4	91
SOUTH WEST	10576	6636	11.4	62.7	99	1957	12.8	18.5	111	1917	10.4	18.1	90	2762	11.3	26.1	98
PACIFIC	15195	9224	15.9	60.7	95	1967	12.9	12.9	78	2723	14.8	17.9	89	4534	18.5	29.8	112
COUNTY SIZE A	38432	24094	41.4	62.7	99	6058	39.6	15.8	94	7057	38.3	18.4	91	10979	44.9	28.6	107
COUNTY SIZE B	27048	16944	29.1	62.6	99	4020	26.3	14.9	89	6000	32.5	22.2	110	6923	28.3	25.6	96
COUNTY SIZE C	13797	8965	15.4	65.0	102	2403	15.7	17.4	104	2784	15.1	20.2	100	3779	15.4	27.4	102
COUNTY SIZE D	12256	8190	14.1	66.8	105	2804	18.3	22.9	137	2593	14.1	21.2	105	2793	11.4	22.8	85
MSA CENTRAL CITY	33107	20455	35.2	61.8	97	5042	33.0	15.2	91	6266	34.0	18.9	94	9147	37.4	27.6	103
MSA SUBURBAN	37441	23693	40.7	63.3	100	5875	38.4	15.7	94	7831	42.5	20.9	104	9986	40.8	26.7	100
NON-MSA	20985	14045	24.1	66.9	105	4368	28.6	20.8	125	4337	23.5	20.7	103	5340	21.8	25.4	95
SINGLE	16130	9798	16.8	60.7	96	2263	14.8	14.0	84	3472	18.8	21.5	107	4063	16.6	25.2	94
MARRIED	53249	34825	59.8	65.4	103	8914	58.3	16.7	100	10838	58.8	20.4	101	15072	61.6	28.3	106
OTHER	22154	13570	23.3	61.3	96	4107	26.9	18.5	111	4124	22.4	18.6	92	5339	21.8	24.1	90
PARENTS	33769	21718	37.3	64.3	101	5259	34.4	15.6	93	6962	37.8	20.6	102	9498	38.8	28.1	105
WORKING PARENTS	21268	12967	22.3	61.0	96	2968	19.4	14.0	84	4180	22.7	19.7	98	5818	23.8	27.4	102
HOUSEHOLD SIZE: 1 PERSON	13148	7645	13.1	58.1	91	2124	13.9	16.2	97	2484	13.5	18.9	94	3038	12.4	23.1	96
2 PERSONS	26230	16956	29.1	64.6	102	4787	31.3	18.3	109	5288	28.7	20.2	100	6881	28.1	26.2	98
3 OR MORE	52155	33591	57.7	64.4	101	8373	54.8	16.1	96	10681	57.8	20.4	101	14557	59.5	27.9	104
ANY CHILD IN HOUSEHOLD	40338	25836	44.4	64.0	101	6388	41.6	15.8	95	8463	45.9	21.0	104	11007	45.0	27.3	102
UNDER 2 YEARS	6825	4216	7.2	61.8	97	998	6.5	14.6	88	1113	6.0	16.3	81	2105	8.6	30.8	115
2-5 YEARS	14954	9426	16.2	63.0	99	2638	17.3	17.6	106	2930	15.9	19.6	97	3858	15.8	25.8	96
6-11 YEARS	18470	11853	20.4	64.2	101	3158	20.6	17.1	102	3680	20.0	19.9	99	5017	20.5	27.2	102
12-17 YEARS	18541	12149	20.9	65.5	103	2819	18.4	15.2	91	4360	23.7	23.5	117	4970	20.3	26.8	100
WHITE	78552	51197	88.0	65.2	103	13309	87.1	16.9	101	16743	90.8	21.3	106	21145	86.4	26.9	101
BLACK	10583	5617	9.7	53.1	83	1665	10.9	15.7	94	1260	6.8	11.9	59	2692	11.0	25.4	95
HOME OWNED	63170	40806	70.1	64.6	102	10761	70.4	17.0	102	13165	71.4	20.8	103	16880	69.0	26.7	100
DAILY NEWSPAPERS: READ ANY	52987	34606	59.5	65.3	103	8822	57.7	16.6	100	11391	61.8	21.5	107	14393	58.8	27.2	102
READ ONE DAILY	42465	27489	47.2	64.7	102	6972	45.6	16.4	98	9282	50.4	21.9	109	11235	45.9	26.5	99
READ TWO OR MORE DAILIES	10522	7117	12.2	67.6	106	1850	12.1	17.6	105	2109	11.4	20.0	100	3159	12.9	30.0	112
SUNDAY NEWSPAPERS: READ ANY	56958	37159	63.9	65.2	103	9601	62.8	16.9	101	11930	64.7	20.9	104	15628	63.9	27.4	103
READ ONE SUNDAY	50164	32735	56.3	65.3	103	8533	55.8	17.0	102	10515	57.0	21.0	104	13688	55.9	27.3	102
READ TWO OR MORE SUNDAYS	6794	4424	7.6	65.1	102	1068	7.0	15.7	94	1415	7.7	20.8	103	1941	7.9	28.6	107
HEAVY MAGAZINES - HEAVY TV	23062	15824	27.2	68.6	108	4612	30.2	20.0	120	4861	26.4	21.1	105	6351	26.0	27.5	103
HEAVY MAGAZINES - LIGHT TV	22703	14427	24.8	63.5	100	3474	22.7	15.3	92	4716	25.6	20.8	103	6237	25.5	27.5	103
LIGHT MAGAZINES - HEAVY TV	22705	13762	23.6	60.6	95	3688	24.1	16.2	97	4361	23.7	19.2	95	5712	23.3	25.2	94
LIGHT MAGAZINES - LIGHT TV	23063	14180	24.4	61.5	97	3511	23.0	15.2	91	4496	24.4	19.5	97	6172	25.2	26.8	100
QUINTILE I - OUTDOOR	18306	11721	20.1	64.0	101	3188	20.9	17.4	104	3875	21.0	21.2	105	4658	19.0	25.4	95
QUINTILE II	18308	11910	20.5	65.1	102	3057	20.0	16.7	100	3759	20.4	20.5	102	5094	20.8	27.8	104
QUINTILE III	18306	11486	19.7	62.7	99	2735	17.9	14.9	89	3720	20.2	20.3	101	5031	20.6	27.5	103
QUINTILE IV	18306	11912	20.5	65.1	102	3219	21.1	17.6	105	3817	20.7	20.9	104	4877	19.9	26.6	100
QUINTILE V	18307	11162	19.2	61.0	96	3088	20.2	16.9	101	3263	17.7	17.8	89	4813	19.7	26.3	98
QUINTILE I - MAGAZINES	18307	12421	21.3	67.8	107	3269	21.4	17.9	107	4108	22.3	22.4	111	5044	20.6	27.6	103
QUINTILE II	18306	11835	20.3	64.7	102	3160	20.7	17.3	103	3702	20.1	20.2	100	4972	20.3	27.2	102
QUINTILE III	18306	11684	20.1	63.8	100	3073	20.1	16.8	101	3522	19.1	19.2	96	5089	20.8	27.8	104
QUINTILE IV	18307	11494	19.8	62.8	99	2792	18.3	15.3	91	3762	20.4	20.5	102	4939	20.2	27.0	101
QUINTILE V	18307	10759	18.5	58.8	92	2990	19.6	16.3	98	3340	18.1	18.2	91	4429	18.1	24.2	90

Exhibit 29–1 (continued)

		ALL				TIMES/LAST 30 DAYS: HEAVY MORE THAN 3				MEDIUM 2 - 3				LIGHT LESS THAN 2			
BASE: WOMEN	TOTAL U.S. '000	A '000	B % DOWN	C % ACROSS	D INDEX	A '000	B % DOWN	C % ACROSS	D INDEX	A '000	B % DOWN	C % ACROSS	D INDEX	A '000	B % DOWN	C % ACROSS	D INDEX
ALL WOMEN	91533	58192	100.0	63.6	100	15285	100.0	16.7	100	18434	100.0	20.1	100	24473	100.0	26.7	100
QUINTILE I - NEWSPAPERS	18308	12259	21.1	67.0	105	3159	20.7	17.3	103	3915	21.2	21.4	106	5185	21.2	28.3	106
QUINTILE II	18306	11451	19.7	62.6	98	2968	19.4	16.2	97	3662	19.9	20.0	99	4824	19.7	26.4	99
QUINTILE III	18306	12015	20.6	65.6	103	3057	20.0	16.7	100	4006	21.7	21.9	109	4951	20.2	27.0	101
QUINTILE IV	18306	11940	20.5	65.2	103	3242	21.2	17.7	106	3754	20.4	20.5	102	4944	20.2	27.0	101
QUINTILE V	18307	10528	18.1	57.5	90	2861	18.7	15.6	94	3097	16.8	16.9	84	4570	18.7	25.0	93
QUINTILE I - RADIO	18297	11679	20.1	63.8	100	3281	21.3	17.8	107	3836	20.8	21.0	104	4581	18.7	25.0	94
QUINTILE II	18305	12069	20.7	65.9	104	2991	19.6	16.3	98	4075	22.1	22.3	111	5003	20.4	27.3	102
QUINTILE III	18308	11238	19.3	61.4	97	2990	19.6	16.3	98	3333	18.1	18.2	90	4915	20.1	26.8	100
QUINTILE IV	18312	11520	19.8	62.9	99	3010	19.7	16.4	98	3501	19.0	19.1	95	5009	20.5	27.4	102
QUINTILE V	18311	11686	20.1	63.8	100	3033	19.8	16.6	99	3689	20.0	20.1	100	4965	20.3	27.1	101
QUINTILE I - TV (TOTAL)	18305	12017	20.7	65.6	103	3952	25.9	21.6	129	3558	19.3	19.4	97	4508	18.4	24.6	92
QUINTILE II	18306	11607	19.9	63.4	100	2975	19.5	16.3	97	3503	19.0	19.1	95	5129	21.0	28.0	105
QUINTILE III	18306	11710	20.1	64.0	101	2584	16.9	14.1	85	4235	23.0	23.1	115	4891	20.0	26.7	100
QUINTILE IV	18308	11684	20.1	63.8	100	3198	20.9	17.5	105	3385	18.3	18.4	91	5120	20.9	28.0	105
QUINTILE V	18308	11175	19.2	61.0	96	2576	16.9	14.1	84	3773	20.5	20.6	102	4825	19.7	26.4	99
RADIO WKDAY: 6-10:00 AM CUME	51628	32533	55.9	63.0	99	8175	53.5	15.8	95	10734	58.2	20.8	103,	13624	55.7	26.4	99
10:00 AM - 3:00 PM	32820	20747	35.7	63.2	99	5406	35.4	16.5	99	6725	36.5	20.5	102·	8615	35.2	26.2	98
3:00 PM - 7:00 PM	33506	21313	36.6	63.6	100	5302	34.7	15.8	95	6549	35.5	19.5	97	9461	38.7	28.2	106
7:00 PM - MIDNIGHT	15646	9977	17.1	63.8	100	2802	18.3	17.9	107	3313	18.0	21.2	105	3862	15.8	24.7	92
RADIO AVERAGE WEEKDAY CUME	71055	45323	77.9	63.8	100	11922	78.0	16.8	100	14394	78.1	20.3	101	19007	77.7	26.7	100
RADIO AVG. WEEKEND DAY CUME	59697	37968	65.2	63.6	100	9961	65.2	16.7	100	12161	66.0	20.4	101	15845	64.7	26.5	99
RADIO FORMATS: ADULT CONTEMP	23734	15998	27.5	67.4	106	3922	25.7	16.5	99	4968	27.0	20.9	104	7108	29.0	29.9	112
ALBUM ORIENTED ROCK (AOR)	9283	5961	10.2	64.2	101	1258	8.2	13.6	81	2087	11.3	22.5	112	2616	10.7	28.2	105
ALL NEWS	2968	1955	3.4	65.9	104	368	2.4	12.3	74	729	4.0	24.6	122	860	3.5	29.0	108
BLACK	2639	1337	2.3	50.7	80	*538	3.5	20.4	122	*203	1.1	7.7	38	596	2.4	22.6	84
CLASSICAL	2137	1343	2.3	62.8	99	*268	1.7	12.4	75	395	2.1	18.5	92	682	2.8	31.9	119
CHR/ROCK	17622	10667	18.3	60.5	95	2443	16.0	13.9	83	3560	19.3	20.2	100	4664	19.1	26.5	99
COUNTRY	16052	10798	18.6	67.3	106	3163	20.7	19.7	118	3413	18.5	21.3	106	4220	17.2	26.3	98
EASY LISTENING	8037	5112	8.8	63.6	100	1205	7.9	15.0	90	1720	9.3	21.4	106	2187	8.9	27.2	102
GOLDEN OLDIES	3232	2040	3.5	63.1	99	575	3.8	17.8	107	658	3.6	20.4	101	807	3.3	25.0	93
MOR/NOSTALGIA	4554	3227	5.5	70.9	111	840	5.5	18.4	110	1069	5.8	23.5	117	1319	5.4	29.0	108
NEWS/TALK	5852	3642	6.3	62.2	98	914	6.0	15.6	94	1221	6.6	20.9	104	1508	6.2	25.8	96
URBAN CONTEMPORARY	4335	2662	4.6	61.4	97	751	4.9	17.3	104	673	3.7	15.5	77	1239	5.1	28.6	107
RADIO NETWORKS: ABC CONTEMP	5589	3615	6.2	64.7	102	883	5.8	15.8	95	1182	6.4	21.1	105	1550	6.3	27.7	104
ABC DIRECTION	3895	2620	4.5	67.3	106	534	3.5	13.7	82	948	5.1	24.3	121	1138	4.7	29.2	109
ABC ENTERTAINMENT	5783	3895	6.7	67.4	106	1000	6.5	17.3	104	1093	5.9	18.9	94	1803	7.4	31.2	117
ABC FM	3795	2243	3.9	59.1	93	*467	3.1	12.3	74	805	4.4	21.2	105	972	4.0	25.6	96
ABC INFORMATION	8156	5641	9.7	69.2	109	1596	10.4	19.6	117	1811	9.8	22.2	110	2234	9.1	27.4	102
ABC ROCK	4239	2661	4.6	62.8	99	552	3.6	13.0	78	1008	5.5	23.8	118	1100	4.5	25.9	97
CBS	5533	3554	6.1	64.2	101	1042	6.8	18.8	113	1168	6.3	21.1	105	1344	5.5	24.3	91
CONCERT MUSIC NETWORK	1026	649	1.1	63.3	99	*120	.8	11.7	70	*216	1.2	21.1	105	313	1.3	30.5	114
INTERNET	27568	17093	29.4	62.0	98	3963	25.9	14.4	86	5419	29.4	19.7	98	7711	31.5	28.0	105
KATZ RADIO GROUP	29876	18916	32.5	63.3	100	4619	30.2	15.5	93	6334	34.4	21.2	105	7962	32.5	26.7	100
MUTUAL	7723	4785	8.2	62.0	97	1281	8.4	16.6	99	1451	7.9	18.8	93	2053	8.4	26.6	99
NBC	5450	3710	6.4	68.1	107	991	6.5	18.2	109	1212	6.6	22.2	110	1507	6.2	27.7	103
NBN	1863	1300	2.2	69.8	110	*511	3.3	27.4	164	*349	1.9	18.7	93	*441	1.8	23.7	89
RADIORADIO	4256	2782	4.8	65.4	103	689	4.5	16.2	97	981	5.3	23.0	114	1111	4.5	26.1	98
SATELLITE MUSIC NETWORK	4229	2822	4.8	66.7	105	825	5.4	19.5	117	862	4.7	20.4	101	1135	4.6	26.8	100
SHERIDAN	2210	1242	2.1	56.2	88	*452	3.0	20.5	122	*208	1.1	9.3	46	584	2.4	26.4	99
THE SOURCE	4479	2876	4.9	64.2	101	553	3.6	12.3	74	1100	6.0	24.6	122	1223	5.0	27.3	102
SUPERNET	19459	12926	22.2	66.4	104	3234	21.2	16.6	100	3965	21.5	20.4	101	5727	23.4	29.4	110
TRANSTAR	4869	3280	5.6	67.4	106	858	5.6	17.6	105	1076	5.8	22.1	110	1348	5.5	27.7	104
US1	5070	3186	5.5	62.8	99	707	4.6	13.9	84	1162	6.3	22.9	114	1317	5.4	26.0	97
US2	4732	3322	5.7	70.2	110	807	5.3	17.1	102	1181	6.4	25.0	124	1334	5.5	28.2	105
WALL STREET JOURNAL NETWORK	3588	2491	4.3	69.4	109	569	3.7	15.9	95	834	4.5	23.2	115	1088	4.4	30.3	113
TV W-DAY AV 1/2 HR:7-10.00AM	8113	5345	9.2	65.9	104	1719	11.2	21.2	127	1645	8.9	20.3	101	1982	8.1	24.4	91
10.00 AM - 4:30 PM	14672	9608	16.5	65.5	103	2777	18.2	18.9	113	2932	15.9	20.0	99	3899	15.9	26.6	99
4:30 PM - 7:30 PM	22790	14571	25.0	63.9	101	4233	27.7	18.6	111	4210	22.8	18.5	92	6129	25.0	26.9	101
7:30 PM - 8:00 PM	35641	22698	39.0	63.7	100	5821	38.1	16.3	98	7139	38.7	20.0	99	9738	39.8	27.3	102
8:00 PM - 11:00 PM	41817	26391	45.4	63.1	99	7118	46.6	17.0	102	8053	43.7	19.3	96	11220	45.8	26.8	100
11:00 PM - 11:30 PM	26221	16670	28.6	63.6	100	4607	30.1	17.6	105	5181	28.1	19.8	98	6882	28.1	26.2	98
11:30 PM - 1:00 AM	7875	5134	8.8	65.2	103	1474	9.6	18.7	112	1660	9.0	21.1	105	1999	8.2	25.4	95
TV PRIME TIME CUME	72347	46500	79.9	64.3	101	12381	81.0	17.1	102	14751	80.0	20.4	101	19368	79.1	26.8	100
PROGRAM-TYPES:DAYTIME DRAMAS	8707	5805	10.0	66.7	105	1869	12.2	21.5	129	1714	9.3	19.7	98	2223	9.1	25.5	95
DAYTIME GAME SHOWS	4462	3291	5.7	73.8	116	978	6.4	21.9	131	1147	6.2	25.7	128	1166	4.8	26.1	98
EARLY MORNING TALK/INFO/NEWS	6405	4362	7.5	68.1	107	1373	9.0	21.4	128	1407	7.6	22.0	109	1583	6.5	24.7	92
EARLY EVE. NETWK NEWS - M-F	13119	8568	14.7	65.3	103	2534	16.6	19.3	116	2851	15.5	21.7	108	3183	13.0	24.3	91
FEATURE FILMS - PRIME	12886	8860	15.2	68.8	108	2473	16.2	19.2	115	2913	15.8	22.6	112	3475	14.2	27.0	101
GENERAL DRAMA - PRIME	13552	8937	15.4	65.9	104	2815	18.4	20.8	124	2969	16.1	21.9	109	3152	12.9	23.3	87
PVT DET/SUSP/MYST/POL.-PRIME	13843	9619	16.5	69.5	109	3015	19.7	21.8	130	2845	15.4	20.6	102	3759	15.4	27.2	102
SITUATION COMEDIES - PRIME	11241	7454	12.8	66.3	104	1737	11.4	15.5	93	2410	13.1	21.4	106	3307	13.5	29.4	110
CABLE TV	42558	27245	46.8	64.0	101	7272	47.6	17.1	102	8508	46.2	20.0	99	11464	46.8	26.9	101
PAY TV	23432	14930	25.7	63.7	100	3933	25.7	16.8	101	4639	25.2	19.8	98	6358	26.0	27.1	101
HEAVY CABLE VIEWING (15+ HR)	13881	9220	15.8	66.4	104	2757	18.0	19.9	119	2633	14.3	19.0	94	3830	15.6	27.6	103
CABLE NETWORKS: A&E	4792	3287	5.6	68.6	108	655	4.3	13.7	82	950	5.2	19.8	98	1682	6.9	35.1	131
BET (BLACK ENTERTAINMENT TV)	1152	679	1.2	58.9	93	*138	.9	12.0	72	*219	1.2	19.0	94	*323	1.3	28.0	105
CNN (CABLE NEWS NETWORK)	15473	9962	17.1	64.4	101	2532	16.6	16.4	98	3263	17.7	21.1	105	4167	17.0	26.9	101
CNN HEADLINE NEWS	10365	6459	11.1	62.3	98	1930	12.6	18.6	112	2094	11.4	20.2	100	2435	9.9	23.5	88
CBN CABLE NETWORK	7664	5070	8.7	66.2	104	1479	9.7	19.3	116	1522	8.3	19.9	99	2069	8.5	27.0	101
THE DISCOVERY CHANNEL	4973	3081	5.3	62.0	97	808	5.3	16.2	97	991	5.4	19.9	99	1281	5.2	25.8	96
ESPN	12830	8412	14.5	65.6	103	2259	14.8	17.6	105	2269	12.3	17.7	88	3884	15.9	30.3	113
FNN (FINANCIAL NEWS NETW'K)	706	425	.7	60.2	95	*93	.6	13.2	79	*120	.7	17.0	84	*213	.9	30.2	113
THE LEARNING CHANNEL	1097	684	1.2	62.4	98	*194	1.3	17.7	106	*234	1.3	21.3	106	*258	1.0	23.3	87
LIFETIME	7134	4474	7.7	62.7	99	1122	7.3	15.7	94	1418	7.7	19.9	99	1934	7.9	27.1	101
MTV	8845	5639	9.7	63.8	100	1432	9.4	16.2	97	1510	8.2	17.1	85	2697	11.0	30.5	114
THE NASHVILLE NETWORK	7937	5338	9.2	67.2	106	1592	10.4	20.1	120	1582	8.6	19.9	99	2161	8.8	27.2	102
NICK AT NITE	3970	2758	4.7	69.4	109	721	4.7	18.2	109	750	4.1	18.9	94	1285	5.3	32.4	121
NICKELODEON	6769	4507	7.7	66.6	105	1146	7.5	16.9	101	1242	6.7	18.3	91	2120	8.7	31.3	117
USA NETWORK	8919	5798	10.0	65.0	102	1575	10.3	17.7	106	1924	10.4	21.6	107	2297	9.4	25.8	96
VH-1 (VIDEO HITS ONE)	2871	2014	3.5	70.1	110	*515	3.4	17.9	107	678	3.7	23.6	117	822	3.4	28.6	107
THE WEATHER CHANNEL	11079	7155	12.3	64.6	102	2158	14.1	19.5	117	2247	12.2	20.3	101	2751	11.2	24.8	93
WTBS	14442	9419	16.2	65.2	103	2616	17.1	18.1	108	2684	14.5	18.4	92	4139	16.9	28.7	107

Exhibit 29–1 (continued)

BASE: WOMEN	TOTAL U.S. '000	ALL A '000	ALL B % DOWN	ALL C % ACROSS	ALL D INDEX	HEAVY MORE THAN 3 A '000	HEAVY B % DOWN	HEAVY C % ACROSS	HEAVY D INDEX	MEDIUM 2 - 3 A '000	MEDIUM B % DOWN	MEDIUM C % ACROSS	MEDIUM D INDEX	LIGHT LESS THAN 2 A '000	LIGHT B % DOWN	LIGHT C % ACROSS	LIGHT D INDEX
						TIMES/LAST 30 DAYS											
ALL WOMEN	91533	58192	100.0	63.6	100	15285	100.0	16.7	100	18434	100.0	20.1	100	24473	100.0	26.7	100
AMERICAN BABY	2544	1528	2.6	60.1	94	*402	2.6	15.8	95	358	1.9	14.1	70	768	3.1	30.2	113
AMERICAN HEALTH	2713	1731	3.0	63.8	100	614	4.0	22.6	136	438	2.4	16.1	80	679	2.8	25.0	94
AMERICAN WAY	455	*304	.5	66.8	105	*60	.4	13.2	79	*57	.3	12.5	62	*186	.8	40.9	153
ARCHITECTURAL DIGEST	1674	1091	1.9	65.2	103	*262	1.7	15.7	94	*351	1.9	21.0	104	478	2.0	28.6	107
AUDUBON	651	490	.8	75.3	118	*172	1.1	26.4	158	*198	1.1	30.4	151	*120	.5	18.4	69
BABY TALK	1720	1141	2.0	66.3	104	*393	2.6	22.8	137	*288	1.6	16.7	83	460	1.9	26.7	100
BARRON'S	290	*222	.4	76.6	120	*48	.3	16.6	99	*73	.4	25.2	125	*101	.4	34.8	130
BASSMASTER	*555	*341	.6	-	-	*124	.8	-	-	*116	.6	-	-	*101	.4	-	-
BETTER HOMES & GARDENS	23452	.18019	27.5	68.3	107	4002	26.2	17.1	102	5308	28.8	22.6	112	6710	27.4	28.6	107
BHG/LHJ COMBO (GR)	38988	26620	45.7	68.3	107	6931	45.3	17.8	106	8908	48.3	22.8	113	10783	44.1	27.7	103
BLACK ENTERPRISE	891	*607	1.0	68.1	107	*147	1.0	16.5	99	*108	.6	12.1	60	*352	1.4	39.5	148
BON APPETIT	3236	2137	3.7	66.0	104	518	3.4	16.0	96	655	3.6	20.2	101	964	3.9	29.8	111
BRIDE'S MAGAZINE	2812	1899	3.3	67.5	106	*493	3.2	17.5	105	*666	3.6	23.7	118	740	3.0	26.3	98
BUSINESS WEEK	1724	1057	1.8	61.3	96	*224	1.5	13.0	78	*446	2.4	25.9	128	387	1.6	22.4	84
BYTE	*290	*174	.3	-	-	*30	.2	-	-	*89	.5	-	-	*54	.2	-	-
THE CABLE GUIDE	8286	5310	9.1	64.1	101	1447	9.5	17.5	105	1856	10.1	22.4	111	2007	8.2	24.2	91
CABLETIME	3030	2025	3.5	66.8	105	*582	3.8	19.2	115	559	3.0	18.4	92	884	3.6	29.2	109
CAR & DRIVER	472	*325	.6	68.9	108	*74	.5	15.7	94	*118	.6	25.0	124	*133	.5	28.2	105
CAR CRAFT	*210	*120	.2	-	-	*11	.1	-	-	*61	.3	-	-	*48	.2	-	-
CHANGING TIMES	1458	905	1.6	62.1	98	*263	1.7	18.0	108	*314	1.7	21.5	107	*329	1.3	22.6	84
CHICAGO TRIBUNE MAGAZINE	1334	821	1.4	61.5	97	*148	1.0	11.1	66	226	1.2	16.9	84	447	1.8	33.5	125
COLONIAL HOMES	1848	1171	2.0	63.4	100	*239	1.6	12.9	77	*448	2.4	24.2	120	485	2.0	26.2	98
CONDE NAST LIMITED (GR)	16987	10874	18.7	64.0	101	2697	17.6	15.9	95	3242	17.6	19.1	95	4934	20.2	29.0	109
CONDE NAST WOMEN (GR)	22647	14269	24.5	63.0	99	3038	19.9	13.4	80	4803	26.1	21.2	105	6428	26.3	28.4	106
CONSUMERS DIGEST	1606	1213	2.1	75.5	119	*369	2.4	23.0	138	*473	2.6	29.5	146	*372	1.5	23.2	87
COSMOPOLITAN	10238	6390	11.0	62.4	98	1352	8.8	13.2	79	2152	11.7	21.0	104	2886	11.8	28.2	105
COUNTRY HOME	3689	2355	4.0	63.8	100	569	3.7	15.4	92	652	3.5	17.7	88	1133	4.6	30.7	115
COUNTRY JOURNAL	1201	776	1.3	64.6	102	*188	1.2	15.7	94	*218	1.2	18.2	90	*370	1.5	30.8	115
COUNTRY LIVING	5369	3246	5.6	60.5	95	858	5.6	16.0	96	998	5.4	18.6	92	1393	5.7	25.9	97
CREATIVE IDEAS FOR LIVING	1455	967	1.7	66.5	105	*257	1.7	17.7	106	*332	1.8	22.8	113	*378	1.5	26.0	97
DELTA SKY (AIR GROUP ONE)	719	*427	.7	59.4	93	*169	1.1	23.5	141	*102	.6	14.2	70	*156	.6	21.7	81
DIAMANDIS MAGAZINE NTWK (GR)	3751	2508	4.3	66.9	105	693	4.5	18.5	111	858	4.7	22.9	114	957	3.9	25.5	95
DISCOVER	1306	872	1.5	66.8	105	*259	1.7	19.8	119	*240	1.3	18.4	91	*372	1.5	28.5	107
DISNEY CHANNEL MAGAZINE	3259	2151	3.7	66.0	104	550	3.6	16.9	101	586	3.2	18.0	89	1015	4.1	31.1	116
EAST/WEST NETWORK (GR)	2585	1615	2.8	62.5	98	411	2.7	15.9	95	*441	2.4	17.1	85	764	3.1	29.6	111
EBONY	5207	2933	5.0	56.3	89	782	5.1	15.0	90	791	4.3	15.2	75	1360	5.6	26.1	98
ELLE	1274	740	1.3	58.1	91	*215	1.4	16.9	101	*129	.7	10.1	50	*396	1.6	31.1	116
ESQUIRE	1134	759	1.3	66.9	105	*225	1.5	19.8	119	*272	1.5	24.0	119	*262	1.1	23.1	86
ESSENCE	2379	1421	2.4	59.7	94	*347	2.3	14.6	87	*458	2.5	19.3	96	615	2.5	25.9	97
FAMILY CIRCLE	21117	14286	24.5	67.7	106	3507	22.9	16.6	99	4826	26.2	22.9	113	5953	24.3	28.2	105
FAMILY COMPUTING	487	*368	.6	75.6	119	*57	.4	11.7	70	*155	.8	31.8	158	*156	.6	32.0	120
FAMILY HANDYMAN	1278	917	1.6	71.8	113	*367	2.4	28.7	172	*234	1.3	18.3	91	*317	1.3	24.8	93
FIELD & STREAM	2602	1837	3.2	70.6	111	*558	3.7	21.4	128	664	3.6	25.5	127	616	2.5	23.7	89
FLOWER & GARDEN	1764	1151	2.0	65.2	103	*261	1.7	14.8	89	*494	2.7	28.0	139	*396	1.6	22.4	84
FOOD & WINE	1281	862	1.5	67.3	106	*199	1.3	15.5	93	*222	1.2	17.3	86	440	1.8	34.3	128
FORBES	740	544	.9	73.5	116	*98	.6	13.2	79	*194	1.1	26.2	130	*252	1.0	34.1	127
FORTUNE	1136	784	1.3	69.0	109	*131	.9	11.5	69	*362	2.0	31.9	158	*292	1.2	25.7	96
4 WHEEL & OFF ROAD	*305	*257	.4	-	-	*87	.6	-	-	*80	.4	-	-	*90	.4	-	-
GLAMOUR	8114	5275	9.1	65.0	102	1126	7.4	13.9	83	1826	9.9	22.5	112	2323	9.5	28.6	107
GOLF DIGEST	1087	800	1.4	73.6	116	*123	.8	11.3	68	*347	1.9	31.9	159	*330	1.3	30.4	114
GOLF DIGEST/TENNIS (GR)	1650	1169	2.0	70.8	111	*216	1.4	13.1	78	481	2.6	29.2	145	*472	1.9	28.6	107
GOLF MAGAZINE	535	424	.7	79.3	125	*52	.3	9.7	58	*200	1.1	37.4	186	*171	.7	32.0	120
GOLF MAGAZINE/SKI (GR)	1250	859	1.5	68.7	108	*104	.7	8.3	50	*359	1.9	28.7	143	*395	1.6	31.6	118
GOOD HOUSEKEEPING	20504	14119	24.3	68.9	108	3444	22.5	16.8	101	4706	25.5	23.0	114	5969	24.4	29.1	109
GOURMET	2036	1325	2.3	65.1	102	*335	2.2	16.5	99	*329	1.8	16.2	80	661	2.7	32.5	121
GQ (GENTLEMEN'S QUARTERLY)	1429	905	1.6	63.3	100	*310	2.0	21.7	130	*204	1.1	14.3	71	*391	1.6	27.4	102
GUNS & AMMO	*501	*391	.7	-	-	*190	1.2	-	-	*64	.3	-	-	*137	.6	-	-
HARPER'S BAZAAR	1943	1322	2.3	68.0	107	*217	1.4	11.2	67	465	2.5	23.9	119	640	2.6	32.9	123
HEALTH	2061	1245	2.1	60.4	95	*251	1.6	12.2	73	*417	2.3	20.2	100	577	2.4	28.0	105
HEARST MAN POWER (GR)	2962	2173	3.7	73.4	115	733	4.8	24.7	148	679	3.7	22.9	114	761	3.1	25.7	96
HEARST WOMAN POWER (GR)	48657	31921	54.9	65.6	103	7692	50.3	15.8	95	10531	57.1	21.6	107	13699	56.0	28.2	105
HG (HOUSE & GARDEN)	6818	4527	7.8	66.4	104	1107	7.2	16.2	97	1432	7.8	21.0	104	1988	8.1	29.2	109
HOME	1562	941	1.6	60.2	95	*226	1.5	14.5	87	*279	1.5	17.9	89	*436	1.8	27.9	104
HOME MECHANIX	797	668	1.1	83.8	132	*228	1.5	28.6	171	*193	1.0	24.2	120	*248	1.0	31.1	116
HOMEOWNER	958	721	1.2	75.3	118	*160	1.0	16.7	100	*348	1.9	36.3	180	*213	.9	22.2	83
HOT ROD	845	652	1.1	77.2	121	*172	1.1	20.4	122	*207	1.1	24.5	122	*273	1.1	32.3	121
HOUSE BEAUTIFUL	4510	2990	5.1	66.3	104	681	4.5	15.1	90	1020	5.5	22.6	112	1289	5.3	28.6	107
HUNTING	*454	*347	.6	-	-	*129	.8	-	-	*53	.3	-	-	*165	.7	-	-
INC.	791	473	.8	59.8	94	*93	.6	11.8	70	*173	.9	21.9	109	*208	.8	26.3	98
INSIDE SPORTS	*577	*389	.7	-	-	*41	.3	-	-	*233	1.3	-	-	*115	.5	-	-
JET	3819	2228	3.8	58.3	92	756	4.9	19.8	119	594	3.2	15.6	77	877	3.6	23.0	86
LADIES' HOME JOURNAL	15536	10601	18.2	68.2	107	2929	19.2	18.9	113	3600	19.5	23.2	115	4073	16.6	26.2	98
LIFE	7704	4973	8.5	64.6	102	1383	9.0	18.0	108	1696	9.2	22.0	109	1893	7.7	24.6	92
MADEMOISELLE	3756	2214	3.8	58.9	93	*376	2.5	10.0	60	829	4.5	22.1	110	1009	4.1	26.9	100
MCCALLS	15887	10684	18.4	67.2	106	3039	19.9	19.1	115	3616	19.6	22.8	113	4028	16.5	25.4	95
MCCALLS NEEDLEWORK & CRAFTS	4581	3284	5.6	71.7	113	907	5.9	19.8	119	1246	6.8	27.2	135	1131	4.6	24.7	92
MCGRAW-HILL NETWORK (GR)	1846	1280	2.2	69.3	109	*363	2.4	19.7	118	*478	2.6	25.9	129	438	1.8	23.7	89
METRO SUNDAY COMICS	15187	10193	17.5	67.1	106	2602	17.0	17.1	103	3352	18.2	22.1	110	4238	17.3	27.9	104
MODERN BRIDE	1648	1083	1.9	65.7	103	*221	1.4	13.4	80	*464	2.5	28.2	140	*398	1.6	24.2	90
MODERN MATURITY	16048	10801	18.6	67.3	106	3137	20.5	19.5	117	3509	19.0	21.9	109	4155	17.0	25.9	97
MODERN PHOTOGRAPHY	985	619	1.1	62.8	99	*82	.5	8.3	50	*216	1.2	21.9	109	*322	1.3	32.7	122
MONEY	2366	1545	2.7	65.3	103	*372	2.4	15.7	94	584	3.2	24.7	123	589	2.4	24.9	93

Exhibit 29–1 (continued)

		ALL				TIMES/LAST 30 DAYS: HEAVY MORE THAN 3				MEDIUM 2 - 3				LIGHT LESS THAN 2			
	TOTAL U.S.	A	B %	C %	D	A	B %	C %	D	A	B %	C %	D	A	B %	C %	D
BASE: WOMEN	'000	'000	DOWN	ACROSS	INDEX	'000	DOWN	ACROSS	INDEX	'000	DOWN	ACROSS	INDEX	'000	DOWN	ACROSS	INDEX
ALL WOMEN	91533	58192	100.0	63.6	100	15285	100.0	16.7	100	18434	100.0	20.1	100	24473	100.0	26.7	100
MOTHER EARTH NEWS	865	569	1.0	65.8	103	*183	1.1	18.8	113	*230	1.2	26.6	132	*178	.7	20.3	76
MOTOR HOME/TRAILER LIFE (GR)	508	*272	.5	53.5	84	*104	.7	20.5	123	*87	.5	17.1	85	*81	.3	15.9	60
MOTOR TREND	*320	*251	.4	-	-	*82	.5	-	-	*105	.6	-	-	*64	.3	-	-
MS.	1320	884	1.5	67.0	105	*118	.8	8.9	54	*324	1.8	24.5	122	*441	1.8	33.4	125
MUSCLE & FITNESS	1069	671	1.2	62.8	99	*112	.7	10.5	63	*194	1.1	18.1	90	*365	1.5	34.1	128
NATIONAL ENQUIRER	11873	8002	13.8	67.4	106	2343	15.3	19.7	118	2649	14.4	22.3	111	3010	12.3	25.4	95
NATIONAL GEOGRAPHIC	13487	9005	15.5	66.8	105	2228	14.6	16.5	99	2843	15.4	21.1	105	3934	16.1	29.2	109
NATIONAL GEOGRAPHIC TRAVELER	1371	829	1.4	60.5	95	*293	1.9	21.4	128	*194	1.1	14.2	70	*342	1.4	24.9	93
NATIONAL LAMPOON	*410	*257	.4	-	-	*59	.4	-	-	*107	.6	-	-	*92	.4	-	-
NATURAL HISTORY	532	348	.6	65.4	103	*54	.4	10.2	61	*83	.5	15.6	77	*212	.9	39.8	149
NEWSWEEK	8307	5678	9.8	68.4	108	1271	8.3	15.3	92	2235	12.1	26.9	134	2172	8.9	26.1	98
NEW WOMAN	2413	1436	2.5	59.5	94	*349	2.3	14.5	87	501	2.7	20.8	103	585	2.4	24.2	91
NEW YORK MAGAZINE	569	*319	.5	56.1	88	*128	.8	22.1	133	*91	.5	16.0	79	*102	.4	17.9	67
NEW YORK TIMES (DAILY)	1043	557	1.0	53.4	84	*155	1.0	14.9	89	*138	.7	13.2	66	*264	1.1	25.3	95
NEW YORK TIMES MAGAZINE	1599	981	1.7	61.4	97	*182	1.2	11.4	68	333	1.8	20.8	103	467	1.9	29.2	109
THE NEW YORKER	1008	608	1.0	60.3	95	*182	1.2	18.1	108	*148	.8	14.7	73	*279	1.1	27.7	104
OMNI	1349	903	1.6	66.9	105	*181	1.2	13.4	80	*286	1.6	21.2	105	*437	1.8	32.4	121
1,001 HOME IDEAS	3058	1909	3.3	62.4	98	430	2.8	14.1	84	655	3.6	21.4	106	823	3.4	26.9	101
ORGANIC GARDENING	1221	869	1.5	71.2	112	*338	2.2	27.7	166	*229	1.2	18.8	93	*302	1.2	24.7	93
OUTDOOR LIFE	2137	1599	2.7	74.8	118	*487	3.2	22.8	136	*604	3.3	28.3	140	*508	2.1	23.8	89
PARADE	32762	21348	36.7	65.2	102	5436	35.6	16.6	99	6764	36.7	20.6	103	9148	37.4	27.9	104
PARENTS' MAGAZINE	7035	4624	7.9	65.7	103	1169	7.6	16.6	100	1306	7.1	18.6	92	2149	8.8	30.5	114
PC MAGAZINE	*353	*223	.4	-	-	*27	.2	-	-	*85	.5	-	-	*112	.5	-	-
PC WORLD	*389	*302	.5	-	-	*49	.3	-	-	*135	.7	-	-	*118	.5	-	-
PENTHOUSE	889	701	1.2	78.9	124	*180	1.2	20.2	121	*171	.9	19.2	96	*350	1.4	39.4	147
PENTON EXECUTIVE NETWK (GR)	1599	1012	1.7	63.3	100	*301	2.0	18.8	113	*318	1.7	9.9	99	395	1.6	24.7	92
PEOPLE	17578	11347	19.5	64.6	102	2933	19.2	16.7	100	3587	19.5	20.4	101	4827	19.7	27.5	103
PERSONAL COMPUTING	633	552	.9	.87.2	137	*63	.4	10.0	60	*165	.9	26.1	129	*324	1.3	51.2	191
PETERSEN MAGAZINE GROUP (GR)	3791	2749	4.7	72.5	114	826	5.4	21.8	130	888	4.8	23.4	116	1035	4.2	27.3	102
PLAYBOY	2978	1878	3.2	63.1	99	615	4.0	20.7	124	568	3.1	19.1	95	694	2.8	23.3	87
POPULAR HOT RODDING	*330	*203	.3	-	-	*84	.5	-	-	*61	.3	-	-	*58	.2	-	-
POPULAR MECHANICS	1264	1029	1.8	81.4	128	*403	2.6	31.9	191	*277	1.5	21.9	109	*349	1.4	27.6	103
POPULAR SCIENCE	1086	719	1.2	66.2	104	*232	1.5	21.4	128	*213	1.2	19.6	97	*274	1.1	25.2	94
PREVENTION	5156	3339	5.7	64.8	102	1012	6.6	19.6	118	1064	5.8	20.6	102	1263	5.2	24.5	92
PSYCHOLOGY TODAY	2709	1751	3.0	64.6	102	531	3.5	19.6	117	462	2.5	17.1	85	759	3.1	28.0	105
PUCK	10316	7210	12.4	69.9	110	1727	11.3	16.7	100	2356	12.8	22.8	113	3128	12.8	30.3	113
READER'S DIGEST	28148	19094	32.8	67.8	107	5436	35.6	19.3	116	6377	34.6	22.7	112	7281	29.8	25.9	97
REDBOOK	10603	6844	11.8	64.5	102	1821	11.9	17.2	103	2212	12.0	20.9	104	2811	11.5	26.5	99
ROAD & TRACK	*396	*273	.5	-	-	*36	.2	-	-	*39	.2	-	-	*198	.8	-	-
RODALE ACTIVE SPORTS (GR)	994	714	1.2	71.8	113	*200	1.3	20.1	120	*189	1.0	19.0	94	*326	1.3	32.8	123
ROLLING STONE	2090	1331	2.3	63.7	100	*197	1.3	9.4	56	*479	2.6	22.9	114	655	2.7	31.3	117
RUNNER'S WORLD	*416	*238	.4	-	-	*53	.3	-	-	*46	.2	-	-	*139	.6	-	-
SATURDAY EVENING POST	2253	1599	2.7	71.0	112	*536	3.5	23.8	142	511	2.8	22.7	113	552	2.3	24.5	92
SCIENTIFIC AMERICAN	541	383	.7	70.8	111	*84	.5	15.5	93	*157	.9	29.0	144	*143	.6	26.4	99
SELF	2449	1418	2.4	57.9	91	*309	2.0	12.6	76	*385	2.1	15.7	78	724	3.0	29.6	111
SEVENTEEN	4631	2732	4.7	59.0	93	813	5.3	17.6	105	895	4.9	19.3	96	1024	4.2	22.1	83
SHAPE	1590	1036	1.8	65.2	102	*173	1.1	10.9	65	*428	2.3	26.9	134	*435	1.8	27.4	102
SKI	715	435	.7	60.8	96	*52	.3	7.3	44	*159	.9	22.2	110	*224	.9	31.3	117
SKIING	677	*423	.7	62.5	98	*47	.3	6.9	42	*131	.7	19.4	96	*245	1.0	36.2	135
SMITHSONIAN	3753	2508	4.3	66.8	105	534	3.5	14.2	85	731	4.0	19.5	97	1243	5.1	33.1	124
SOAP OPERA DIGEST	4320	2846	4.9	65.9	104	893	5.8	20.7	124	978	5.3	22.6	112	975	4.0	22.6	84
SOUTHERN LIVING	7313	4974	8.5	68.0	107	1299	8.5	17.8	106	1577	8.6	21.6	107	2097	8.6	28.7	107
SPORT	797	527	.9	66.1	104	*158	1.0	19.6	117	*137	.7	17.2	85	*234	1.0	29.4	110
THE SPORTING NEWS	*512	*375	.6	-	-	*92	.6	-	-	*173	.9	-	-	*110	.4	-	-
SPORTS AFIELD	564	*385	.7	68.3	107	*105	.7	18.6	111	*130	.7	23.0	114	*150	.6	26.6	99
SPORTS ILLUSTRATED	3751	2520	4.3	67.2	106	535	3.5	14.3	85	902	4.9	24.0	119	1083	4.4	28.9	108
STAR	6991	4611	7.9	66.0	104	1436	9.4	20.5	123	1533	8.3	21.9	109	1642	6.7	23.5	88
SUNDAY MAG/NET	20379	13474	23.2	66.1	104	3333	21.8	16.4	98	4366	23.7	21.4	106	5775	23.6	28.3	106
SUNSET	2554	1746	3.0	68.4	108	*469	3.1	18.4	110	391	2.1	15.3	76	887	3.6	34.7	130
TENNIS	563	*369	.6	65.5	103	*93	.6	16.5	99	*134	.7	23.8	118	*142	.6	25.2	94
TIME	10909	7196	12.4	66.0	104	1900	12.4	17.4	104	2268	12.3	20.8	103	3028	12.4	27.8	104
TOWN & COUNTRY	1342	840	1.4	62.6	98	*231	1.5	17.2	103	*280	1.5	20.9	104	*329	1.3	24.5	92
TRAVEL & LEISURE	1471	968	1.7	65.8	104	*347	2.3	23.6	141	*274	1.5	18.6	92	*347	1.4	23.6	88
TRAVEL/HOLIDAY	700	545	.9	77.9	122	*119	.8	17.0	102	*235	1.3	33.6	167	*191	.8	27.3	102
TRUE STORY	4740	2902	5.0	61.2	96	1127	7.4	23.8	142	752	4.1	15.9	79	1023	4.2	21.6	81
TV GUIDE	24968	16454	28.3	65.9	104	4468	29.2	17.9	107	5226	28.3	20.9	104	6760	27.6	27.1	101
U.S. AIR MAGAZINE	580	*378	.6	65.2	103	*97	.6	16.7	100	*173	.9	29.8	148	*109	.4	18.8	70
U.S. NEWS & WORLD REPORT	4366	2901	5.0	66.4	105	677	4.4	15.5	93	990	5.4	22.7	113	1233	5.0	28.2	106
US	2935	2045	3.5	69.7	110	*389	2.5	13.3	79	752	4.1	25.6	127	905	3.7	30.8	115
USA TODAY	1336	854	1.5	63.9	101	*222	1.5	16.6	100	*263	1.4	19.7	98	370	1.5	27.7	104
USA WEEKEND	13436	8725	15.0	64.9	102	2046	13.4	15.2	91	3000	16.3	22.3	111	3679	15.0	27.4	102
VANITY FAIR	1188	654	1.1	55.1	87	*211	1.4	17.8	106	*180	1.0	15.2	75	*262	1.1	22.1	82
VOGUE	5516	3483	6.0	62.8	99	734	4.8	13.3	80	1097	6.0	19.9	99	1632	6.7	29.6	111
WALL STREET JOURNAL	1291	913	1.6	70.7	111	*252	1.6	19.5	117	*265	1.4	20.5	102	396	1.6	30.7	115
WEIGHT WATCHERS	3273	2221	3.8	67.9	107	799	5.2	24.4	146	594	3.2	18.1	90	828	3.4	25.3	95
WOMAN	1672	1128	1.9	67.3	106	*320	2.1	19.1	115	*431	2.3	25.8	128	376	1.5	22.5	84
WOMAN'S DAY	20114	13512	23.2	67.2	106	3689	24.1	18.3	110	4363	23.7	21.7	108	5459	22.3	27.1	102
WOMAN'S WORLD	4799	3071	5.3	64.0	101	939	6.1	19.6	117	1015	5.5	21.2	105	1118	4.6	23.3	87
THE WORKBASKET	3006	2261	3.9	75.2	118	769	5.0	25.6	153	736	4.0	24.5	122	756	3.1	25.1	94
WORKBENCH	782	582	1.0	74.4	117	*177	1.2	22.6	136	*128	.7	16.4	81	*277	1.1	35.4	132
WORKING MOTHER	2010	1505	2.6	74.9	118	*388	2.5	19.3	116	*522	2.8	26.0	129	595	2.4	29.6	111
WORKING WOMAN	2799	1826	3.1	65.2	103	*322	2.1	11.5	69	649	3.5	23.2	115	855	3.5	30.5	114
YANKEE	1636	1001	1.7	61.2	96	*285	1.9	17.4	104	*273	1.5	16.7	83	443	1.8	27.1	101

Assignment 30

How a Professional Media Planner Solved a Marketing/Media Problem

An Annotated Media Plan for Lux Liquid

Objective: To provide you with the opportunity to review and study a media plan for a given problem.

Discussion

Presented here are media plan recommendations for the restaging and introduction of Lux Liquid dishwashing detergent. (Details of the brand and product category have been altered to protect the confidential nature of existing products.) Media objectives, strategies, schedules, and the rationale for these recommendations are included. This is an edited version of both problem and recommendations.

First read the problem so that you know the marketing situation that this media planner faced. Then read the solutions. As you read, make sure that you understand the logic of the strategy. Try to determine where the media planner had to make decisions on rather subjective bases and where relevant data allowed objectivity. Perhaps you can use some of these planning ideas in your next media plan.

Problem

Background

Lux Liquid is a light-duty detergent used primarily to wash dishes. The product is manufactured by a major company and has been on the market since 1940. Lux Liquid is in a highly competitive product category that includes several major competing liquid detergent brands including Ivory, Dove, Palmolive, and Joy.

Over the years, Lux's product users have grown older. As other brands repackaged and reformulated their products, Lux experienced a continuous erosion in its market share, which is now 9 share points.

To correct this situation and move to a 13-share level, the brand is attempting a restage. *Restaging* means making changes in package design (from white to floral pink), reformulating the product to generate more suds, and adding a pleasant aroma to heighten the image of mildness and cleansing.

Lux Liquid faces short-term and long-term inroads on its business from three sources:

- Other aggressively advertised and promoted light-duty liquids
- Concentrated detergents, such as Cascade, that are used in automatic dishwashers
- The threat of a new product category, Ajax Liquid, which began its national roll-out last year and should be national by next year. (Ajax's spending rate is $8 million in advertising and $10 million in trade allowance and dealer promotion activity.)

Lux Liquid's advertising budget next year is $4,725,000, of which $225,000 will be set aside for production. The brand will invest $3,700,000 in promotion to the retail trade. With these funds the brand is expected to successfully restage next year and offset Ajax's roll-out as well as defend itself against heavy category activity.

Lux's New Marketing Plan

Objective. To optimize Lux Liquid's brand volume within minimum profit requirements that will permit the brand to support its restage while defending against counter-category activity in the face of Ajax Liquid's roll-out.

Strategy. To achieve the objective, Lux Liquid will assume an essentially offensive posture in all its marketing efforts. The brand must retain the financial flexibility to adopt defensive tactics to combat Ajax Liquid's launch.

Brand positioning. Lux Liquid will be positioned as a brand that offers superlative mildness for hands that do dishes. Thus, Lux Liquid will be distinguished from Ivory and Thrill, which feature economy, or Palmolive and Joy, which stress cleaning of dishes. By emphasizing the product benefit of mildness to hands, the focus is on the glamour of the women using the product, rather than on the drudgery of cleaning dishes.

Target group. Psychographically, Lux Liquid users are basically narcissistic, self-conscious, glamour-oriented women who are not particularly interested in washing dishes beyond the practical need for clean dishes and avoiding the guilt associated with not doing them.

Seasonality. Category sales and competitive advertising are flat throughout the year.

Creative Objectives and Strategy

Objectives. The objective of Lux Liquid copy is to convince women that Lux is a superlatively mild dishwashing liquid.

Strategy. Lux Liquid gives women cared-for hands that are admired by others. The tone of the advertising will be feminine, cosmetic, and contemporary. This will serve to reinforce the superlative mildness position that Lux is seeking to establish.

Marketing Data

Brand	Share (%)	Brand loyalty (%)
	Relative share of market and comparative loyalty to brand	
Dove	7%	21%
Ivory	22	37
Joy	18	32
Lux	9	26
Palmolive	16	39
Thrill	5	22
Vel	2	18
All others	21	
	100%	

Seasonal sales pattern

Quarter	Lux Liquid	LDL category
1st	24	25
2nd	26	25
3rd	26	26
4th	24	24
Annual	100	100

Estimated sales of Lux Liquid and LDL category by company sales districts

Sales districts	U.S. TV HHs (%)	Lux sales (%)	Brand index	Category sales (%)	Category index
Atlanta	10%	12%	120%	9%	90%
Baltimore	5	6	120	5	100
Chicago	20	22	110	15	75
Detroit	5	3	60	6	120
New England	10	10	100	10	100
Florida	5	6	120	5	100
New York	15	15	100	15	100
Los Angeles	10	8	80	12	120
San Francisco	15	12	80	18	120
Texas	5	6	120	5	100
Total U.S.	100%	100%	100%	100%	100%

Category quarter spending pattern (last year)

Brand	First quarter	Second quarter	Third quarter	Fourth quarter	Total
Dove	$ 700.0	$ 600.0	$ 800.0	$ 500.0	$ 2,600.0
Ivory	1,860.0	1,290.0	1,500.0	2,050.0	6,700.0
Joy	1,200.0	1,080.0	1,260.0	1,300.0	4,840.0
Lux	900.0	1,200.0	900.0	600.0	3,600.0
Palmolive	1,350.0	1,700.0	1,300.0	1,300.0	5,650.0
Thrill	500.0	500.0	400.0	450.0	1,850.0
Vel	300.0	200.0	400.0	150.0	1,800.0
Ajax (40% roll-out)	—	—	800.0	600.0	1,400.0
	$6,810.0	$6,570.0	$7,360.0	$6,950.0	$27,690.0
Without Ajax	6,810.0	6,570.0	6,560.0	6,350.0	26,290.0
% by quarter	26%	25%	25%	24%	100%

Category allocation by medium (%)						
Brand	Day network	Night network	Spot TV	Radio	Magazines	Total
Dove	50%	25%	25%	—	—	100%
Ivory	47	30	15	—	8%	100
Joy	35	50	15	—	—	100
Lux	60	—	40	—	—	100
Palmolive	25	25	30	—	20	100
Thrill	65	—	35	—	—	100
Ajax	—	—	100	—	—	100

Recommended Media Plan[1]

Each media planner, department, or agency will approach media planning differently. Although there are some generally accepted guidelines, there is no standard format or approach for developing or presenting final media recommendations. Accordingly, the following recommendation is not presented as the best solution, but rather as a good solution that a media planner (given certain perceptions and information) might confidently recommend. There is some merit in reviewing this recommendation for its strengths and media planning insights, but there is even greater value in looking for lapses in rationale, better strategies, or stronger tactical approaches or rationale for selected strategies.

Marketing Objectives

The market situation clearly sets forth the challenge and requirements for introducing reformulated Lux Liquid. As a light-duty liquid (LDL) detergent used primarily to wash dishes, Lux Liquid must restage its product and positioning more strongly in this highly competitive but mature and declining category, in which usage is shrinking rapidly due to growth in automatic dishwashing soaps.

The restage of Lux Liquid with new package design, higher sudsing formula, more pleasant aroma, and intrusive new creative approach to convince women that Lux is a superlatively mild dishwashing liquid admittedly will not be earthshaking news to the homemaker. The Lux Liquid media budget (increased 25 percent to $4.5 million) remains fourth, behind the brand leaders. With a relatively small share of category spending (15 percent of total), and at a rate of only 75 percent of average spending for each of the three leading brands, Lux Liquid might need more than one year to reach its 13-share goal. If Lux

[1]Recommended media plan presented at an *Ad Age* Media Workshop by Robert Reuschle, formerly at Henderson Advertising Agency. Media schedule, costs, and various numbers are based on this presentation. Please note that this is an edited version of Reuschle's original plan.

Liquid is to achieve this share, it must do so largely at the expense of the three leading brands (which account for 56 percent of total LDL volume and 62 percent of the non-Lux LDL volume).

Impressions must be concentrated against selected user segments to achieve a realistic, but fair, share of the noise level against key users. If a 45 percent increase in market share is to be achieved, the initial period of restage must receive very strong support, rather than generate a slow buildup of impressions over the year.

To achieve the marketing objectives, an essentially offensive posture is needed (strong effort in areas with high category volume). However, more data (market-by-market share, distribution, etc.) must be reviewed to determine final allocation of effort to high-opportunity markets versus markets where Lux Liquid volume is high (and industry is at least average). It is assumed that advertising messages are designed to effectively work against less frequent and non-users of Lux Liquid, but new package-reformulated product messages also reinforce attitudes of current Lux Liquid users.

Finally, further review of promotion spending is needed. Analysis of regional brand shares, distribution, and competitive promotional efforts against the trade might show overexpenditure in trade promotion by Lux Liquid. If so, this is at the expense of weakening (or providing an inadequate base for building) a stronger consumer franchise. (Note: Lux Liquid brand loyalty versus major competition is relatively low.)

Obviously, a strong distribution base is needed, especially in opportunity areas where Lux Liquid volume lags behind strong category sales. For this reason, a strong initial promotional effort against the trade is recommended as a base for successful advertising effort. Rather than the more typical spending rate of 25 percent each quarter, 35 percent of promotional budget is recommended in the first quarter. Thus, the first-through-fourth-quarter spending of promotional funds would be: 35 percent, 25 percent, 20 percent, and 20 percent. If the promotional budget for the restage year has been increased 25 percent (comparable to increase in media budget), the first-quarter promotional level would be at a rate 75 percent greater than the first quarter of the past year.

Media Objectives

The following media objectives are recommended for the restage of Lux Liquid:

1. **Use strong introductory effort, especially in the first three to six months, to achieve immediate high levels of reach and awareness of reformulation message and to achieve product trial.**

   Discussion. Big changes in a brand's marketing and advertising plans represent big news that consumers should know. In this situation, Lux's restaging effort is news and deserves special treatment to dramatize it. Theoretically, this news could be started in a small way and build up to a climax at the end of the year. But it is generally accepted as a better strategy to start big, with a powerful introduction, so the objective established was to set the stage for a big introduction of the restaging news. The planner intends for the introduction to last from three to six months with extra heavy advertising. However, it remains for the strategy to explain precisely how long the introduction will last.

Also, the consequence of a strong introduction is that reach will be high. As a result, relatively high brand awareness should be attained. Brand awareness can be achieved through high reach, or high reach and frequency (gross rating points). Chances are that the reach level for this plan will be higher than the awareness goal, because not everyone reached will see ads for Lux.

2. **Efficiently deliver impressions on a national basis to the target universe of homemakers—the medium and heavy users of LDL detergents, especially those who do not currently use Lux Liquid.** The 12 percent of homemakers who are heavy users account for 33 percent of LDL volume, and the 48 percent of homemakers considered medium to heavy in usage account for over 69 percent of volume.

   Discussion. The targets for advertising can be found by analyzing the volume usage data at the bottom of Table 30–1. The media planner decided that both heavy and medium users of dishwashing detergents should be targets. From these two groups of users, the planner hopes to find enough homemakers who will switch brands after they are exposed to Lux's advertising and thereby enable Lux to achieve a 13 percent market share.

   Heavy users account for 33 percent of sales volume, and moderate users account for 36 percent of sales volume. Alone, each user group would not be large enough to find enough people to switch to Lux. Together, they represent a substantial amount of potential users who might switch brands.

   Also note that this will be a national, rather than a regional or local, plan. Finally, the planner pointed out that advertising impressions (meaning gross impressions) should be delivered efficiently. This means that the cost of reach target groups should be relatively low, or having relatively low cost-per-thousand target reach.

3. **Direct media weight to those homemakers most likely to be important targets.** (See Table 30–1.)

   - Primary target: Women aged 35–49, \$5,000–\$8,000 income, not employed, who did not attend college, larger households (5+)
   - Secondary target: Women 18–34 and 50–64, less than \$25,000 income, medium-size households (3+), and employed part-time

   Discussion. The precise delineation of targets is made on a demographic segment basis obtained from Table 30–1. Segments with the highest index numbers are the ones selected.

4. **Given the need for a strong initial effort, provide high frequency and good continuity levels (as budget permits) to stimulate trial and acceptance.** High exposure and noise level are needed against selected targets to build awareness versus competition.

   Discussion. This objective provides an additional dimension to reach: frequency and continuity. The reasons for requiring both are explained. Note that by stating this objective, the planner is explaining that brand awareness will be achieved by having a large number of gross rating points (reach times frequency) and consistent advertising over the year.

5. **Additionally support opportunity markets representing greatest volume and growth potential.**

Discussion. This statement represents a plan for geographic weighting. In other words, this media plan will cover not only the entire country (a national effort), but also concentrate in geographic areas where there is the greatest opportunity for growth. The implications are: (1) not every geographic market is equally valuable in terms of sales; and (2) more advertising dollars (or gross rating points) should be placed where sales are more likely to grow.

Table 30-1 Usage Comparisons by Demographic Groups

Demographics	Heavy and medium users of Lux Liquid %	Heavy and medium users of Lux Liquid Index	Heavy and medium users of LDL, and non-Lux users Index	I=Primary II=Secondary III=Tertiary
Age				
18–24	13.0%	95	103	II
25–34	19.2	95	95	II
35–49	29.1	108	108	I
50–64	22.7	99	98	II
65+	16.1	98	93	III
Income				
Under $5,000	22.3	113	114	II
$ 5,000–7,900	20.8	122	118	I
$ 8,000–9,900	9.9	108	109	II
$10,000–14,900	28.4	100	102	II
$15,000–24,900	14.5	75	75	III
$25,000+	4.1	67	68	III
Education				
Not high school graduate	38.5	125	124	I
High school	40.0	104	105	II
Attend college	13.5	75	75	III
College graduate	8.0	63	62	III
Household size				
5+	28.8	128	127	I
3–4	38.1	103	104	II
1–2	33.1	82	81	III
Employed homemaker				
Not employed	68.2	110	110	I
Part time	12.5	100	110	II
Full time	19.3	73	73	III

Volume of Dishwashing Usage
Heavy users account for 33 percent of volume sold.
Medium users account for 36 percent of volume sold.
Light users account for 31 percent of volume sold.

6. **Use media that will most effectively deliver messages of the reformulated product: high sudsing and cosmetic/mildness appeals.**

   Discussion. The creative strategy is very important in the media planning process. Not every medium is equally desirable to deliver a given style of message. The best media will be the ones that most effectively show the high sudsing and cosmetic/mildness messages. At this point, the planner has to examine all media classes to see which are most appropriate. The planner will explain which are best in the strategy statements.

7. **Provide vehicles for immediate and broad delivery of coupons to promote trial purchases.**

   Discussion. Advertising messages describing the product changes alone cannot do the entire selling job. Sales promotion is also necessary, in the form of coupons. Advertising will therefore serve another purpose in addition to delivering the key sales messages: It will announce the promotion and deliver the coupons as well. This latter requirement requires a print medium.

8. **Provide flexibility to adjust to changing market opportunities and budgetary considerations.**

   Discussion. Once an advertising campaign starts, sales develop in a manner that requires quick changes in the media plan. For example, some markets that were not expected to do well begin to show very high sales. A media plan, therefore, has to be flexible enough to move money around from markets where sales are not doing well to those areas where they are. Flexible media are local, such as spot television, newspapers, etc. Network television and magazines are not very flexible.

Media Strategy

Each strategy statement is related to a media objective. The following strategies are recommended:

1. **Employ daytime network television to efficiently deliver impressions nationally and to achieve adequate reach and frequency levels for high awareness among key user groups.** (The heavy-viewing quintile is also the heavy-user group of LDL.)

   Discussion. The strategy here calls for network television because it is a national medium. But within the framework of network, the most cost-efficient daypart is daytime. Table 30–2 shows just how efficient daytime is when compared to the other dayparts. Note that data on television viewing quintiles are not shown, but are available from syndicated research companies. Also note from Table 30–2 that magazines are not as cost efficient as are network television commercials used in daytime.

2. **During the first quarter, use network early evening television to effectively extend reach to target homemakers on a national basis.**

Discussion. The problem with using daytime television is that it cannot build enough reach of the target market. But by adding another daypart, such as early fringe news, it is possible to extend the reach. In the early evening daypart, many more homemakers are available to watch television than during the day, and this extra viewing extends the reach.

3. **During the first half of the introductory year, and thereafter as budget permits, efficiently provide additional support via use of spot television in key opportunity markets to extend reach and build impressions and awareness among homemakers in these important markets.**

   Discussion. Now spot television has been added to the strategy of network. However, spot television is to be used only in geographic markets that show good sales potential (called *opportunity markets*). It is obvious that if spot is added over an umbrella of network, many persons will be reached more than once, and this will contribute some gains in reach but more gains in frequency in the local markets.

4. **Use national Sunday supplements (plus independents in key markets) to efficiently deliver coupons, with immediate high reach exposure of coupons and package to promote awareness and trial.**

   Discussion. Conceivably, the planner could have opted for national magazines to deliver coupons nationally. Or daily newspapers could have been used to do the same in the opportunity markets. However, by selecting supplements, the planner has a medium that combines the qualities of both. The editorial material of supplements is primarily feature material, and the delivery is both local (with newspapers) and national. Some markets have independent supplements, and wherever they are located, they may be purchased if the market sales potential is high.

Table 30–2 How Media Compare in Efficiency in Reaching Dishwashing Liquid Users

	Media concentration, non-Lux and heavy/medium LDL users		HH CPM	Media efficiency, non-Lux and heavy/medium LDL users		
	Total homemakers (%)	Index		VPS*	CPM	Index
Network television (:30s)						
Daytime	37.6%	117	$ .92	.24	$ 3.83	100
Early news	33.2	103	1.20	.25	4.80	125
Prime time	31.5	98	2.76	.23	12.00	313
Late fringe	30.8	96	1.52	.22	6.91	180
Spot television (:30s)						
Early news	30.5	95	1.88	.23	8.17	213
Early fringe movies and game shows	34.5	107	1.50	.25	6.00	157
Magazines (four-color page)						
Women's shelter	28.1	88	—	NA	8.28	216
Screen/romance	36.9	115	—	NA	6.03	157

*Viewers per set.

Source: TGI.

Plan Tactics

The tactics of a media plan are sometimes part of strategy statements and sometimes spelled out separately, as they are here. There is no one presentation method that is always correct.

How network television is to be used

1. During the first quarter, use high GRP levels in network television to provide strong noise levels (strong reach *and* frequency). Use 140 target GRPs during the daytime and 100 target GRPs during early evening per week each. This will translate to 560 GRPs per month for daytime TV and 400 GRPs per month for early fringe TV.

   Discussion. How does a planner know how many GRPs to plan for? This was discussed earlier in Assignment 20, which discussed estimating the reach and frequency of competitors. But, essentially, the planner must decide how the brand will compare with the competition's. A planner's goal usually is to equal or beat the competition's reach and/or frequency. Table 30–3 shows how the category of dishwashing liquid spends dollars on the average. It also shows how Ivory, one of the leaders, spends its dollars. The planner now tries to relate the plan to both the category and Ivory brand spending, and the reach and frequency competitors' dollars will buy.

   Using Lux's spending plan as a guide, it is now possible to estimate how many GRPs can be purchased for that given dollar amount. The cost per rating point for an average television program is easily calculated and widely known. A planner only has to divide the rating point cost into the dollar amount available to estimate how many GRPs can be purchased.

Once the number of GRPs that can be purchased is known, then it is a matter of trying various alternative GRP levels to find which one will provide the correct reach and/or frequency that is needed.

Table 30–3 Competitive Budget Levels[a]

	1st	2nd	3rd	4th	Total
Network TV ($000) per quarter					
Category[b]	$4,970	$4,450	$4,490	$4,570	$18,480
Ivory	1,430	995	1,155	1,580	5,160
Lux	1,675	680	680	680	3,715
Spot TV ($000) per quarter					
Category[b]	$1,510	$1,465	$1,370	$1,350	$ 5,695
Ivory	280	195	225	310	1,010
Lux	80	460	70	—	610
Total media ($000) per quarter including print					
Category[b]	$6,960	$6,420	$6,285	$6,375	$26,040
Ivory	1,860	1,290	1,500	2,050	6,700
Lux	1,910	1,148	756	686	4,500

[a]Dollars can be converted to impressions (use CPM per daypart) or GRPs (relate to equivalent coverage of impressions). Original presentation used GRPs as basis for comparison. Dollars used here for convenience, as given in media case problem.

[b]Category includes Ivory, Ajax, and all brands except Lux for comparative purposes versus Lux effort.

The planner first started with a daytime television plan of 60 GRPs a week (240 GRPs a month). Using a reach and frequency table or a computer, the planner arrived at a 61 percent reach and 3.9 frequency for four weeks. Then two other alternatives were tried, one that developed a 73 percent reach and another with an 88 percent reach.

At this point, the planner interjected another criterion into the decision: how to get as much frequency of exposure with the same reach. To learn which alternative was best, the planner had to create a frequency distribution table as shown at the bottom of Table 30–4. This portion of Table 30–4 clearly showed that the third alternative (88 percent reach) had the most frequency per four-week period (or 64 percent compared to 26 percent and 28 percent for the other alternatives). The planner's final decision, however, was to increase the GRP level for early evening network television from 60 GRPs per week to 100. The final decision then increased reach only 1 percent, but the frequency level went to 10.8.

Table 30–4 Reach and Frequency of Alternative Network TV Plans

Alternative plan number	Weekly GRPs: Day	Weekly GRPs: Early evening	Weekly GRPs: Weekly total	Total monthly GRPs	Reach	Frequency
1	60	0	60	240	61%	3.9
2	60	20	80	320	73	4.5
3	145	60	205	820	88	9.5
Final plan	140	100	240	960	89	10.8

Frequency distributions of alternatives

Number of times audience was reached in four weeks	Alternative number 1 (61% reach)	Alternative number 2 (73% reach)	Alternative number 3 (88% reach)	Final reach (89%)
1 time	13%	23%	6%	6%
2–3 times	22	22	18	18
4+ times	26	28	64	65
Total reached	61%	73%	88%	89%

Use daytime (primarily) and early news (secondarily) as these dayparts provide greater concentration of impressions to non-Lux heavy/medium LDL users (see Table 30–2) and more efficient reach than prime time and late fringe.

Discussion. This section is self-explanatory, with the exception of the phrase about cost efficiency. The cost efficiency of the various dayparts is shown in Table 30–2. Clearly daytime and early evening programming had the lowest cost per thousand.

Continue strong GRP levels in daytime network for the rest of the year. (One hundred and ten GRPs a week will achieve maximum reach levels within day network and high levels of frequency to competitively restage the product against the leading brands. Heavy viewers of daytime television are heavy LDL users and relatively light Lux Liquid users. See Tables 30–5 through 30–7 for additional research data.)

Discussion. The first quarter of the year was the most important for planning purposes. Now the remaining three-quarters were covered. Both reach and frequency are key criteria in making decisions here, but the levels of both are not as high as they were for the introduction. Data for viewing by daypart are to be found in syndicated audience research studies.

Provide short hiatus periods (two to three weeks) each quarter to allow somewhat greater concentration of GRPs and impressions during flights.

Discussion. The planner could have planned for advertising in each of the 52 weeks but chose instead to have higher concentrations of GRPs at various times of the year by not advertising for short periods of time (two to three weeks). These nonadvertising times are called *hiatuses*. By having hiatuses at four different times of the year, the planner is using a *flighting* strategy. It allows concentration of advertising firepower at the best times of the year in order to be heard over the noise level of competitors. The planner knows that the product will not lose much impact by not advertising during the short hiatuses.

How spot television is to be used

1. Approximately 12.5–15 percent of budget will be allocated to high-potential and opportunity markets. Opportunity markets are considered those with 115–120 CDI and 60–80 BDI, accounting for 30 percent of U.S. TV homes and 36 percent of category sales. (It should be noted that Ajax has recently entered those regions accounting for the bulk [83 percent] of volume in opportunity markets.)

   Although not included in the current spot TV recommendation, further analysis should review those high Lux Liquid regions (115–120 index) with at least average (100+) CDI. These three regions account for 15 percent of TV homes and LDL volume and 18 percent of Lux Liquid volume. (Ajax has already entered two of these three regions.)

   Discussion. It is important to note how the planner defines an opportunity market. Essentially it is a geographic marketing area where the BDI is low but the category is doing well. What this means is that because the competition is doing well, Lux should also do well, especially because it has restaged the product and therefore has something new to say and has a better selling proposition for customers than it had before. By spending more money in opportunity markets, it is hoped that the market will respond with increased sales for Lux. See marketing data to find opportunity markets. They are markets within the Detroit, Los Angeles, and San Francisco sales districts.

   Recommendations are also given for studying markets with high Lux BDI and at least 100 CDI. These too might receive extra weight in the near future if the planner believes the time is ripe to place more dollars or GRPs in these markets. (Study marketing data for BDI and CDI.)

2. Spot TV should be scheduled with late fringe commercials early in the restaging campaign as a means of strengthening the brand's position in these key regions, especially against the homemaker not reached by daytime or early news television.

   Discussion. There are some targets who, for various reasons, do not see much daytime or early evening television but do watch at late fringe periods. These people should be reached with late fringe commercials.

3. After five weeks of first quarter spot TV (at medium GRP levels as an overlay to network—140 GRPs/week day and 100/week early news), increase early evening spot TV to 150 GRPs/week for ten weeks in second quarter (as an overlay to 110 GRPs/week day network only). This provides adequate and substantial levels of spot TV to extend and strengthen the strong day network TV effort. Spot TV will run concurrent with the full network schedule to further emphasize impression levels against TV viewers during the entire second-quarter flight.

   Discussion. In the first part of the introductory period, the spot TV portion of the plan will use 50 GRPs a week for five weeks in the opportunity markets. (See Exhibit 30–1.) Spot TV is used as a supplement to network, which is carrying most of the burden of delivering messages. But in the second quarter as network television is given fewer GRPs (only 110 per week), spot television GRPs will be increased from 50 to 150 per week. The reason is that by this time, brand awareness should be high nationally, and now special effort is necessary to win new customers in the best markets.

4. In the third quarter, and as the budget permits, extend spot TV effort in key regions at first-quarter levels (50 GRPs a week) as an overlay to daytime network only.

   Discussion. Again, daytime network is the basic advertising medium. Early evening network was used only in the first quarter. At the third quarter the campaign begins to taper off under the assumption that by now the key consumers have already been bombarded with advertising and only continuing reminders are needed. However, the best potential markets are the ones getting the extra weight.

5. Depending on individual market programming opportunities, use early movies and game shows to further extend reach to target audiences on an efficient basis.

   Discussion. This statement provides direction in selecting the kinds of spot television programming that should be selected. The planner is saying: Either select the time slots "in" local programming or "adjacent to" certain kinds of programs that will reach new and different segments of the target audiences.

How Sunday supplements are to be used

1. Use four-color supplements with high reach to provide package design registration and early and immediate delivery of coupons to homemakers in these markets. All three major syndicated supplements are used for broad coverage of targets (including *Family Weekly* for important C and D counties) plus independents, especially in the key West Coast markets.

2. Supplements provide high reach immediately and more efficiently in these markets than do magazines. Supplements provide rates favorable to national use of local newspapers and also provide reproduction quality to enhance the image of package, scent, and reformulated product (mildness/sudsing).

   Discussion. The planner here explains why supplements were recommended. As in all good media plans, this kind of statement helps establish the credibility of a planner's decision. Most likely someone on the client's side would have asked this question in a plan's board meeting. By stating it now, there is no need to ask the question later.

Spending plan

1. Fifty-eight percent of the budget is spent in the second through fourth quarters, one-third of budget in last half of year. All flexible media dollars are in day network and spot TV. (Eighty percent of spot TV budget is in the second and third quarters.)

Exhibit 30–1 Lux Liquid Advertising Schedule

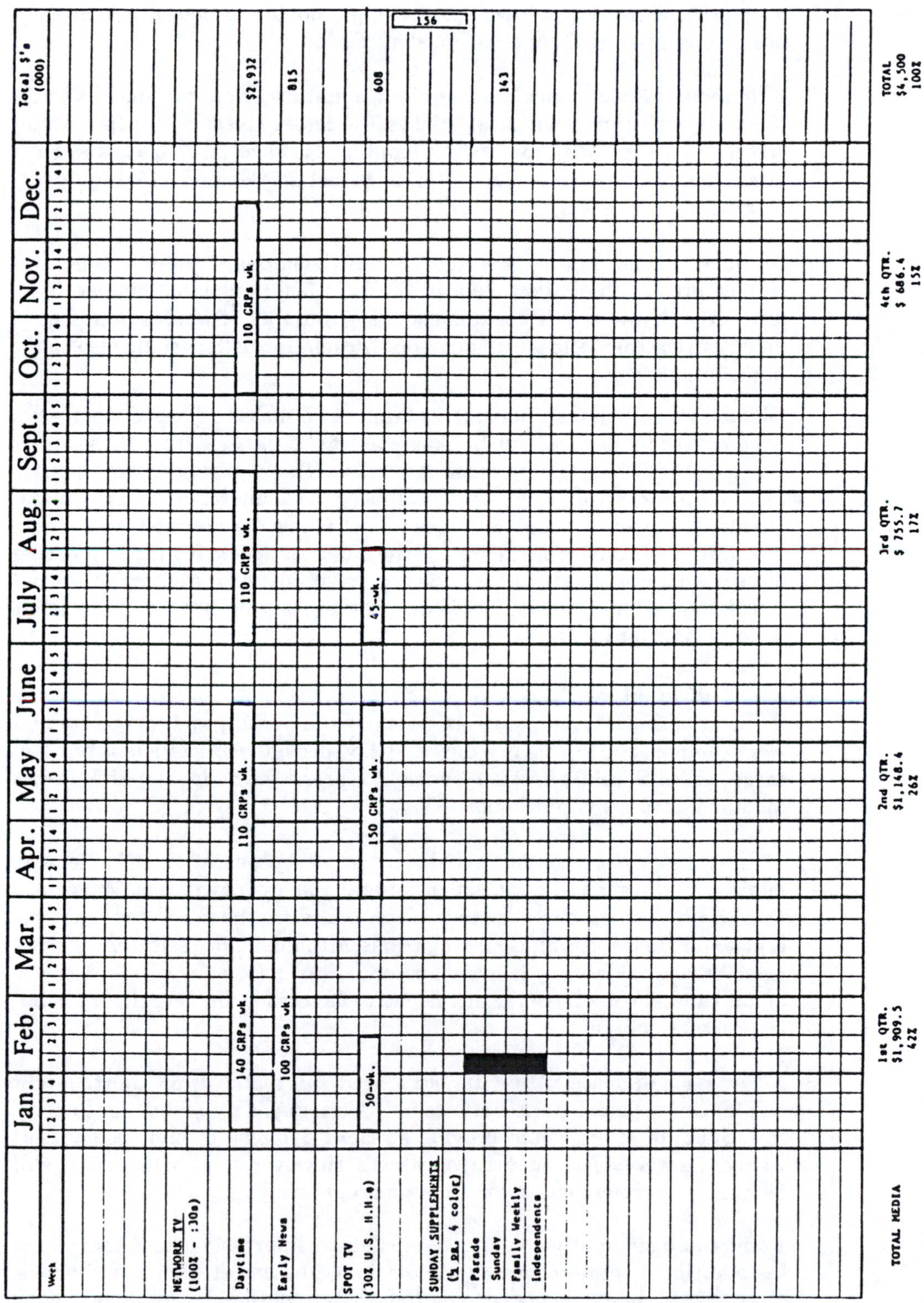

Day and spot TV provide good flexibility for financial adjustments. Day network time could be "sold" to other company brands or advertisers or back to the network if needed. Spot TV might not be purchased or, if already purchased, can be sold or reassigned as needed.

2. If financial cutbacks should be required, a mature brand such as Lux could probably withstand six months' hiatus if necessary (especially after strong restage introduction in the first six months). However, if share goals are to be achieved, a strong introductory effort to restage the product is highly recommended.

3. A final comment: The heavy weight in television might result in talent residuals greater than allowed for in the $225,000 production budget. If so, day network and spot TV media spending (number of weeks) could be reviewed in the third and fourth quarters. (Promotion dollars could also be cut in the second half.)

Discussion. Perhaps other media planners would have devised other ways to spend media dollars. But the key point to be gleaned from these statements is that the spending must be flexible. Talent residuals are the payments to actors on or off camera who appear in commercials. The method of payment is covered by union contracts that are renewed from time to time. There are two kinds of payments to actors: one for appearing in the shooting of a filmed commercial (or videotaped commercial) and the other for use and reuse. Every time a commercial is shown, there is usually a set amount that must be paid for its use.

Use of additional media

1. Prime time and late fringe are not recommended, as day and early news network (and in spot TV, early fringe and day) provide more efficient reach of target users. Special effort is made not to spread the budget too thin across media and too many markets.

2. Magazines are not recommended due to lack of concentration and efficiency against the target audience, which generally skews downscale. Magazines that reach this audience, such as *Screen Magazine*, have limited reach potential due to low circulation. Magazines, although more selective, are not used for coupon delivery to avoid audience duplication and slower delivery of total audience (believed highly negative factors for coupon delivery in initial restage effort).

3. Medium-small space ROP will not be used, but distribution efforts might call for some special market efforts in ROP (see spot TV budget for flexibility). Such an effort would provide efficient delivery of impressions, but likely at lower effectiveness to consumers. However, most of this effort will be handled through a retail promotion program.

4. Radio could efficiently and selectively deliver impressions to homemakers (as additional reinforcement to television), but not at high reach levels. Such efforts should be tested prior to full-scale national or regional implementation. Admittedly, radio delivers proportionately more impressions to

light viewers of day and early news television programs than does additional early fringe television.

Discussion. After a media plan has been prepared, it is almost inevitable that someone will ask: "Why did you not use this or that medium?" or, "Why did you not use a medium in a certain way?" This discussion tries to cover such questions before they are asked. Of course, it does not cover every possible alternative medium or media usage. But by answering these questions now, the client and other interested persons can concentrate their thinking on the logic of what was proposed as compared to what was not proposed. This should be a part of a media plan.

Conclusion

The beginner should note that specific media vehicles were not mentioned. There is no need to do that. This plan was spelled out in enough detail for media buyers to implement without much question. Also, when the plan is initially developed, it is not always possible to know what specific TV programs will be available when the planner is ready to make the buy. It would not be wrong to select media vehicles, but it is not necessary. If the reasoning and logic are good and complete for a media plan, then implementation of the plan is simply a matter of following directions.

Table 30–5 Lux Weight Level Delivery

Network TV

	GRPs per quarter		
	First	Second–fourth (each quarter)	Total
Category	4,400	4,400	17,600
Ivory	1,600	1,600	6,400
Lux objective	2,200	1,467	6,600

Lux's plan: 1st qtr.: Spend 50% of category and equal Ivory. 2nd, 3rd, 4th qtrs.: Spend 33% of category.

Spot Markets

	GRPs per quarter				
	First	Second	Third	Fourth	Total
Category	5,280	5,280	5,280	5,280	21,120
Lux objective	2,640	2,640	1,430	1,320	7,920

Table 30–6 Lux Total Spending by Quarter

	First (000)	Second (000)	Third (000)	Fourth (000)	Total (000)
Media	$1,910	$1,148	$ 756	$ 686	$4,500
Promotion	1,300	900	750	750	3,700
Total	$3,210	$2,048	$1,506	$1,436	$8,200
Percentages	39%	25%	18%	18%	100%
Category percentages	26	25	25	24	100

Table 30–7 Lux Spending by Medium

	Dollars (000)	Percentage
Network television	$3,715	82.6%
Spot television	610	13.6
Supplements	175	3.9
Totals	$4,500	100.1%

Section Four

Miscellaneous Problems

Assignment 31

Developing a Complete Media Plan

Objective: To present a case for which you are to devise a complete media plan, using your understanding of all the principles discussed previously.

Discussion

Up to this point you have been working on parts of media plans (e.g., objectives, strategies, strategic impressions, etc.). You also had the opportunity to study how a professional thinks through and solves media problems.

Now you are to develop a complete media plan, including strategies and other details, for a line of low-calorie frozen meals.

The media plan will include recommendations for media selection and usage, a rationale for all decisions, a flowchart to show how the money will be spent, and various other kinds of media plan information, such as tables and data, that make it easy for anyone to understand.

Background

More than one-third of U.S. adults are involved in dieting. The reasons range from medical (need to reduce intake of sodium, sugar, or saturated fat) to a desire to lose weight to a general concern with physical fitness. Over half of the dieters give the need to lose weight as their reason for dieting.

Product. Low-Cal International—a line of packaged, frozen, low-calorie meals—was developed to appeal to dieters concerned with losing weight. The principle advantage of the line, other than reduced calories, is taste. The line stresses international meals. This allows the use of exotic spices and flavorings that enhance taste while adding few, if any, calories. Although the line also contains lower levels of sodium and fat than regular frozen entrees, the company does not consider them low enough to merit stressing that fact in advertising. The line includes entrees such as stir fry meals from China, chicken specialties from Japan and Italy, and fish dishes from Polynesia.

Distribution. National distribution is planned, although stronger in cities of 200,000 population than in smaller markets. Brand strength (as well as category strength) is in A and B counties and metropolitan areas. The company has a very small sales force and relies heavily on brokers and wholesalers to promote its line to food stores.

Nationally, distribution is near 70 percent but varies a great deal by region of the country. Indices indicating the incidence of weight loss dieting, brand development, and brand distribution by Nielsen territory are shown below.

Nielsen territory	Weight loss dieting	BDI	Brand ACV* distribution (%)
New England	102	95	68%
Middle Atlantic	108	113	73
East Central	95	88	60
West Central	121	117	75
South East	90	71	58
South West	91	95	67
Pacific	92	90	63

*All commodity volume (ACV) measures distribution based on the total volume of business done by stores selling the brand rather than on a simple store-count basis.

Competition. The brand enjoys a fairly good market position, considering that it was introduced three years ago. The competition includes all low-calorie food products. Media spending among the chief competitors includes the following:

Brand	Medium	Last year's expenditures
Healthy Choice	Magazines	$ 4,830,000
(Conagra)	Network TV	10,795,000
	Spot TV	5,790,000
	Cable TV	361,000
	Sunday magazines	475,000
	Total	$22,251,000
Lean Cuisine	Magazines	$ 1,631,000
(Stouffers)	Network TV	9,519,000
	Spot TV	2,763,000
	Cable TV	280,000
	Spot radio	1,617,000
	Total	$15,810,000
Le Menu Light Style	Spot TV	$ 1,936,000
(Swanson)	Spot radio	301,000
	Total	$ 2,237,000
Weight Watchers	Magazines	$ 658,000
(Heinz)	Network TV	909,000
	Network radio	1,002,000
	Total	$ 2,569,000

Consumers. The primary purchasers are college-educated, female homemakers aged 25–54, living in urban areas. They are employed, at least part-time, and have household incomes of $35,000 or higher.

Seasonality. Brand sales by bimonthly reporting periods follow:

Period	Index
January–February	82
March–April	112
May–June	130
July–August	110
September–October	88
November–December	78

Copy platform. Advertising for the brand emphasizes the international aspect of the line and the outstanding taste of the entrees. The product has enough visual appeal to encourage the use of appetizing illustrations.

Promotion plans. The brand plans two national promotions: a coupon effort in March and a sweepstakes in July.

Budget. The "working media" budget is $8,000,000. This is to cover all media costs—including media to support promotions—but does not include production or other promotion costs.

Media usage by dieters. Exhibit 31–1 contains MRI media usage data for dieters. Although not specifically reporting media use by users of low-calorie meals, it does report media use by dieters, who are important targets for the brand. You should find this of value as you begin selecting media classes and vehicles.

Marketing Objectives

1. Continue to support national distribution and sales with a sales goal of a 10 percent increase next year.
2. Consolidate sales position in those metropolitan markets located in above-average sales territories.
3. Provide a strong kick-off at the beginning of and maintain a good effort throughout the peak sales season.
4. Continue to maintain strong communication with food store managers and buyers at food chain headquarters.
5. Expand food store distribution in areas where it is below 70 percent.

Exhibit 31–1 MRI: Media Use by Dieters

BASE: ADULTS	TOTAL U.S. '000	ALL DIETERS A '000	B % DOWN	C % ACROSS	D INDEX
ALL ADULTS	178281	57277	100.0	32.1	100
MEN	85035	21042	36.7	24.7	77
WOMEN	93246	36235	63.3	38.9	121
HOUSEHOLD HEADS	101395	29585	51.6	29.2	91
HOMEMAKERS	102573	37272	65.1	36.3	113
GRADUATED COLLEGE	31271	11198	19.5	35.8	111
ATTENDED COLLEGE	32228	11152	19.5	34.6	108
GRADUATED HIGH SCHOOL	69392	22507	39.3	32.4	101
DID NOT GRADUATE HIGH SCHOOL	45389	12422	21.7	27.4	85
18-24	26460	6288	11.0	23.8	74
25-34	43285	12576	22.0	29.1	90
35-44	34153	10931	19.1	32.0	100
45-54	23496	8834	15.4	37.6	117
55-64	22626	8727	15.2	38.6	120
65 OR OVER	28262	9923	17.3	35.1	109
18-34	69744	18882	32.9	27.0	84
18-49	115832	34310	59.9	29.6	92
25-54	100933	32342	56.5	32.0	100
EMPLOYED FULL TIME	101695	31953	55.8	31.4	98
PART-TIME	11602	4348	7.6	37.5	117
SOLE WAGE EARNER	33693	10164	17.7	30.2	94
NOT EMPLOYED	64984	20977	36.6	32.3	100
PROFESSIONAL	15286	5728	10.0	37.5	117
EXECUTIVE/ADMIN./MANAGERIAL	14533	5061	8.8	34.8	108
CLERICAL/SALES/TECHNICAL	34157	12553	21.9	36.8	114
PRECISION/CRAFTS/REPAIR	13836	3041	5.3	22.0	68
OTHER EMPLOYED	35484	9920	17.3	28.0	87
H/D INCOME $60,000 OR MORE	23842	9030	15.8	37.9	118
$50,000 - 59,999	16373	5709	10.0	34.9	109
$35,000 - 49,999	38392	13281	23.2	34.6	108
$25,000 - 34,999	31792	10476	18.3	33.0	103
$15,000 - 24,999	32570	9113	15.9	28.0	87
LESS THAN $15,000	35312	9668	16.9	27.4	85
CENSUS REGION: NORTH EAST	38166	12650	22.1	33.1	103
NORTH CENTRAL	43768	14846	25.9	33.9	106
SOUTH	60933	17825	31.1	29.3	91
WEST	35414	11957	20.9	33.8	105
MARKETING REG.: NEW ENGLAND	9686	3271	5.7	33.8	105
MIDDLE ATLANTIC	31069	10171	17.8	32.7	102
EAST CENTRAL	25139	7195	12.6	28.6	89
WEST CENTRAL	28755	10488	18.3	36.5	114
SOUTH EAST	31991	9777	17.1	30.6	95
SOUTH WEST	20167	5791	10.1	28.7	89
PACIFIC	31474	10585	18.5	33.6	105
COUNTY SIZE A	75038	24500	42.8	32.7	102
COUNTY SIZE B	52854	16490	28.8	31.2	97
COUNTY SIZE C	26664	8837	15.4	33.1	103
COUNTY SIZE D	23725	7450	13.0	31.4	98
MSA CENTRAL CITY	63360	19693	34.4	31.1	97
MSA SUBURBAN	73656	24451	42.7	33.2	103
NON-MSA	41265	13133	22.9	31.8	99
SINGLE	37775	9527	16.6	25.2	79
MARRIED	108540	37008	64.6	34.1	106
OTHER	31965	10742	18.8	33.6	105
PARENTS	60645	19062	33.3	31.4	98
WORKING PARENTS	45672	14693	25.7	32.2	100
SOLE PARENT	9134	2844	5.0	31.1	97
HOUSEHOLD SIZE: 1 PERSON	21914	6781	11.8	30.9	96
2 PERSONS	55277	19106	33.4	34.6	108
3 OR MORE	101090	31392	54.8	31.1	97
ANY CHILD IN HOUSEHOLD	73418	22544	39.4	30.7	96
UNDER 2 YEARS	14139	3589	6.3	25.4	79
2-5 YEARS	25587	7492	13.1	29.3	91
6-11 YEARS	33017	10811	18.9	32.7	102
12-17 YEARS	33793	10713	18.7	31.7	99
WHITE	154028	50598	88.3	32.8	102
BLACK	19599	5308	9.3	27.1	84
SPANISH SPEAKING	10301	3273	5.7	31.8	99
HOME OWNED	121083	40971	71.5	33.8	105
DAILY NEWSPAPERS: READ ANY	104357	35993	62.8	34.5	107
READ ONE DAILY	79732	27582	48.2	34.6	108
READ TWO OR MORE DAILIES	24625	8411	14.7	34.2	106
SUNDAY NEWSPAPERS: READ ANY	115283	39811	69.2	34.4	107
READ ONE SUNDAY	100418	34233	59.8	34.1	106
READ TWO OR MORE SUNDAYS	14865	5379	9.4	36.2	113
HEAVY MAGAZINES - HEAVY TV	45040	16083	28.0	35.7	111
HEAVY MAGAZINES - LIGHT TV	44101	14543	25.4	33.0	103
LIGHT MAGAZINES - HEAVY TV	44104	13615	23.8	30.9	96
LIGHT MAGAZINES - LIGHT TV	45036	13058	22.8	29.0	90
QUINTILE I - OUTDOOR	35657	12884	22.5	36.1	112
QUINTILE II	35656	11758	20.5	33.0	103
QUINTILE III	35655	11644	20.3	32.7	102
QUINTILE IV	35656	10951	19.1	30.7	96
QUINTILE V	35657	10060	17.6	28.2	88
QUINTILE I - MAGAZINES	35658	12657	22.1	35.5	110
QUINTILE II	35657	12224	21.3	34.3	107
QUINTILE III	35658	11615	20.3	32.6	101
QUINTILE IV	35656	11176	19.5	31.3	98
QUINTILE V	35652	9605	16.8	26.9	84

BASE: ADULTS	TOTAL U.S. '000	ALL DIETERS A '000	B % DOWN	C % ACROSS	D INDEX
ALL ADULTS	178281	57277	100.0	32.1	100
QUINTILE I - NEWSPAPERS	35656	12679	22.1	35.6	111
QUINTILE II	35652	12646	22.1	35.5	110
QUINTILE III	35655	11885	20.8	33.3	104
QUINTILE IV	35659	10656	18.6	29.9	93
QUINTILE V	35659	9412	16.4	26.4	82
QUINTILE I - RADIO	35645	11919	20.8	33.4	104
QUINTILE II	35661	10878	19.0	30.5	95
QUINTILE III	35660	11352	19.8	31.8	99
QUINTILE IV	35656	11998	20.9	33.6	105
QUINTILE V	35659	11129	19.4	31.2	97
QUINTILE I - TV (TOTAL)	35648	11757	20.5	33.0	103
QUINTILE II	35653	12149	21.2	34.1	106
QUINTILE III	35655	11827	20.6	33.2	103
QUINTILE IV	35657	11203	19.6	31.4	98
QUINTILE V	35667	10343	18.1	29.0	90
RADIO WKDAY: 6-10:00 AM CUME	103038	33542	58.6	32.6	101
10:00 AM - 3:00 PM	66025	20852	36.4	31.6	98
3:00 PM - 7:00 PM	73616	23608	41.2	32.1	100
7:00 PM - MIDNIGHT	33775	10542	18.4	31.2	97
RADIO AVERAGE WEEKDAY CUME	140818	45258	79.0	32.1	100
RADIO AVG. WEEKEND DAY CUME	114034	37420	65.3	32.8	102
RADIO FORMATS: ADULT CONTEMP	33761	11752	20.5	34.8	108
ALBUM ORIENTED ROCK (AOR)	21313	5556	9.7	26.1	81
ALL NEWS	9016	3230	5.6	35.8	112
BLACK	2205	673	1.2	30.5	95
CLASSICAL	5626	2011	3.5	35.7	111
CHR/ROCK	32031	10019	17.5	31.3	97
COUNTRY	31604	10138	17.7	32.1	100
EASY LISTENING	10918	4354	7.6	39.9	124
GOLDEN OLDIES	11167	3284	5.7	29.4	92
MOR/NOSTALGIA	8273	3036	5.3	36.7	114
NEWS/TALK	14640	4789	8.4	32.7	102
SOFT CONTEMPORARY	4583	1614	2.8	35.2	110
URBAN CONTEMPORARY	8889	2347	4.1	26.4	82
RADIO NETWORKS: ABC CONTEMP	9683	3112	5.4	32.1	100
ABC DIRECTION	8228	2932	5.1	35.6	111
ABC ENTERTAINMENT	11398	4287	7.5	37.6	117
ABC FM	6947	2087	3.6	30.0	94
ABC INFORMATION	19042	6470	11.3	34.0	106
ABC ROCK	11398	3353	5.9	29.4	92
CBS	14089	5121	8.9	36.3	113
CONCERT MUSIC NETWORK	1992	738	1.3	36.9	115
INTERNET	52122	16589	29.0	31.8	99
KATZ RADIO GROUP	64388	20500	35.8	31.8	99
MUTUAL	16749	5753	10.0	34.3	107
NBC	13650	4453	7.8	32.6	102
NBN	2701	641	1.1	23.7	74
RADIORADIO	7828	2402	4.2	30.7	96
SATELLITE MUSIC NETWORK	6820	2143	3.7	31.4	98
SHERIDAN	2753	730	1.3	26.5	83
THE SOURCE	11470	3164	5.5	27.6	86
SUPERNET	30916	10087	17.6	32.6	102
TRANSTAR	12743	4475	7.8	35.1	109
US1	11733	3978	6.9	33.9	106
US2	7537	2690	4.7	35.7	111
WALL STREET JOURNAL NETWORK	9207	2946	5.1	32.0	100
TV WKDAY AV 1/2 HR:7-10:00AM	12769	4441	7.8	34.8	108
10:00 AM - 4:30 PM	19624	6158	10.8	31.4	98
4:30 PM - 7:30 PM	40869	13777	24.1	33.7	105
7:30 PM - 8:00 PM	63337	21438	37.4	33.8	105
8:00 PM - 11:00 PM	76991	26167	45.7	34.0	106
11:00 PM - 11:30 PM	49720	16438	28.7	33.1	103
11:30 PM - 1:00 AM	17239	5728	10.0	33.2	103
TV PRIME TIME CUME	136315	44641	77.9	32.7	102
PROGRAM-TYPES:DAYTIME DRAMAS	9698	3183	5.6	32.8	102
DAYTIME GAME SHOWS	6423	2145	3.7	33.4	104
EARLY MORNING TALK/INFO/NEWS	13789	5432	9.5	39.4	123
EARLY EVE. NETWK NEWS - M-F	26010	9883	17.3	38.0	118
FEATURE FILMS - PRIME	22330	8325	14.5	37.3	116
GENERAL DRAMA - PRIME	14633	4990	8.7	34.1	106
PVT DET/SUSP/MYST/POL.-PRIME	18335	6101	10.7	33.3	104
SITUATION COMEDIES - PRIME	18238	6346	11.1	34.8	108
CABLE TV	93824	31787	55.5	33.9	105
PAY TV	50951	16849	29.4	33.1	103
HEAVY CABLE VIEWING (15+ HR)	36246	11864	20.7	32.7	102
CABLE NETWORKS: A&E	16109	5551	9.7	34.5	107
BET (BLACK ENTERTAINMENT TV)	4067	1216	2.1	29.9	93
CNN (CABLE NEWS NETWORK)	39830	13174	23.0	33.1	103
CNN HEADLINE NEWS	27851	9577	16.7	34.4	107
CBN FAMILY CHANNEL	13483	4425	7.7	32.8	102
THE DISCOVERY CHANNEL	18948	6535	11.4	34.5	107
ESPN (ENT. & SPORTS NETWORK)	40099	12550	21.9	31.3	97
FNN (FINANCIAL NEWS NETW'K)	3158	715	1.2	22.6	70
THE LEARNING CHANNEL	2728	845	1.5	31.0	96
LIFETIME	14654	5145	9.0	35.1	109
MTV	22237	6713	11.7	30.2	94
THE NASHVILLE NETWORK	15928	5270	9.2	33.1	103
NICK AT NITE	11014	3584	6.3	32.5	101
NICKELODEON	14877	4850	8.5	32.6	101
THE TRAVEL CHANNEL	1776	538	.9	30.3	94
USA NETWORK	21973	7280	12.7	33.1	103
VH-1 (VIDEO HITS ONE)	9727	2746	4.8	28.2	88
THE WEATHER CHANNEL	27233	9362	16.3	34.4	107
WTBS	35763	11744	20.5	32.8	102

Exhibit 31–1 (continued)

BASE: ADULTS	TOTAL U.S. '000	ALL DIETERS A '000	B % DOWN	C % ACROSS	D INDEX
ALL ADULTS	178281	57277	100.0	32.1	100
AMERICAN BABY	3478	1359	2.4	39.1	122
AMERICAN HEALTH	4156	1927	3.4	46.4	144
AMERICAN WAY	999	415	.7	41.5	129
ARCHITECTURAL DIGEST	3607	1389	2.4	38.5	120
AUDUBON	1934	657	1.1	34.0	106
BABY TALK	2264	822	1.4	36.3	113
BARRON'S	1214	349	.6	28.7	89
BASSMASTER	3619	978	1.7	27.0	84
BETTER HOMES & GARDENS	31746	12307	21.5	38.8	121
BHG/LHJ COMBO (GR)	50571	20410	35.6	40.4	126
BLACK ENTERPRISE	1613	*393	.7	24.4	76
BON APPETIT	5225	2273	4.0	43.5	135
BRIDE'S MAGAZINE	3846	1470	2.6	38.2	119
BUSINESS WEEK	5665	1566	2.7	27.6	86
THE CABLE GUIDE	14547	4804	8.4	33.0	103
CAR & DRIVER	4879	1270	2.2	26.0	81
CAR CRAFT	2876	*572	1.0	19.9	62
CHANGING TIMES	4236	1772	3.1	41.8	130
CHICAGO TRIBUNE MAGAZINE	2717	960	1.7	35.3	110
COLONIAL HOMES	2029	820	1.4	40.4	126
CONDE NAST LIMITED (GR)	21590	8070	14.1	37.4	116
CONDE NAST WOMEN (GR)	29172	10815	18.9	37.1	115
CONSUMERS DIGEST	5098	2174	3.8	42.6	133
COSMOPOLITAN	12795	4861	8.5	38.0	118
COUNTRY HOME	5204	2053	3.6	39.5	123
COUNTRY JOURNAL	1536	706	1.2	46.0	143
COUNTRY LIVING	8333	3399	5.9	40.8	127
CREATIVE IDEAS FOR LIVING	2519	980	1.7	38.9	121
DELTA SKY (AIR GROUP ONE)	1311	543	.9	41.4	129
DIAMANDIS MAGAZINE NTWK (GR)	23600	5452	9.5	23.1	72
DISCOVER	4848	1513	2.6	31.2	97
DISNEY CHANNEL MAGAZINE	6289	1940	3.4	30.8	96
DUCKS UNLIMITED	2367	902	1.6	38.1	119
EAST/WEST NETWORK (GR)	5776	2456	4.3	42.5	132
EBONY	8712	2586	4.5	29.7	92
ELLE	2597	944	1.6	36.3	113
ESQUIRE	3308	1071	1.9	32.4	101
ESSENCE	3687	989	1.7	26.8	83
FAMILY CIRCLE	24628	10845	18.9	44.0	137
FAMILY HANDYMAN	3849	1291	2.3	33.5	104
FIELD & STREAM	13136	3947	6.9	30.0	94
FINANCIAL WORLD	1014	347	.6	34.2	107
FLOWER & GARDEN	3337	1456	2.5	43.6	136
FLOWER & GRDN/WORKBENCH (GR)	6099	2382	4.2	39.1	122
FOOD & WINE	2419	966	1.7	39.9	124
FORBES	4139	1492	2.6	36.0	112
FORTUNE	3961	1318	2.3	33.3	104
4 WHEEL & OFF ROAD	3450	773	1.3	22.4	70
FOUR WHEELER	2355	*550	1.0	23.4	73
GAMES	2145	896	1.6	41.8	130
GLAMOUR	9445	3400	5.9	36.0	112
GOLF DIGEST	4955	1461	2.6	29.5	92
GOLF DIGEST/TENNIS (GR)	6293	1938	3.4	30.8	96
GOLF MAGAZINE	3764	1407	2.5	37.4	116
GOOD HOUSEKEEPING	25743	10684	18.7	41.5	129
GOURMET	3412	1584	2.8	46.4	145
GQ (GENTLEMEN'S QUARTERLY)	4303	1020	1.8	23.7	74
GRIT/CAPPERS (GR)	2286	993	1.7	43.4	135
GUNS & AMMO	4751	1066	1.9	22.4	70
HARPER'S BAZAAR	2867	1097	1.9	38.3	119
HEALTH	3802	1481	2.6	39.0	121
HEARST MAN POWER (GR)	17549	4993	8.7	28.5	89
HEARST WOMAN POWER (GR)	62016	25184	44.0	40.6	126
HG (HOUSE & GARDEN)	4643	2008	3.5	43.2	135
HOME	3415	1115	1.9	32.7	102
HOME MECHANIX	3411	874	1.5	25.6	80
HOMEOWNER	1896	601	1.0	31.7	99
HOT ROD	5847	1389	2.4	23.8	74
HOUSE BEAUTIFUL	6719	2997	5.2	44.6	139
HUNTING	3572	931	1.6	26.1	81
INC.	2453	945	1.6	38.5	120
INSIDE SPORTS	4005	1040	1.8	26.0	81
JET	6755	2002	3.5	29.6	92
THE KNAPP COLLECTION (GR)	12247	4777	8.3	39.0	121
LADIES' HOME JOURNAL	18825	8103	14.1	43.0	134
LIFE	16823	5748	10.0	34.2	106
MADEMOISELLE	4591	1556	2.7	33.9	105
MCCALLS	17548	7593	13.3	43.3	135
MCGRAW-HILL NETWORK (GR)	10418	3262	5.7	31.3	97
METROPOLITAN HOME	1767	630	1.1	35.7	111
METRO-PUCK COMICS NETWORK	50576	17255	30.1	34.1	106
MODERN BRIDE	2616	897	1.6	34.3	107
MODERN MATURITY	32797	13481	23.5	41.1	128

BASE: ADULTS	TOTAL U.S. '000	ALL DIETERS A '000	B % DOWN	C % ACROSS	D INDEX
ALL ADULTS	178281	57277	100.0	32.1	100
MODERN PHOTOGRAPHY	2614	781	1.4	29.9	93
MONEY	7523	2899	5.1	38.5	120
MOTHER EARTH NEWS	2658	859	1.5	32.3	101
MOTOR TREND	4338	1232	2.2	28.4	88
MS.	1950	865	1.5	44.4	138
MUSCLE & FITNESS	4263	1286	2.2	30.2	94
NATIONAL ENQUIRER	19248	6431	11.2	33.4	104
NATIONAL GEOGRAPHIC	30240	10980	19.2	36.3	113
NATIONAL GEOGRAPHIC TRAVELER	3379	1063	1.9	31.5	98
NATURAL HISTORY	1482	413	.7	27.9	87
NEWSWEEK	19792	6968	12.2	35.2	110
NEW WOMAN	3156	1535	2.7	48.6	151
NEW YORK MAGAZINE	1359	407	.7	29.9	93
NEW YORK TIMES (DAILY)	2634	878	1.5	33.3	104
NEW YORK TIMES MAGAZINE	3613	1241	2.2	34.3	107
THE NEW YORKER	2569	964	1.7	37.5	117
OMNI	4320	1234	2.2	28.6	89
1,001 HOME IDEAS	5142	1896	3.3	36.9	115
ORGANIC GARDENING	3775	1355	2.4	35.9	112
OUTDOOR LIFE	9364	2840	5.0	30.3	94
PARADE	69610	24087	42.0	34.6	108
PARENTS' MAGAZINE	9586	3231	5.6	33.7	105
PC MAGAZINE	2446	683	1.2	27.9	87
PC WORLD	2487	876	1.5	35.2	110
PENTHOUSE	5323	1335	2.3	25.1	78
PENTON EXECUTIVE NETWK (GR)	7452	2074	3.6	27.8	87
PEOPLE	29380	10765	18.8	36.6	114
PERSONAL COMPUTING	1966	635	1.1	32.3	101
PERSONAL MEDIA GROUP (GR)	11187	4392	7.7	39.3	122
PETERSEN MAGAZINE GROUP (GR)	37383	9053	15.8	24.2	75
PLAYBOY	11565	3210	5.6	27.8	86
POPULAR HOT RODDING	3409	666	1.2	19.5	61
POPULAR MECHANICS	8222	2274	4.0	27.7	86
POPULAR SCIENCE	6715	2000	3.5	29.8	93
PRACTICAL HOMEOWNER	1441	480	.8	33.3	104
PREVENTION	7606	3536	6.2	46.5	145
PSYCHOLOGY TODAY	4373	1606	2.8	36.7	114
READER'S DIGEST	48561	17603	30.7	36.2	113
REDBOOK	12278	5143	9.0	41.9	130
ROAD & TRACK	4123	930	1.6	22.6	70
RODALE ACTIVE SPORTS (GR)	4003	1324	2.3	33.1	103
ROLLING STONE	7180	1972	3.4	27.5	85
RUNNER'S WORLD	1351	427	.7	31.6	98
SATURDAY EVENING POST	4314	1764	3.1	40.9	127
SCIENTIFIC AMERICAN	2211	600	1.0	27.1	84
SELF	3689	1675	2.9	45.4	141
SESAME STREET MAGAZINE	4979	1967	3.4	39.5	123
SEVENTEEN	6070	2009	3.5	33.1	103
SHAPE	2564	1145	2.0	44.7	139
SMITHSONIAN	9076	3458	6.0	38.1	119
SOAP OPERA DIGEST	5396	2231	3.9	41.3	129
SOUTHERN LIVING	10413	4679	8.2	44.9	140
SPORT	4774	1277	2.2	26.7	83
THE SPORTING NEWS	3441	910	1.6	26.4	82
SPORTS AFIELD	6019	1648	2.9	27.4	85
SPORTS ILLUSTRATED	19734	5486	9.6	27.8	87
STAR	9657	3244	5.7	33.6	105
SUNDAY MAG/NET	38810	12782	22.3	32.9	103
SUNSET	4948	1606	2.8	32.5	101
TENNIS	1338	475	.8	35.5	110
TIME	23701	8145	14.2	34.4	107
TOWN & COUNTRY	2076	848	1.5	40.8	127
TRAILER LIFE/MOTOR HOME (GR)	2097	745	1.3	35.5	111
TRAVEL & LEISURE	3023	1314	2.3	43.5	135
TRUE STORY	5974	2378	4.1	39.8	124
TV GUIDE	46336	15580	27.2	33.6	105
U.S. AIR MAGAZINE	1810	643	1.1	35.5	111
U.S. NEWS & WORLD REPORT	13306	4401	7.7	33.1	103
US	5083	1784	3.1	35.1	109
USA TODAY	3987	1508	2.6	37.8	118
USA WEEKEND	25947	9029	15.8	34.8	108
VANITY FAIR	1631	744	1.3	45.6	142
VOGUE	7601	2714	4.7	35.7	111
WALL STREET JOURNAL	3882	1294	2.3	33.3	104
WEIGHT WATCHERS	4354	2711	4.7	62.3	194
WOMAN	2362	976	1.7	41.3	129
WOMAN'S DAY	21978	9313	16.3	42.4	132
WOMAN'S WORLD	5678	2741	4.8	48.3	150
THE WORKBASKET	3319	1561	2.7	47.0	146
WORKBENCH	2762	926	1.6	33.5	104
WORKING MOTHER	2535	1108	1.9	43.7	136
WORKING WOMAN	3247	1542	2.7	47.5	148
YANKEE	3185	1001	1.7	31.4	98

Problem

Based on the foregoing information, you are to develop a complete written media plan following the outline contained in the media plan checklist in Assignment 28. You may recommend any media class/vehicle for which you have cost information taken from the appendix, Assignment 32 (spot TV), or Assignment 29 (Grocery Trade Magazines). Specifically, do the following :

1. Spell out the media objectives (refer to Assignment 26).
2. State the media strategies to be followed (refer to Assignments 27 and 29).
3. List media selections and rationales including audience data, reach/frequency, CPM, etc.
4. Provide a flowchart showing specific media scheduling. A blank flowchart has been included as Exhibit 31–2.
5. Include a budget recap showing cost analysis of the plan.

Exhibit 31–2 Advertising Flowchart

Month	Week	Monthly REACH	Monthly FREQUENCY	GRPs	Dollars per month	Budget monthly (%)
Jan.	1 2 3 4					
Feb.	1 2 3 4					
Mar.	1 2 3 4 5					
Apr.	1 2 3 4					
May	1 2 3 4					
June	1 2 3 4 5					
July	1 2 3 4					
Aug.	1 2 3 4					
Sept.	1 2 3 4 5					
Oct.	1 2 3 4					
Nov.	1 2 3 4					
Dec.	1 2 3 4 5					
Total						

Assignment 32

Spot TV Planning

Objective: To help you understand the special problem of planning for spot television. In this assignment you will set market weights and plan for the allocation of a budget to those markets.

Discussion

In a previous assignment you selected markets for added advertising weight. In that assignment, however, no attempt was made to determine what advertising weight levels would be used or what the budget per market would be.

Market weighting can be accomplished in a number of ways. The number of gross rating points run each week can be varied. The number of weeks the schedule runs can be varied. The length of commercials (60 or 30 seconds) can be varied. Of course, combinations of the foregoing methods can be used.

Budgeting by market is done in several ways; however, a common method is to set the total budget for the spot buy and then apportion it among the markets based on desired gross rating point levels and the cost per rating point in each market. If necessary, GRP levels will be adjusted to fit budget constraints, or length of schedules might have to be altered.

Another concern in spot market planning is determining how much weight is needed or deserved in each market. Obviously, much depends on the reason for providing extra weight. If the added weight is to make up for deficiencies in network ratings, the task is relatively easy—just add enough spot weight to bring the market up to the national average. However, the weighting often is based on personal judgment. Take, for example, a case involving markets selected because of sales strength and markets selected because of sales potential. The planner must decide whether to treat them equally or to give some markets more weight than others, and how much. Often the marketing plan will provide some direction to the planner regarding the weight for markets.

In order to establish budgets for planning purposes, media planners often use estimated costs per rating point that have been developed for each daypart in each television market. The larger advertising agencies and advertisers developed these estimates based on their actual buying experience in each market. Some of the station representative firms also provide this information. Recently, several companies have been organized to develop such cost-per-point information, and they make it available to advertisers and agencies for a monthly fee.

One such company is Spot Quotations and Data, Inc. It provides not only estimated costs per household rating point, but also estimated costs per rating point for specific demographic groups, such as women aged 25–54. Spot Quotations and Data (SQAD) reports include estimated future costs by quarter. The reports are updated on a monthly basis.

The data in Exhibit 32–1 are from a SQAD report. It lists cost per household rating point in the top 100 ADIs. The estimates are for 30-second commercials and are based on actual buying experiences as reported by cooperating advertising agencies.

Problems

Suppose you have been asked to determine spot market weights and budgets for the following markets.

	Annual sales volume (000)
Philadelphia	$895
Boston	807
Detroit	786
Atlanta	743
Seattle–Tacoma	645
Tampa–St. Petersburg	607
Miami	592
Nashville	578
Kansas City	553

The following guidelines have been included in the media plan:

a. Minimum weight in any market is to be 50 GRPs a week.
b. Markets with annual sales of $700,000 or more are to receive 50 percent more GRPs than the other markets on the list.
c. Thirty-second commercials are to be used for all spots.
d. The heavy-up period is for 13 weeks. The schedule, however, may be flighted if necessary for budgetary reasons. Nevertheless, a major goal of this plan is to have good continuity throughout the 13-week period. *All markets should receive the same number of weeks, and the goal is to maximize the number of weeks.*
e. Market-by-market budgeting is to be based on the GRP levels assigned to each market and at the cost per point shown in Exhibit 32–1.
f. The total budget for this project is $950,000. You are not to exceed this figure.

---

1. Assume that the purpose of the spot TV heavy-up is to provide added reach to a daytime network TV plan and that the preferred daypart for spot is early fringe. Your assignment is to decide the GRP weight for each market, establish the number of weeks the schedule is to run, and develop market-by-market budgets.

   To assist you in getting started, here is a method used by many media planners. First, establish the cost per market for one GRP in the selected daypart. Next, establish GRP levels for each market and figure the

Exhibit 32–1 Cost per Household Rating Point: 30-Second Commercials (Spot TV)

QuickView : May, 1995 (NSI TV DMA)
Qtr/Yr : 2nd Qtr, 1995
Level : Average
Target : Tv Households
Group : Top 100 DMA's
Data : CPP

Market	EM	DA	EF	EN	PA	PR	LN	LF
NEW YORK	229	230	365	512	570	1415	783	534
LOS ANGELES	250	325	405	591	629	1260	652	444
CHICAGO	127	136	175	229	357	503	484	222
PHILADELPHIA	121	90	150	179	236	544	271	182
SAN FRANCISCO-OAK-SAN JOS	123	133	257	342	366	594	351	218
BOSTON	128	102	183	209	285	593	388	223
WASHINGTON, DC	95	80	144	164	242	495	302	194
DALLAS-FT. WORTH	54	73	94	204	198	379	378	169
DETROIT	56	62	92	108	121	289	210	118
ATLANTA	52	56	92	103	130	334	207	111
HOUSTON	62	74	87	145	164	324	287	132
SEATTLE-TACOMA	71	61	114	153	144	330	177	138
CLEVELAND	41	57	79	107	138	223	172	124
MINNEAPOLIS-ST. PAUL	52	58	85	144	138	210	224	156
TAMPA-ST. PETE.-SARASOTA	55	56	85	137	140	264	174	94
MIAMI-FT. LAUDERDALE	59	88	135	159	208	404	239	122
PITTSBURGH	32	43	68	73	86	171	122	80
DENVER	44	56	87	89	120	181	148	121
PHOENIX	61	59	82	163	174	227	214	153
ST. LOUIS	25	35	54	87	102	143	165	93
SACRAMENTO-STKN-MODESTO	36	48	85	145	118	219	119	70
ORLANDO-DAYTONA BCH-MELBR	58	45	75	94	114	198	134	78
BALTIMORE	34	45	85	116	124	259	149	106
INDIANAPOLIS	23	34	56	76	81	167	93	43
PORTLAND, OR	43	35	71	96	87	188	87	69
HARTFORD-NEW HAVEN	43	38	74	91	110	180	146	86
SAN DIEGO	56	76	118	163	182	233	199	114
CHARLOTTE	21	27	50	60	68	119	63	37
MILWAUKEE	28	36	50	93	76	122	138	74
CINCINNATI	30	29	46	65	64	150	87	58
KANSAS CITY	31	37	50	75	95	142	98	84
RALEIGH-DURHAM	22	29	53	76	67	138	101	76
NASHVILLE	32	33	46	80	90	112	113	85
COLUMBUS, OH	46	47	68	93	93	176	121	99
GREENVILLE-SPART-ASHEVILL	22	19	35	59	50	82	79	46
BUFFALO	27	30	54	47	56	124	69	60
SALT LAKE CITY	23	38	77	80	85	126	124	118
GRAND RAPIDS-KALMZOO-B.CR	24	26	50	59	48	98	75	48
SAN ANTONIO	24	28	39	66	67	92	110	44
NORFOLK-PORTSMTH-NEWPT NW	28	22	50	61	71	101	63	53
NEW ORLEANS	19	23	26	51	57	80	82	46
MEMPHIS	22	23	25	40	48	72	63	43
OKLAHOMA CITY	21	26	32	43	56	77	66	49
HARRISBURG-LNCSTR-LEB-YOR	26	29	57	75	101	117	86	53
WEST PALM BEACH-FT. PIERC	37	43	61	78	93	116	74	49
PROVIDENCE-NEW BEDFORD	23	22	45	51	62	98	66	50
WILKES BARRE-SCRANTON	19	18	28	39	39	62	44	32
GREENSBORO-H.POINT-W.SALE	12	15	34	45	33	96	54	38
ALBUQUERQUE-SANTA FE	26	30	43	68	62	83	63	44
LOUISVILLE	20	24	37	42	45	84	53	43
BIRMINGHAM	24	26	32	40	51	81	67	53
ALBANY-SCHENECTADY-TROY	26	24	36	47	45	82	66	43
DAYTON	20	26	39	43	47	105	72	55
RICHMOND-PETERSBURG	16	18	29	43	45	80	59	35
JACKSONVILLE, BRUNSWICK	30	31	45	73	65	88	71	49
CHARLESTON-HUNTINGTON	12	13	25	34	31	56	39	31
FRESNO-VISALIA	17	19	32	52	46	76	34	28
LITTLE ROCK-PINE BLUFF	17	18	20	33	39	49	62	37
TULSA	23	21	28	41	42	58	67	44
FLINT-SAGINAW-BAY CITY	15	17	21	33	24	52	39	26
MOBILE-PENSACOLA	17	22	22	35	40	58	44	33
WICHITA-HUTCHINSON PLUS	14	14	21	34	33	41	46	26
KNOXVILLE	18	17	27	41	36	61	59	41
TOLEDO	15	19	31	37	31	52	48	36

Exhibit 32–1 (continued)

Market	EM	DA	EF	EN	PA	PR	LN	LF
AUSTIN	22	26	35	52	55	65	69	64
ROANOKE-LYNCHBURG	12	14	31	35	36	68	52	37
SYRACUSE	16	19	28	30	36	59	38	36
LEXINGTON	13	13	18	31	23	54	40	28
HONOLULU	11	14	20	37	43	65	52	29
GREEN BAY-APPLETON	12	12	18	23	31	37	37	29
ROCHESTER	18	21	25	38	45	67	55	34
LAS VEGAS	29	34	48	56	57	93	77	48
DES MOINES-AMES	8	13	14	22	27	37	30	26
OMAHA	13	16	19	29	38	46	44	43
SPOKANE	19	25	34	42	39	63	54	43
SHREVEPORT	10	11	14	23	26	34	30	21
PADUCAH-C.GIRARDEAU-HARRB	10	9	12	19	17	28	28	14
CHAMPAIGN-SPRNGFLD-DECATU	15	14	13	24	27	46	35	32
PORTLAND-AUBURN	15	24	32	52	50	89	63	46
SPRINGFIELD, MO	10	11	11	23	20	30	32	21
TUCSON(NOGALES)	20	16	23	33	41	54	42	42
CHATTANOOGA	13	12	19	24	24	44	35	26
HUNTSVILLE-DECATUR-FLORNC	12	14	15	24	30	45	45	33
CEDAR RAPIDS-WATERLOO-DUB	9	13	17	33	29	41	36	37
MADISON	14	18	14	24	31	43	46	33
SOUTH BEND-ELKHART	9	14	17	33	29	37	32	24
COLUMBIA, SC	14	19	17	28	26	47	38	24
DAVENPRT-ROCK ISLND-MOLIN	8	9	10	25	24	31	38	34
FT. MYERS-NAPLES	22	24	23	35	30	47	39	29
JACKSON, MS	8	11	15	21	21	31	30	16
JOHNSTOWN-ALTOONA	8	10	14	23	19	37	27	19
BURLINGTON-PLATTSBURGH	13	18	27	35	33	63	48	49
TRI-CITIES, TN-VA	10	11	16	28	22	33	35	26
YOUNGSTOWN	11	15	18	28	20	41	31	23
EVANSVILLE	9	8	13	18	22	32	30	17
BATON ROUGE	11	13	15	21	27	35	36	29
COLORADO SPRINGS-PUEBLO	12	14	16	22	22	31	24	26
WACO-TEMPLE	11	14	15	23	21	28	34	24
SPRINGFIELD-HOLYOKE, MA	13	17	22	36	29	73	33	37
EL PASO	11	13	17	23	25	29	27	23
Top 50 Markets	2589	2849	4453	6125	6890	12794	8767	5533
Top 100 Markets	3348	3693	5576	7784	8560	15436	10982	7182

Key to dayparts:*

EM= Early morning (6:30–9:00 a.m.)
DA = Daytime (10:00 a.m.–4:30 p.m.)
EF = Early fringe (4:30–6:00 p.m.)
EN = Early news (6:00–7:00 p.m.)
PA = Prime time access (7:00–8:00 p.m.)
PR = Prime time (8:00–11:00 p.m.)
LN = Late news (11:00–11:30 p.m.)
LF = Late fringe (11:30 p.m.–1:00 a.m.)

*Times approximate based on EST.

one-week cost in each market. Total the one-week cost in each market and divide this total into the budget to determine the number of weeks you can afford. If necessary, adjust GRP levels to provide more or fewer weeks of advertising.

Note: In establishing GRP levels you should use multiples of five (e.g., 50, 55, 60, 65). Do not use GRP goals such as 57, 63, etc. Remember you are setting goals for the buyer, not exact GRP levels.

List on a separate sheet the markets, weekly GRP level for each, number of weeks scheduled (include specific flights and hiatus periods, if used), the budget for each market, and the total budget.

2. Assume that a decision has been made to schedule the spots in prime time access (PA) (instead of fringe). How would you adjust the GRP levels and number of weeks? List the markets, weekly GRP level for each, number of weeks scheduled (include specific flights and hiatus periods, if used), the budget for each market, and the total budget.

Assignment 33

Allocating an Advertising Budget to Spot TV Markets

Objective: To understand the concept of allocating dollars needed for spot television by determining the most overdelivered market from network television usage.

Discussion

One weakness of using network television is that it rarely delivers rating points in proportion to the value of the sales in any given market. The reason audiences tune in to network television is that they like certain programs. They tend not to watch programs they dislike. But their program preferences have little to do with sales in markets where they live.

Therefore, network television is often used as an umbrella to achieve national coverage. Spot television is used to achieve heavier weights in underdelivered markets. This can be called an *adjustment strategy*. It is used by most ad agency media departments, in many different formats. The format used here simply explains the concept, so that anyone who sees any other format can understand the underlying concept.

Also, most agencies have these techniques done by computer. The Interactive Media Service Company (IMS, a media computer company) also has a computer program called "Pal" that does the same thing, but again in a somewhat different style.

Let us simulate a marketing situation in which we want to adjust network dollars to determine how much to spend in five spot television markets. What kind of adjustment needs to be made?

The first step is to determine sales in each of the five markets and then allocate the budget to each market. (Although sales percentages were used here, BDIs are often preferred because they indicate sales potential.) Dollars are allocated to markets proportionally, based on sales. Therefore, if a market does 25 percent of the business, it should get 25 percent of the advertising budget.

Market	Total sales	Allocation of $1 million budget
A	20%	$ 200,000
B	15	150,000
C	30	300,000
D	25	250,000
E	10	100,000
	100%	$1,000,000

The next step is to compare sales per market with network television delivery. This requires that the number of GRPs delivered into each market be known for every program. If a company bought three network television programs, then the sum of GRPs for all programs in each market should be known, and that sum would then be converted to a percentage of the total GRPs for all markets. The percentages of delivery shown in the following chart have been gathered as described earlier.

Market	Total sales	Network delivery
A	20%	10%
B	15	25
C	30	15
D	25	30
E	10	20
	100%	100%

It is obvious that some markets are overdelivered (meaning that they get too much network television advertising), and others are underdelivered. Market A, for example, does 20 percent of the business but gets only 10 percent of network delivery. On the other hand, market D does 25 percent of the business but gets more network TV than it needs. The solution is to adjust the differences.

The first step in making adjustments is to divide each network delivery percentage by sales to get an index of the two:

$$\text{Index} = \frac{\text{Network delivery}}{\text{Sales percentages}}$$

Here are the indices that resulted:

Market	Index
A	50
B	167
C	50
D	120
E	200

The market most overdelivered, therefore, is E.

Now we want to determine what the total budget for each market would be if it were based on the most overdelivered market (E). One simply divides the budget for E by the network delivery percentage, or .20:

$$\frac{100{,}000}{.20} = 500{,}000$$

If we used the relationship of network delivery to budget in E, then the base is $500,000 (or $100,000 ÷ .20). Now we know how much to spend in network ($500,000 of the $1 million) and how much to spend in spot TV (the other $500,000).

We multiply each delivery percentage by the total network budget to find what the new allocation dollars should be in each individual market:

Market	Network delivery					Adjusted network budget
A	10%	.10	×	$500,000	=	$ 50,000
B	25	.25	×	500,000	=	125,000
C	15	.15	×	500,000	=	75,000
D	30	.30	×	500,000	=	150,000
E	20	.20	×	500,000	=	100,000
	100%					$500,000

Now, simply subtract the adjusted network budget from the original prorata budget to find how much to spend in spot TV.

Market	Original budget	Adjusted network budget	New spot TV budget
A	$ 200,000	$ 50,000	$150,000
B	150,000	125,000	25,000
C	300,000	75,000	225,000
D	250,000	150,000	100,000
E	100,000	100,000	0
	$1,000,000	$500,000	$500,000

Note that the key point about this procedure is that market E gets no spot TV dollars because network overdelivered it (index 200). Other markets get some dollars for spot TV. It is also important to note that the technique does not end here. Although the dollar amounts have been determined by a computer, adjustments still have to be made, because some of these markets will cost more or less than the amounts shown here. Some might be so overpriced that they do not represent a good buy.

Problem

Here is a list of six markets for which sales, delivery data, and a total budget have been shown. Using the technique explained earlier, determine how much should be spent for adjusted network and spot TV in each market, and as a total amount. Show your work.

Market	Sales	Network delivery	Pro-rata budget	Index of delivery	Adjusted network budget	New spot TV budget
A	15%	19%				
B	10	7				
C	30	23				
D	15	11				
E	20	24				
F	10	16				
	100%	100%	$2,500,000			

Assignment 34

Spot TV Buying Problem

Objective: To help you understand the use of TV station availabilities in making a spot television buy. The media planner usually develops the goals and budgets for the buy. It is important to understand how buys are executed. This assignment will also require you to calculate CPMs, allocate a budget, and buy to specified goals.

Discussion

In a media plan calling for the use of spot television, the planner establishes the markets, budget per market, target audience, and GRP weights to be used. Once approved, the plan must be executed by the television buyer. This requires the buyer to select the actual spots to be purchased from among those that are available on the stations in the market.

The buyer contacts the stations, usually through their representatives, and asks for spot availabilities (*avails*, in the jargon of the industry) in the dayparts that are to be purchased. The buyer also specifies when the buy is to run, the target audience, and any specific audience information that will be of help in selecting the best spots. The station representative submits the avails along with the audience data and costs.

In actual practice the costs submitted are somewhat negotiable, and the buyer and rep will haggle over the actual price to be charged for each spot. Often the buy is for a time in which no audience measurements are made, and the buyer must estimate what the programs will actually deliver in the season being purchased. Estimates of program audience are based on trends established for the program and/or time period, HUT levels by season, experience, and judgment.

Refer to *Advertising Media Planning*, 5th ed., by Sissors and Bumba, Chapter 14.

Problem

As a buyer, you are to execute a spot TV buy in the Columbia, South Carolina, market. The buying specifications for this buy are as follows:

1. The product is a laundry detergent purchased by women. All women purchase the product, but the primary target audience is women aged 25–54.

2. Sixty GRPs/week are to be purchased with 30 in daytime and 30 in fringe time.
3. Reach is an important consideration. A spread throughout the dayparts is desirable. Although two spots per week may be purchased in a program that airs Monday through Friday, no more than one spot per week should be purchased in a program that airs once a week.
4. Cost efficiency is important, but it is equally important to buy to the GRP goal and to reach as many target audience women as possible within the budget limitations.
5. Weekly budget for the market is $800.

Based on the foregoing specifications, you have asked the station reps to submit avails for the four stations in the Columbia market. These avails are listed in Exhibit 34–1. You are to review these avails, calculate CPM for your target audience for each program, and list the spots you would buy based on the buying specifications. For purposes of this assignment, assume that the costs given are the lowest you could negotiate and that the audience data is an acceptable estimate for the period of the buy.

Station	Day	Time	Program	DMA rating	Total women (000)	Women aged 25–54 (000)	Cost	CPM women 25–54

Complete the following information for your buy:
Number of stations used: ______________ Total GRPs/week: ______________
Daytime GRPs/week: ______________ Fringe GRPs/week: ______________
Total women impressions: ______________
Women 25–54 impressions: ______________
CPM women 25–54 impressions: ______________ Weekly cost: ______________

Exhibit 34–1 Spot TV Availabilities (Columbia, SC)

Station/Net	Day	Time	Program	Rating (%)	Homes (000)	Total women (000)	Women 25–54 (000)	Cost
WIS–TV/NBC	M–F	9–11A	Live with Regis and Kathy Lee	8%	23	19	10	$ 70
WIS–TV/NBC	M–F	11A–12Noon	One on One/Concentration	6	18	15	7	70
WIS–TV/NBC	M–F	1–4P	NBC Rotation (Soaps)	17	49	51	26	225
WIS–TV/NBC	M–F	530–6P	Jeopardy	17	49	41	14	200
WIS–TV/NBC	Sat.	1130P–100A	Saturday Night Live	8	23	16	12	125
WIS–TV/NBC	Sun.	6–630P	Six O'Clock Report	18	52	37	13	250
WLTX–TV/CBS	M–F	9–10A	Donahue	6	17	16	10	90
WLTX–TV/CBS	M–F	10–11A	Mama's Family/Gimme A Break	5	14	14	7	60
WLTX–TV/CBS	M–F	11A–1P	Midday Rotation	7	20	17	9	100
WLTX–TV/CBS	M–F	1130P–12Mid	Sanford and Son	9	26	24	16	250
WLTX–TV/CBS	M–F	12–1A	CBS Late Nite	3	9	5	3	50
WOLO–TV/ABC	M–F	1–4P	Day Rotation (Soaps)	9	26	24	18	130
WOLO–TV/ABC	M–F	4–5P	Oprah Winfrey	8	23	23	9	105
WOLO–TV/ABC	M–F	7–730P	Cheers	12	35	25	18	310
WOLO–TV/ABC	M–F	11–1130P	News	11	32	20	14	150
WACH–TV/FOX	M–F	1–2P	Sally Jesse Raphael	5	14	15	10	80
WACH–TV/FOX	M–F	2–230P	The People's Court	4	12	10	6	50
WACH–TV/FOX	M–F	6–630P	Full House	7	20	17	7	80
WACH–TV/FOX	M–F	1030P–12Mid	Arsenio Hall	7	20	15	8	80

Assignment 35

Developing a Regional Media Plan

Objective: To present a case for which you will develop a complete media plan for a small regional advertiser, using your understanding of all of the principles discussed in this workbook and the course.

Discussion

Developing a media plan for a regional client is a bit different from developing a plan for a large national client. Although the plans contain the same types of information, the media choices are limited for a regional advertiser. Network television and radio are not appropriate, and national magazines might not have regional editions that precisely fit the marketing territory of the client. Also, regional advertisers have considerably smaller budgets to work with. You will develop media plan recommendations within these constraints.

Background

The Charleston Tea Plantation, Charleston, South Carolina, is a relatively new company, which grows and markets American Classic Tea—the only tea grown in the United States. The package proudly states:

> Over 100 years ago, tea planters brought their finest ancestral tea bushes from China, India, and Ceylon to the verdant Lowcountry of South Carolina.
>
> Now the direct descendants of those very plants have been lovingly restored to their former grandeur at Charleston Tea Plantation—a lush, subtropical tea farm nestled on a balmy barrier island near the historic, old city.
>
> It is within this context of great natural beauty, legendary Charleston civility, and colonial pride that we bring you **AMERICAN CLASSIC—the only tea grown in America.** A noble cup—proud of its exotic past and native heritage—ready to claim its rightful place as one of the world's great teas.

The brand was introduced a year ago and has built distribution with food stores in North and South Carolina. Little advertising has been done in support of the brand.

Product. The company produces regular tea that is sold in tea bag form in several different package sizes. They do not market instant, decaffeinated, flavored, or herbal versions of the product.

Distribution. American Classic Tea is currently distributed through grocery stores in North and South Carolina. The client wants to mount an advertising campaign designed to increase consumer awareness (and ultimately usage) of the product in this region. Grocery store distribution is adequate to support a consumer advertising program. There are no immediate plans to expand distribution, but that certainly is a future possibility once brand sales are firmly established in the present distribution area.

Competition. American Classic Tea competes against all the imported teas normally found in food stores. There are no specific sales or share data for North and South Carolina. Nationally, the major competitors are Lipton with 44 percent, Tetley with 10 percent, and Luzianne with 6 percent of users. Luzianne is marketed primarily in the South, so it is a stronger competitor than its 6 percent national share of users indicates.

In terms of reported advertising spending, Lipton is the leader, spending in excess of $20 million annually in magazines, network television, spot television, and spot radio. Lipton spot markets in North and South Carolina include Charleston (SC), Greensboro (NC), Greenville (SC), and Raleigh (NC). Lipton's spot dollars are spent primarily in the second and third quarters. Tetley spends $4.7 million, primarily in magazines, with a small amount ($787,000) in spot TV. Tetley's spot TV markets do not include any in North or South Carolina. Luzianne spends about $3.7 million annually, almost all of which is in spot television concentrated in the second and third quarters. Luzianne spot markets include Charlotte (NC), Charleston (SC), Columbia (SC), and Raleigh (NC).

Seasonality. There is relatively little seasonality of tea consumption in the South, where iced tea is considered a year-round drink. However, bimonthly sales indices do show a slight increase in consumption during the summer months.

Period	Index
January–February	94
March–April	96
May–June	105
July–August	110
September–October	101
November–December	94

Regionality. There is little regionality in the two-state region where American Classic Tea is marketed. Distribution is adequate throughout both states, although it tends to be concentrated in the metropolitan markets of the ADIs, which are listed here:

ADI	TV HH (000)	Percentage of Total*
Charlotte, NC	775	24.6%
Raleigh–Durham, NC	754	24.0
Greenville–Spartanburg, SC; Asheville, NC	669	21.3
Greensboro–Winston Salem, NC	538	17.1
Columbia, SC	296	9.4
Charleston,SC	115	3.6
	3,147	100.0%

*Based on North and South Carolina TV homes.

User profile. Demographically, there are not many differences among all users of regular tea. However, there is a slight tendency for regular tea users to be older (35+) and to live in MSA suburban areas of A and B counties. Regular tea usage is above average (index 111) in the Southeast. When heavy users of tea (four or more cups per day) are profiled, some stronger differences emerge. Heavy tea users tend to be aged 35–54, married with families of three or more, and living in B and D counties in the Southeast. In fact, the Southeast has the highest user index (162) among heavy users. This is a plus for American Classic Tea, which is marketed only in two southeastern states.

Creative/promotion. Creative for the brand will stress the southern background and American heritage of this tea grown in Charleston. This theme is adaptable to both print and broadcast executions. Promotion plans call for extensive sampling of the product in supermarkets. The client has also indicated a desire to distribute coupons early in the advertising program.

Budget. The "working media" budget for American Classic Tea is $300,000. This budget is for media only and does not have to include costs for production or promotion. Production and promotion costs will be covered in another budget.

Marketing Objectives

1. Support the brand in markets throughout the two-state marketing area.
2. Provide a strong kick-off to the two-state marketing effort for the brand.
3. Build a strong consumer franchise for the brand.
4. Promote retail stocking and trade support of the brand.

Advertising/Communications Objectives

1. Build consumer awareness of the brand with a goal of 40 percent unaided recall and 60 percent total recall by the end of the introductory period.
2. Promote consumer trial of the brand.
3. Create trade awareness of and encourage trade support for the brand.

Available media vehicles. Not all media vehicles are available. For this project, two regional editions of consumer magazines, spot radio, spot television, and newspapers in the key ADI markets may be used. Ad units available and costs are shown in Table 35–1.

Table 35–1 Media Vehicles

Magazines (regional edition)	Circulation	Cost of four-color units: Page	Half page	One-third page
Better Homes & Gardens (North and South Carolina)	312,000	$16,850	$9,779	N/A
Southern Living (North and South Carolina)	335,000	$23,150	$13,080	$9,260

Newspapers*	Circulation	Cost per inch (black-and-white)
Charlotte Observer	236,579	$126.98
Raleigh News–Observer	148,618	76.48
Durham Herald–Sun	53,842	40.96
Fayetteville Observer–Times	70,002	36.22
Greenville News–Piedmont	117,798	89.59
Asheville Citizen–Times	68,454	54.76
Spartanburg Herald–Journal	61,450	36.96
Greensboro News–Record	97,100	58.20
Winston Salem Journal	89,893	50.15
Columbia State	133,917	77.86
Charleston Post–Courier	111,236	69.27

*Listing includes all newspapers with 50,000 or greater circulation in each ADI.

	Cost per rating point			
Spot TV ADI	Day	News (average)	Prime	Fringe (average)
Charlotte	25	60	117	42
Raleigh–Durham	26	85	135	63
Greenville–Spartanburg–Asheville	17	67	80	39
Greensboro–Winston Salem	14	48	94	35
Columbia	18	32	46	20
Charleston	12	22	39	16

	Cost per rating point	
Spot radio metro markets	AM/PM drive time	10 a.m.–3 p.m.
Charlotte	55	44
Greensboro	29	24
Raleigh	45	37
Greenville–Spartanburg–Asheville	31	26
Columbia	25	21
Charleston	24	20
Fayetteville	19	14

Problem

Based on the foregoing information, you will develop a complete written media plan following the outline contained in the media plan checklist in Assignment 28. You may select only those media alternatives listed in Table 35–1 of this assignment. Specifically, you are to:

1. Spell out the media objectives (refer to Assignment 26).
2. State the media strategies to be followed (refer to Assignments 27 and 29).
3. List media selections and rationales.
4. Provide a flowchart showing specific media scheduling. Keep in mind that you are to decide when the advertising launch should be scheduled. Also indicate monthly reach and frequency levels as well as monthly budget levels on the flowchart. A blank flowchart has been included as Exhibit 35–1.
5. Include a budget recap showing cost analysis of the plan. Show a breakdown of costs by market as well as a breakdown of the total budget.

Exhibit 35–1 Advertising Flowchart

	Jan.				Feb.				Mar.					Apr.				May				June					July				Aug.				Sept.					Oct.				Nov.				Dec.					Total
Week	1	2	3	4	1	2	3	4	1	2	3	4	5	1	2	3	4	1	2	3	4	1	2	3	4	5	1	2	3	4	1	2	3	4	1	2	3	4	5	1	2	3	4	1	2	3	4	1	2	3	4	5	
Monthly REACH																																																					
Monthly FREQUENCY																																																						
GRPs																																																						
Dollars per month																																																						
Budget monthly (%)																																																						

Assignment 36

Evaluating a Media Plan

Objective: To help you think about how to evaluate a media plan. Some guidelines for beginning planners are presented in the form of a rating scale.

Discussion

How shall we evaluate a media plan? Shall we evaluate it on the basis of adequacy in following all of the rules and principles of media planning as agreed upon by most media experts? That certainly is one option. However, we also might evaluate it on the basis of effectiveness. Effectiveness is the degree to which media contributes optimally to the success of marketing and advertising objectives. There might also be other methods of evaluating media plans, but these two are most often used.

The concept that appeals to many media experts is to find a way to measure a medium's contribution to sales. Such a way represents the "ideal" means of evaluation. Unfortunately, the ideal has not been reached, because there are so many variables that affect the success of marketing and advertising campaigns that it is difficult to parse out, with precision, a media vehicle's contribution to it. To some extent, the effective reach/effective frequency concepts discussed earlier are attempts at answering the question of effectiveness. But the weaknesses of these methods overshadow their strengths, and, at present, only a limited number of media planners are using them for evaluation purposes.

In the meantime, students and beginners who plan media need a practical and valid method of evaluating a media plan. This assignment presents a measuring instrument, which, if applied carefully, can serve the purpose.

General Thoughts about Evaluation

Almost any decision about the selection and use of media can at times be acceptable, provided that it is well thought out, reasonable, and logical. When a decision is made it must be proved to whatever extent proof is possible. Beginners often recommend media actions that represent more of a gut feeling than a rational approach to decision making. The ability of a planner to solve problems is expressed by a good media plan. The planner explains the problems and shows how planning decisions solve them.

All media decisions must take the competition into consideration. This does *not* mean that our brand has to follow competition. But it is inconceivable that a planner would ignore the competitors. So there must be evidence in the plan that competitors' media actions have been taken into consideration.

Along these same lines, it does not make sense to try to counteract the effect of all competitors, but only those that would affect the planner's marketing and media efforts. Sometimes, this is one competitor whom we must attack directly. At other times, it is a small number of competitors who are vulnerable to our marketing and media attack. So the plan must reflect these considerations, and they must be spelled out in detail.

A Rating Scale for Measuring Media Plans

Exhibit 36–1 is a rating scale of various criteria by which a media plan can be judged. The perfect media plan would receive a 100 score. Plans less than perfect would receive anywhere from 1 to 99 as scores. Please note that there are certain criteria in this scale that would not appear in a professional scale, such as a rating for accuracy of calculations, or perhaps the communication of the plan itself. It is assumed that professionals do not have such problems, as beginners might have.

Exhibit 36–1 Values and Criteria for Judging Media Plans

The 100-point scale: There are 11 items in this 100-point rating scale, with each item representing more or less importance in evaluating a good media plan. Please note the value of each item and how it is judged.

10 points: Media Objectives

a. How well do media objectives relate to marketing objectives and strategies?
b. Are the target audiences identified and proven to be the best ones?
c. Are objectives complete? (None missing?)

20 points: Media Strategies (and Tactics)

a. How well do the strategies attain media objectives?
b. How thoughtfully were they chosen? (Adequacy of proof)
c. Were all viable alternatives considered before strategies were selected?
d. Are they complete? (None missing?)

10 points: Reach/Frequency/GRPs

a. Are the correct levels chosen for each? (Proof?)
b. Are the correct relationships between reach and frequency chosen? (Proof?)

10 points: Media Vehicle Selection

a. Are the correct vehicles selected?
b. Is there statistical audience-data proof provided? Target CPM?
c. Have all appropriate alternatives been considered?
d. Are there subjective evaluations of vehicles (quality) that are also needed?

9 points: Weighting Geographically

a. How well was the geographic weighting done?
b. Is the weighting concept used reasonable and defendable?
c. Is weighting complete?

8 points: Timing and Scheduling

a. How well have the reach/frequency/GRPs and dollars been distributed throughout the year?
b. Is the logic for timing reasonable and valid?

5 points: Spending Plan

a. Related to timing is the spending plan. How well does the planner spend available money?
b. Is the concept of spending reasonable and valid?

5 points: Creative Strategy Input

a. How well does the plan take into consideration the creative strategy of the campaign?

5 points: Calculations and Accuracy

a. How accurate are the calculations of data that are needed as evidence?
b. How complete are the data?

8 points: Innovativeness of the Plan

a. Does the plan show evidence that it is not just another "me-too" effort?
b. To what extent does the plan meet all other criteria and yet serve as an innovative solution to the problem?

10 points: Mechanical Structure and Communicability of the Plan

a. Is the plan well organized?
b. Are all the details there?
c. Have the statistical data been presented in an easy-to-read and understandable manner?
d. Is the plan itself easy to read and easy to understand?

The Rating Scale

	Maximum number of points	Points for plan being evaluated
Media objectives	10	______
Media strategies (and tactics)	20	______
Reach/frequency/GRPs	10	______
Media vehicle selection	10	______
Weighting geographically	9	______
Timing and scheduling	8	______
Spending plan	5	______
Creative strategy input	5	______
Calculations and accuracy	5	______
Innovativeness of the plan	8	______
Mechanical structure and communicability of the plan	10	______
Total	100	Total ______

Problem

Using the criteria in Exhibit 36–1, explain why each criterion is important in media planning. Also, if there are any other criteria not listed that should be considered, explain why each should be included.

Appendix

Media Rates and Other Data

Conversion Factors

Table 1 Spot Television Dayparts

Dayparts	TVHH Rtg %	Men 18+	Men 18–34	Men 18–49	Men 25–54	Men 55+	Women 18+	Women 18–34	Women 18–49	Women 25–54	Women 55+	Teens 12–17	Children 2–11	Children 6–11
Persons per TVHH		94	34	64	57	24	103	35	65	59	31	22	40	23
Early Morning (M-F 7:00A-9:00A)														
Rtg/VPVH	3.9	41	6	17	19	21	74	12	31	35	37	3	5	3
Conversion Factor		44	18	26	33	88	72	35	40	59	120	12	12	12
Daytime (M-F 9:00A-4:00P)														
Rtg/VPVH	4.5	30	8	14	13	15	81	25	42	38	34	4	6	2
Conversion Factor		32	24	23	23	61	78	70	64	64	111	19	15	11
Early Fringe (M-F 4:00P-6:00P)														
Rtg/VPVH	5.6	43	10	20	20	19	76	18	36	35	34	8	9	6
Conversion Factor		45	30	32	35	81	74	52	56	59	111	35	23	25
Early News (M-F 6:00P-7:30P)														
Rtg/VPVH	10.1	56	12	27	27	25	71	15	31	32	34	7	10	6
Conversion Factor		59	36	41	47	105	69	41	48	54	111	32	25	28
Prime Access (M-F 7:30P-8:00P)														
Rtg/VPVH	8.6	58	15	31	30	23	80	19	38	38	35	9	14	9
Conversion Factor		62	44	49	53	97	77	53	59	64	114	42	36	40
Primetime (M-Sat 8:00P-11:00P;Sun 7:00P-11:00P)														
Rtg/VPVH	10.3	59	18	36	35	18	80	23	46	45	28	11	15	10
Conversion Factor		63	52	57	62	76	77	67	71	75	90	50	38	44
Late News (M-F 11:00P-11:30P)														
Rtg/VPVH	9.2	61	14	33	34	23	76	17	39	40	31	4	3	2
Conversion Factor		65	42	52	59	96	74	48	59	67	101	16	8	8
Late Fringe (M-F 11:30P-1:00A)														
Rtg/VPVH	3.5	59	18	37	34	18	69	18	38	37	26	4	3	2
Conversion Factor		62	54	58	60	74	67	52	59	63	83	20	7	7
Weekend Children's (Sat 8:00A-Noon)														
Rtg/VPVH	2.9	35	13	22	19	11	42	14	24	22	15	19	64	38
Conversion Factor		38	38	34	34	48	41	41	38	38	49	85	161	164

Note: Data reflects the mix of affiliate and independent stations that is typically bought in each daypart. Source: NSI Planners Reports, 1993; DMA Demographic Rank Report, September 1993. Reprinted with permission of Grey Advertising, Inc.

Table 2 Network Dayparts

	Men					Women						Teens		Children	
Dayparts	**18+**	**18–34**	**18–49**	**25–54**	**55+**	**WW**	**18+**	**8–34**	**18–49**	**25–54**	**55+**	**Total**	**Female**	**2–11**	**6–11**
Early Morn.	48	24	34	40	83	56	66	37	49	59	103	9	9	10	9
Daytime	29	24	20	19	50	44	83	77	68	64	120	32	45	25	22
Early News	61	29	38	46	120	49	73	31	42	51	140	18	18	15	13
Primetime	59	50	53	56	71	67	73	63	65	68	93	50	45	38	43
Late Night	57	56	58	60	54	62	63	57	62	63	73	32	36	13	13
Child Daytime	27	41	33	26	17	27	32	49	38	34	23	86	64	165	165
Wknd News/Info.	59	26	38	46	113	47	63	26	35	42	123	14	9	13	13
Weekend Spts.	84	71	73	77	113	40	45	34	35	37	67	41	27	25	26

Source: Network conversion factors developed by authors by dividing VPVH (Viewers Per Viewing Houshold) by PPH (Persons Per Household) using Nielsen Ranking Plus data, September 1992–September 1993.

Media Rate and Audience Data

Table 3 Annual Network TV Average Cost Data

Average TV Home Ratings

	1st Qtr.	2nd Qtr.	3rd Qtr.	4th Qtr.
Daytime (M-F 10 AM-4:30 PM)	5.1	4.8	5.4	5.2
Early News (M-F 6:30-7:30 PM)	11.5	9.9	9.8	11.4
Prime Time (M-S 8-11 PM)	13.5	11.6	9.3	13.1
Late Eve. (M-F 11:30-1 AM)	4.0	4.0	4.1	4.2
Weekend Children's Shows	3.5	3.3	3.0	3.6

Average Cost Per 30-Second Commercial
(In thousands)

	1st Qtr. ($)	2nd Qtr. ($)	3rd Qtr. ($)	4th Qtr. ($)
Early Morning (M-F 6:30-9 AM)	24.9	20.0	20.6	22.4
Daytime (M-F 10 AM-4:30 PM)	20.3	21.4	17.1	22.0
Early News (M-F 6:30-7:30 PM)	82.9	91.8	64.8	83.9
Prime Time (M-S 8-11 PM)	155.7	179.3	128.8	175.0
Late Eve. (M-F 11:30-1 AM)	38.3	41.4	29.4	37.9
Weekend Children's Shows	16.9	22.3	14.9	30.4

Cost Per TV Home Rating Point

	1st Qtr. ($)	2nd Qtr. ($)	3rd Qtr. ($)	4th Qtr. ($)
Early Morning (M-F 6:30-9 AM)	6,213	6,655	5,150	5,599
Daytime (M-F 10 AM-4:30 PM)	3,971	4,450	3,168	4,223
Early News (M-F 6:30-7:30 PM)	7,207	9,272	6,615	7,358
Prime Time (M-S 8-11 PM)	12,978	16,916	14,000	14,583
Late Eve. (M-F 11:30-1 AM)	9,587	10,350	7,177	9,033
Weekend Children's Shows	4,821	6,763	4,965	8,441

Source: Editor's estimates

Spot TV

Table 4 Top 100 DMAs for Television by Market

DMAs by Rank	TV HH (000)	% US	Cume % US
1. New York	6716	7.0	7.0
2. Los Angeles	4936	5.2	12.2
3. Chicago	3102	3.3	15.5
4. Philadelphia	2682	2.8	18.3
5. San Francisco/Oakland	2251	2.4	20.7
6. Boston	2105	2.2	22.9
7. Washington, D.C.	1876	2.0	24.9
8. Dallas/Ft. Worth	1821	1.9	26.8
9. Detroit	1748	1.8	28.6
10. Atlanta	1567	1.6	30.2
11. Houston	1562	1.6	31.8
12. Seattle/Tacoma	1469	1.5	33.3
13. Cleveland	1460	1.5	34.8
14. Minneapolis/St. Paul	1411	1.5	36.3
15. Tampa/St. Petersburg	1390	1.5	37.8
16. Miami/Ft. Lauderdale	1309	1.4	39.2
17. Pittsburgh	1151	1.2	40.4
18. Denver	1142	1.2	41.6
19. Phoenix	1133	1.2	42.8
20. St. Louis	1120	1.2	44.0
21. Sacramento/Stockton	1109	1.2	45.2
22. Orlando/Daytona Beach	983	1.0	46.2
23. Baltimore	979	1.0	47.2
24. Indianapolis	926	1.0	48.2
25. Portland, OR	920	1.0	49.2
26. Hartford/New Haven	917	1.0	50.2
27. San Diego	915	1.0	51.2
28. Charlotte	794	.8	52.0
29. Milwaukee	789	.8	52.8
30. Cincinnati	782	.8	53.6
31. Kansas City	781	.8	54.4
32. Raleigh/Durham	763	.8	55.2
33. Nashville	749	.8	56.0
34. Columbus, OH	722	.8	56.8
35. Greenville/Spartanburg/Asheville	672	.7	57.5
36. Buffalo	639	.7	58.2
37. Salt Lake City	638	.7	58.9
38. Grand Rapids	634	.7	59.6
39. San Antonio	628	.7	60.3
40. Norfolk	620	.6	60.9
41. New Orleans	615	.6	61.5
42. Memphis	606	.6	62.1
43. Oklahoma City	578	.6	62.7
44. Harrisburg/Lebanon/Lancaster/York	578	.6	63.3
45. West Palm Beach	571	.6	63.9
46. Providence/New Bedford	567	.6	64.5
47. Wilkes Barre/Scranton	555	.6	65.1
48. Greensboro/Winston Salem/High Point	548	.6	65.7

Table 4 (continued)

DMAs by Rank	TV HH (000)	% US	Cume % US
49. Albuquerque	541	.6	66.3
50. Louisville	539	.6	66.9
51. Birmingham	530	.6	67.5
52. Albany/Schenectady/Troy	514	.5	68.0
53. Dayton	513	.5	68.5
54. Richmond	494	.5	69.0
55. Jacksonville	488	.5	69.5
56. Charleston/Huntington, WV	479	.5	70.0
57. Fresno/Visalia	478	.5	70.5
58. Little Rock	472	.5	71.0
59. Tulsa	463	.5	71.5
60. Flint/Saginaw	452	.5	72.0
61. Mobile/Pensacola	433	.5	72.5
62. Witchita/Hutchinson	426	.4	72.9
63. Knoxville	418	.4	73.3
64. Toledo	411	.4	73.7
65. Austin	398	.4	74.1
66. Roanoke/Lynchburg	390	.4	74.5
67. Syracuse	388	.4	74.9
68. Lexington, KY	384	.4	75.3
69. Honolulu	380	.4	75.7
70. Green Bay/Appleton	369	.4	76.1
71. Rochester, NY	369	.4	76.5
72. Las Vegas	368	.4	76.9
73. Des Moines/Ames	365	.4	77.3
74. Omaha	361	.4	77.7
75. Spokane	353	.4	78.1
76. Shreveport/Texarkana	353	.4	78.5
77. Paducah/Cape Girardeau/Harrisburg	347	.4	78.9
78. Champaign/Springfield/Decatur	346	.4	79.3
79. Portland/Auburn, ME	343	.4	79.7
80. Springfield, MO	338	.4	80.1
81. Tucson/Nogales	334	.4	80.5
82. Chattanooga	318	.3	80.8
83. Huntsville/Decatur	304	.3	81.1
84. Cedar Rapids	303	.3	81.4
85. Madison	303	.3	81.7
86. South Bend/Elkhart	302	.3	82.0
87. Columbia, SC	302	.3	82.3
88. Davenport/Rock Island/Moline	303	.3	82.6
89. Ft. Myers/Naples	299	.3	82.9
90. Jackson, MS	291	.3	83.2
91. Johnstown/Altoona	286	.3	83.5
92. Burlington/Plattsburgh	284	.3	83.8
93. Tri-Cities, VA–TN	281	.3	84.1
94. Youngstown	277	.3	84.4
95. Evansville	275	.3	84.7
96. Baton Rouge	261	.3	85.0
97. Colorado Springs/Pueblo	259	.3	85.3
98. Waco/Temple	252	.3	85.6
99. Springfield, MA	249	.3	85.9
100. El Paso	249	.3	86.2

Source: SQAD Report Projections as of September 1995.

Cable

Table 5 Cable TV Penetration: Top 100 DMAs

Rank	Market	DMA TV HH (000)	DMA Cable HH (000)	Cable % of DMA	Ad Ins* CATV HH (000)	Ad Ins* HH's % of DMA TV HH	Number of Systems	Cost per :30
	Puerto Rico	1029	270	26.2	214	20.8	6	240.00
1.	New York	6716	4453	66.3	4389	65.4	53	1,328.70
2.	Los Angeles	4936	2940	59.6	2560	51.9	69	1,753.67
3.	Chicago	3102	1766	56.9	1563	50.4	60	1,110.38
4.	Philadelphia	2682	1966	73.3	2024	75.5	50	1,381.54
5.	San Francisco–Oakland	2251	1530	68.0	1376	61.1	19	1,146.30
6.	Boston	2105	1589	75.5	1574	74.8	58	1,084.95
7.	Washington, D.C.	1876	1221	65.1	1151	61.4	27	828.15
8.	Dallas–Ft. Worth	1821	895	49.2	731	40.2	43	174.55
9.	Detroit	1748	1123	64.2	991	56.7	31	699.15
10.	Atlanta	1567	983	62.7	930	59.4	39	646.25
11.	Houston	1562	834	53.4	702	44.9	34	250.38
12.	Seattle–Tacoma	1469	1018	69.3	1127	76.7	13	78.81
13.	Cleveland	1460	960	65.7	904	61.9	35	432.00
14.	Minneapolis–St. Paul	1411	686	48.7	590	41.8	33	389.30
15.	Tampa–St. Petersburg	1390	963	69.2	946	68.0	18	425.37
16.	Miami–Ft. Lauderdale	1309	883	67.4	887	67.7	16	674.00
17.	Pittsburgh	1151	873	75.8	783	68.0	36	523.30
18.	Denver	1142	663	58.1	573	50.1	27	549.00
19.	Phoenix	1133	612	54.0	583	51.5	21	281.25
20.	St. Louis	1120	565	50.4	469	41.9	15	436.50
21.	Sacramento–Stockton	1109	688	62.0	630	56.8	26	632.60
22.	Orlando–Daytona Beach	983	727	73.9	634	64.4	14	324.57
23.	Baltimore	979	597	60.9	589	60.2	14	415.43
24.	Indianapolis	926	564	61.0	481	51.9	30	462.10
25.	Portland, OR	920	536	58.3	519	56.4	17	377.75
26.	Hartford–New Haven	917	766	83.6	786	85.7	20	636.40
27.	San Diego	915	725	79.3	687	75.1	4	245.00
28.	Charlotte	794	511	64.4	492	62.0	21	529.50
29.	Milwaukee	789	431	54.6	448	56.8	15	255.00
30.	Cincinnati	782	464	59.3	394	50.4	17	259.57
31.	Kansas City	781	490	62.8	422	54.0	12	372.50
32.	Raleigh–Durham	763	458	60.0	462	60.5	18	457.75
33.	Nashville	749	442	59.0	383	51.1	29	317.28
34.	Columbus, OH	722	439	60.9	398	55.2	19	266.16
35.	Greenville–Spartanburg–Asheville	672	386	57.5	339	50.5	23	288.28
36.	Buffalo	639	458	71.8	429	67.2	20	250.08
37.	Salt Lake City	638	333	52.2	285	44.6	6	168.48
38.	Grand Rapids	634	380	60.0	349	55.0	22	256.00
39.	San Antonio	628	402	64.0	338	53.8	9	185.38
40.	Norfolk	620	441	71.1	432	69.7	11	294.00
41.	New Orleans	615	426	69.2	398	64.7	11	279.43
42.	Memphis	606	360	59.4	262	43.3	16	162.24
43.	Oklahoma City	578	340	58.9	293	50.7	13	208.00
44.	Harrisburg–Lebanon–Lancaster–York	578	415	71.7	400	69.1	13	426.72
45.	West Palm Beach	571	447	78.2	502	87.9	12	341.40
46.	Providence–New Bedford	567	416	73.5	404	71.4	11	293.35
47.	Wilkes Barre–Scranton	555	434	78.2	434	78.3	27	323.91
48.	Greensboro–Winston Salem–High Point	548	330	60.3	302	55.1	21	333.00
49.	Albuquerque	541	301	55.6	255	47.1	20	180.60

Table 5 (continued)

Rank	Market	DMA TV HH (000)	DMA Cable HH (000)	Cable % of DMA	Ad Ins* CATV HH (000)	Ad Ins* HH's % of DMA TV HH	Number of Systems	Cost per: 30
50.	Louisville	539	330	61.2	284	52.8	9	198.00
51.	Birmingham	530	336	63.4	289	54.5	19	315.66
52.	Albany–Schenectady–Troy	514	352	68.6	342	66.6	17	277.70
53.	Dayton	513	345	67.2	336	65.4	13	298.25
54.	Richmond	494	289	58.5	258	52.2	9	152.20
55.	Jackonsville	488	355	72.8	310	63.5	9	200.88
56.	Charleston–Huntington	479	350	73.0	240	50.1	18	195.75
57.	Fresno–Visalia	478	246	51.5	218	45.7	8	149.00
58.	Little Rock	472	278	58.9	202	42.7	22	132.75
59.	Tulsa	463	285	61.7	223	48.2	9	92.00
60.	Flint–Saginaw	452	269	59.5	238	52.7	17	198.16
61.	Mobile–Pensacola	433	294	67.9	273	63.0	14	256.50
62.	Wichita–Hutchinson	426	288	67.5	200	46.9	14	180.25
63.	Knoxville	418	271	64.9	227	54.2	15	168.35
64.	Toledo	411	275	67.0	239	58.1	14	209.70
65.	Austin	398	258	64.8	252	63.1	13	113.59
66.	Roanoke–Lynchburg	390	245	62.8	217	55.5	17	217.00
67.	Syracuse	388	278	71.5	249	64.2	13	199.90
68.	Lexington	384	264	68.6	205	53.3	22	252.00
69.	Honolulu	380	323	85.2	330	86.9	5	184.00
70.	Green Bay–Appleton	369	202	54.7	174	47.1	16	241.25
71.	Rochester, NY	369	255	69.2	257	69.6	3	130.80
72.	Las Vegas	368	240	65.2	222	60.3	2	140.00
73.	Des Moines–Ames	365	208	57.0	128	35.1	4	95.00
74.	Omaha	361	234	64.9	170	47.1	5	100.40
75.	Spokane	353	216	61.0	167	47.1	10	92.40
76.	Shreveport–Texarkana	353	206	58.5	148	42.1	13	169.75
77.	Paducah–Cape Girardeau–Harrisburg	347	197	56.7	138	39.7	21	202.44
78.	Champaign–Springfield–Decatur	346	249	72.0	218	63.1	21	207.85
79.	Portland–Auburn	343	251	73.3	220	64.1	19	225.42
80.	Springfield, MO	338	164	48.4	121	35.7	11	97.06
81.	Tucson–Nogales	334	199	59.7	195	58.4	5	100.50
82.	Chattanooga	318	210	66.0	180	56.8	11	167.05
83.	Huntsville–Decatur	304	212	69.8	181	59.4	13	212.26
84.	Cedar Rapids	303	186	61.4	125	41.2	5	92.50
85.	Madison	303	179	59.2	160	52.7	7	117.00
86.	South Bend–Elkhart	302	169	55.9	141	46.6	11	130.90
87.	Columbia, SC	302	168	55.7	137	45.4	6	145.00
88.	Davenport–Rock Island–Moline	300	192	64.2	145	48.5	8	130.16
89.	Ft. Myers–Naples	299	231	77.2	267	89.2	8	189.00
90.	Jackson, MS	291	165	56.9	125	42.9	6	79.80
91.	Johnstown–Altoona	286	228	79.6	189	66.2	21	174.05
92.	Burlington–Plattsburgh	284	170	59.9	136	48.0	19	127.67
93.	Tri-Cities TN–VA	281	204	72.5	143	50.7	12	124.35
94.	Youngstown	277	190	68.6	156	56.3	9	135.80
95.	Evansville	275	163	59.3	125	45.4	15	160.61
96.	Baton Rouge	261	192	73.6	167	64.0	9	144.00
97.	Colorado Springs–Pueblo	259	170	65.7	138	53.5	3	57.80
98.	Waco–Temple	252	170	67.3	147	58.5	10	80.80
99.	Springfield, MA	249	195	78.1	184	73.7	9	123.20
100.	El Paso	249	147	58.8	147	59.2	3	69.00

*Ad Ins = Advertising Insertable. These figures indicate those CATV households that can be reached through cable operators capable of inserting advertising messages.

Source: Cable Track Planning Guide 1995, Advanced Media Systems.

Radio

Table 6 Spot Radio

Cost Per Metro Rating Point (60-second commercials)
Qtr/Yr: SPARC, 2nd Quarter, 1995
Level: Average
Target: Adults 25–54
Group: Top 100 Metro
Data: CPP

Market (Metro's)	AM	DA	PM	EV
Akron	37	31	38	40
Albany-Schenectady-Troy	35	30	38	40
Albuquerque	25	21	27	27
Allentown-Bethlehem	21	18	22	23
Anaheim-Santa Ana	213	175	231	240
Atlanta	121	102	127	133
Austin	28	24	29	32
Bakersfield	25	21	27	29
Baltimore	88	76	93	102
Baton Rouge	21	18	23	24
Birmingham	42	36	44	47
Boston	156	130	165	170
Buffalo-Niagara Falls	40	33	41	45
Charleston, SC	24	20	25	27
Charlotte-Gastonia-Rock H	54	44	57	61
Chattanooga	18	15	18	19
Chicago	200	173	213	219
Cincinnati	69	60	76	80
Cleveland	64	53	67	72
Columbia, SC	25	21	26	28
Columbus, OH	56	47	60	63
Dallas–Ft. Worth	159	136	169	182
Dayton	42	36	44	47
Daytona Beach	25	21	27	29
Denver-Boulder	101	84	108	115
Detroit	115	99	122	127
El Paso	20	17	22	23
Fresno	27	23	28	30
Ft. Wayne	18	15	19	20
Grand Rapids	33	28	35	37
Greensboro–WS–High Point	28	24	30	31
Greenville–Spartanburg	30	26	32	34
Greenville/New Bern, NC	19	17	20	22
Harrisburg–Lebanon–Carlisle	23	20	25	26
Hartford–New Britain–Midd	87	74	92	96
Honolulu	29	25	32	33
Houston–Galveston	140	122	150	160
Indianapolis	47	39	50	53
Jacksonville	32	28	34	36
Johnson City-Kingsport–Br	23	19	24	25
Kansas City	49	40	51	55
Knoxville	22	19	23	25
Las Vegas	35	30	39	40
Little Rock	25	22	27	29
Los Angeles	433	363	460	494

Table 6 (continued)

Market (Metro's)	AM	DA	PM	EV
Louisville	35	30	37	41
McAllen–Brownsville	21	17	22	23
Melbourne–Titusville–Coco	14	11	15	15
Memphis	49	42	51	54
Miami–Ft. Lauderdale–Holl	99	83	106	111
Milwaukee–Racine	56	47	61	64
Minneapolis–St. Paul	77	65	79	86
Mobile	19	16	21	21
Monmouth–Ocean, NJ	30	24	32	33
Monterey–Salinas–Santa Cr	25	22	27	29
Nashville	49	43	52	55
Nassau–Suffolk (Long Island)	118	98	123	131
New Bedford–Fall River, M	27	22	28	30
New Haven	54	44	56	59
New Orleans	53	45	55	59
New York	328	276	350	376
Norfolk–Virginia Beach–NW	47	39	50	53
Oklahoma City	30	26	32	34
Omaha–Council Bluffs	23	19	24	26
Orlando	65	54	68	71
Philadelphia	167	138	179	189
Phoenix	76	63	82	87
Pittsburgh	69	58	72	76
Portland, OR	71	61	76	81
Providence–Warwick–Pawtuc	57	50	60	63
Raleigh–Durham	43	37	47	47
Richmond	36	31	39	41
Riverside–San Bernardino	57	49	60	64
Rochester, NY	44	38	47	49
Sacramento	85	72	90	96
Salt Lake City–Ogden–Providence	52	45	56	58
San Antonio	49	42	51	55
San Diego	103	90	107	116
San Francisco	262	220	282	301
San Jose	95	79	100	107
Sarasota–Bradenton	35	30	37	39
Seattle–Talcoma	123	103	131	139
Spokane	14	12	15	16
Springfield, MA	24	21	27	28
St. Louis	69	58	73	78
Stockton	40	34	42	45
Syracuse	47	40	51	53
Tampa–St. Petersburg–Clea	67	57	72	73
Toledo	37	31	39	41
Tucson	24	20	26	27
Tulsa	30	26	32	34
Washington, DC	194	164	207	219
West Palm Beach–Boca Rato	46	40	49	51
Wichita	17	14	18	19
Wilkes Barre–Scranton	27	23	29	31
Wilmington, DE	17	15	19	20
Youngstown–Warren	19	16	21	22
Top 100 Markets Totals	6239	5275	6635	7026

Key to dayparts:

AM = Morning drive (6:00–10:00 a.m.)
DA = Daytime (10:00 a.m.–3:00 p.m.)
PM = Evening drive (3:00–7:00 p.m.)
EV = Evening (7:00 p.m.–Midnight)

Source: Spot Quotations and Data, Inc. Copyright SPARC Partners, 1993–1995.

Table 7 Network Radio—Interconnected Networks

AFFILIATES, FORMATS AND TARGET GROUPS

	No. of Affils.	Principal Types of Station Formats	Key Demo Target
ABC Excel	105	● Various Young Adult Targeted Formats	18-34
ABC Galaxy	990	● Various Adult Targeted Formats	25-54
ABC Genesis	330	● Various Young Adult Targeted Formats	12-34
ABC Platinum	1,580	● Various Adult Targeted Formats	25-54
ABC Prime	1,640	● Various Adult Targeted Formats	25-54
ABC Special Programming	2,000	● Various	12-54
AURN — American Urban Radio Network	214	● Urban & Black Adult Contemporary ● R&B/Oldies/Gospel/Inspirational	12-49 25-54
AURN STRZ Entertainment Ntwk	290	● Urban Contemporary/R&B ● Urban Adult Contemporary	12-49
AURN — SBN Sports Network	200	● News/Talk/Sports ● Urban Contemporary ● Various Formats	18-34 25-54
AURN — Urban Public Affairs Network	250	● News/Talk/Information ● Urban Contemporary	12-54
BEI — Broadcast Equities, Inc.	392	● News/Talk ● Special Programming/Urban Music	25-54
BRN Business Radio Network	235	● Financial News & Reports/Talk ● Entertainment Talk/Weather	25-54
BRN BRN's American Forum	235	● Sports Talk/Play-by-Play ● General/Entertainment Talk	25-54
CBN Radio Network	408	● News/Talk/Call-In ● Adult Contemporary Christian	25-54
CBS Radio Network	440	● News/Talk/Sports ● Variety	25-54
CBS Spectrum Radio Net.	600	● Various	25-54
CMN "Concert Music"	41	● Classical	25-54
CNBC — Business Radio	—	● News/Talk ● Full Services AC	25-54
Dow Jones Report	55	● Easy Listening/Classical ● New Adult Contemporary	25-54[1]
NBC Talknet	300	● Talk/Music	25-64
Standard News	225	● News/Information	25-54
Unistar Power	200	● Adult Contemporary ● Contemporary Hit Radio	18-49

Table 7 (continued)

AFFILIATES, FORMATS AND TARGET GROUPS (con't)

	No. of Affils.	Principal Types of Station Formats	Key Demo Target
Unistar Programming	2,000	● Various	12-54
Unistar Super	1,250	● Various	25-54
Unistar Ultimate	1,120	● Various	25-54
Wall Street Journal Radio Network	105	● News/Talk ● Classical	25-54[1]
Westwood MBS (Mutual)	1,000	● Various	25-49
Westwood NBC	500	● Various Adult Targeted Formats	25-49
Westwood Source	110	● Various Young Adult Targeted Formats	18-34
Westwood One	4,450*	● Various	Various
Westwood WONE	1,400	● News/Entertainment	25-54

Source: All data supplied by the various radio networks.
[1]Men *Cumulative total of network programs.

C/RP RATIOS FOR NETWORK RADIO*

a) By Dayparts and Demographic Segments

	Mon.-Sun. 6 AM-Mid.	M-F 6-10 AM	M-F 3-7 PM	Sat./Sun. 6AM-Mid.
	($)	($)	($)	($)
Adults 18 +	2,832	3,051	3,476	2,819
Men 18 +	2,787	3,212	3,593	2,758
Men 18-34	2,428	2,220	2,399	2,946
Men 25-54	2,937	2,979	3,292	2,905
Women 18 +	2,609	2,830	3,179	2,585
Women 18-34	2,542	3,000	3,173	2,531
Women 25-54	2,937	2,970	3,460	3,132
Teens 12-17	2,054	2,211	1,740	1,977

*C/RP's are for 30 second units.

b) Seasonal Cost Per Point Indices

	Cost Per Point Indices
1st Quarter	90
2nd Quarter	110
3rd Quarter	105
4th Quarter	95
Annual Average	100

Magazines

Table 8 Consumer Magazine Rate Data

	Yrly. Freq.	Rate Base (000)	One Time Rate Pg. 4/C ($)	Pg. B/W ($)	Eff. Date	B/W Close (wks)	4/C Close (wks)
American Health	10	800	25,050	18,130	1/92	8	8
American Legion	12	2,900	32,315	23,815	1/92	8	8
American Photo	6	250	21,000	13,200	1/92	8	8
American Way	24	304[1]	16,680	12,855	1/92	6	6
Architectural Digest	12	625	37,400	27,000	1/93	12	12
Automobile	12	550	40,720	28,510	10/92	9	9
Better H&G	12	8,000	147,500	121,930	9/92	12	12
Black Enterprise	12	240	16,735	12,560	1/93	10	10
Bon Appetit	12	1,200	38,705	27,145	1/92	8	8
Boys' Life	12	1,300	22,840	17,510	1/92	6	6
Bride's	6	425	30,190	24,260	2/92	12	12
Business Week	52	870	59,800	39,500	1/92	4	5
Cable Guide	12	6,000	71,965	53,905	8/91	6	7
Car & Driver	12	1,000	65,710	42,690	10/91	10	10
Car Craft	12	425	20,315	11,830	1/92	9	9
Chicago Tribune Mag.	60	1,133	29,530	25,080	10/92	4	5
Colonial Homes	6	575	34,140	24,395	1/92	8	8
Conde Nast Traveler	12	675	35,400	23,880	9/92	8	8
Cooking Light	7	950	25,500	19,630	1/92	8	8
Cosmopolitan	12	2,500	69,170	51,395	1/92	9	9
Country America	10	950	36,855	25,900	9/92	8	8
Country Gardens	3	450	15,000	12,000	3/93	11	11
Country Home	6	1,000	49,175	39,425	2/92	10	10
Country Living	12	1,700	56,080	40,990	1/92	10	10
Discover	12	1,100	32,995	22,745	1/91	7	7
Ebony	12	1,800	41,913	31,024	1/93	8	8
Elk's	10	1,473	12,795	8,558	2/92	6	6
Elle	12	825	41,135	28,575	1/92	12	12
Endless Vacation	6	900	21,000	16,800	11/92	6	6
Entertainment Weekly	50	800	29,985	22,910	7/92	4	4
Episodes Magazine	6	1,000	14,000	11,200	6/92	7	7
Esquire	12	700	38,370	25,580	1/92	8	8
Essence	12	950	30,730	20,470	1/93	12	12
Family Circle	17	5,000	96,990	81,510	1/92	3	3
Family Handyman	10	1,000	29,740	20,510	1/92	9	9
Field & Stream	12	2,000	64,775	43,725	1/92	8	8
Financial World	25	500	34,330	22,885	1/92	1	1
Flower & Garden	6	600	13,645	9,735	2/92	8	8
Food & Wine	12	725	31,025	22,160	1/93	8	8
Forbes	28	735	49,550	32,600	1/92	4	5
Fortune	27	675	56,260	37,130	7/92	4	4
GQ	12	600	36,180	24,100	1/93	9	9
Glamour	12	2,000	67,730	48,070	1/93	12	12
Golf Digest	12	1,400	68,610	45,740	1/92	8	8
Golf Illustrated	10	425	11,630	17,430	1/92	8	8
Golf Magazine	12	1,125	49,935	33,265	1/92	10	10
Good Housekeeping	12	5,000	122,035	97,260	1/92	8	8
Gourmet	12	750	32,450	20,560	1/92	8	8
Guns & Ammo	12	575	22,890	13,980	1/92	8	8
Harper's Bazaar	12	700	36,105	25,025	1/92	8	8
Home	10	925	35,800	26,900	1/92	12	12
Home Mechanix	10	1,000	26,000	18,330	2/92	8	8

[1] No rate base, figure represents BPA circulation.

Table 8 (continued)

	Yrly. Freq.	Rate Base (000)	One Time Rate Pg. 4/C ($)	Pg. B/W ($)	Eff. Date	B/W Close (wks)	4/C Close (wks)
Hot Rod	12	850	39,155	23,375	1/92	8	8
HG	12	550	36,770	26,820	1/92	12	12
House Beautiful	12	950	56,265	38,329	1/93	10	10
Inc.	12	640	54,455	35,590	1/92	8	8
Inside Sports	12	675	26,130	17,510	1/93	7	7
Insight	52	200	9,000	7,500	1/92	4	4
Kiplinger's Personal Finance Magazine	12	1,000	32,920	23,165	1/92	6	6
Ladies' Home Journal	12	5,000	92,100	77,400	2/92	4	4
Life	12	1,700	73,660	57,085	2/92	7	7
Los Angeles Times Magazine	48	1,532	33,970	26,390	1/92	5	5
Mademoiselle	12	1,100	44,540	30,660	1/93	12	12
McCall's	12	4,600	83,315	70,615	1/92	10	10
Metro-Puck Comics Network	52	46,161	730,882	—	1/92	—	6
Metropolitan Home	12	700	39,740	29,800	1/92	12	12
Modern Maturity	6	22,450	226,970	204,840	1/92	12	12
Money	13	1,800	77,110	49,705	1/92	6	6
Motorland	6	2,000	19,950	15,750	9/92	7	7
Motor Trend	12	900	55,440	33,000	1/92	8	8
National Enquirer	52	3,500	49,800	39,500	1/93	5	5
Nat'l Geographic	12	7,400	142,915	109,935	1/92	8	8
Nat'l Geo. Traveler	6	700	26,655	19,990	1/92	7	7
National Star	52	3,100	40,300	33,450	1/93	5	5
Nation's Business	12	850	38,600	25,820	1/92	6	6
Natural History	12	510	18,655	12,755	10/92	6	6
New Choices	10	575	23,750	17,450	1/92	8	8
New York Magazine	50	415	30,280	19,240	1/92	3	3
New York Times Sunday Magazine	52	1,701	44,910	30,790	1/92	5	6
New Yorker	52	600	38,195	23,950	1/92	3	3
Newsweek	52	3,100	114,535	73,620	1/92	5	5
Omni	12	700	30,165	21,730	10/90	8	8
Organic Gardening	9	735	24,998	18,113	11/92	8	8
Outdoor Life	12	1,500	48,580	32,790	1/92	8	8
Parade	52	36,324	486,400	393,800	7/92	5	5
Parenting	11	875	33,850	25,390	3/93	10	10
Parents	12	1,725	55,210	43,125	1/93	10	10
Penthouse	12	1,500	31,355	27,970	7/91	12	12
People	52	3,150	97,090	75,325	1/92	3	7
Playboy	12	3,400	73,340	52,370	1/92	12	12
Popular Mechanics	12	1,600	58,390	41,145	1/92	8	9
Popular Photography	12	650	53,170	41,200	1/92	8	8
Popular Science	12	1,800	48,590	34,250	1/92	8	9
Prevention	12	3,000	49,280	39,425	2/93	10	10
Reader's Digest	12	16,250	151,900	130,634	1/93	8	8
Redbook	12	3,200	69,755	52,750	1/92	10	10
Rolling Stone	24	1,200	49,970	37,510	8/92	7	7

Table 8 (continued)

	Yrly. Freq.	Rate Base (000)	Pg. 4/C ($)	One Time Rate Pg. B/W ($)	Eff. Date	B/W Close (wks)	4/C Close (wks)
Saturday Evening Post	6	525	14,414	11,011	4/91	8	8
Scholastic Teen Ntwk.	16	2,300[2]	38,695	30,960	1/92	9	9
Scientific American	12	500[3]	31,300[3]	20,850[2]	10/92	7	7
Scouting	6	900	13,035	8,905	1/92	8	7
Self	12	1,100	47,310	31,670	1/93	8	8
Sesame Street	10	1,175	38,525	37,222	1/92	10	10
Seventeen	12	1,800	48,966	33,786	1/92	10	10
Smithsonian	12	2,100	56,180	37,805	1/92	6	6
Soap Opera Digest	26	1,300	25,480	20,910	1/92	6	8
Southern Living	12	2,275	63,400	44,960	1/92	8	8
Spin	12	315	16,605	11,620	1/93	4	4
Sport	12	850	29,640	19,760	1/92	11	11
Sporting News	62	625	19,610	15,850	3/92	17	17
Sports Afield	12	500	27,650	19,200	1/92	8	8
Sports Illustrated	52	3,150	127,600	84,260	1/92	5	7
Stereo Review	12	500	35,630	25,455	1/93	8	8
Sunday Mag. Ntwk.	52	16,321	226,380	183,450	1/92	6	6
Sunset	12	1,375	43,510	31,400	1/93	8	8
'Teen	12	1,100	26,095	17,395	1/92	9	9
Tennis	12	755	39,450	26,300	1/92	7	7
Time	52	4,000	134,400	91,000	1/92	4	4
Town & Country	12	475	34,555	26,859	6/92	8	8
Travel & Leisure	12	1,100	44,865	38,010	1/92	7	7
Travel Holiday	10	550	19,807	14,464	1/92	7	7
TV Guide	52	14,000	112,700	95,750	3/92	17[1]	4
Us	12	1,100	37,615	29,140	1/93	8	8
U.S. News & W.R.	50	2,150	77,100	51,650	1/92	17[1]	5
USA Today (M-Th.)	254	1,740	74,757	57,505	1/91	2[1]	4[1]
USA Today (Fri.)		2,162	85,552	65,810			
USA Weekend	52	15,900	217,035	183,645	8/92	4	4
Vanity Fair	12	800	52,490	35,020	1/93	8	8
Vogue	12	1,100	52,680	36,590	1/93	8	8
Wall St. Journal	256	1,852	—	110,627	1/92	2[1]	—
Weight Watchers	12	1,000	25,730	18,405	1/92	12	12
Woman's Day	17	4,500[2]	84,320	70,435	1/92	12	12
Workbasket	6	1,065	17,500	13,900	2/92	8	8
Workbench	6	860	17,500	14,200	2/92	8	8
Working Mother	12	850	30,725	25,185	4/92	10	10
Working Woman	12	900	30,725	25,185	4/92	8	8
Yankee	12	700	17,925	14,405	7/92	8	8
YM	10	1,300	37,865	24,265	2/93	9	9

[1] Figure given in days.
[2] Rate Base and rates vary during the academic year. See publisher for complete information.
[3] North American figures.